Berg Women's Series

George Sand

A Brave Man — The Most Womanly Woman

Donna Dickenson

BERG *Oxford / New York / Hamburg*
Distributed exclusively in the US and Canada by
St. Martin's Press, New York

Published in 1988 by
Berg Publishers Limited
Market House, Deddington, Oxford OX5 4SW, UK
175 Fifth Avenue / Room 400, New York, NY 10010, USA
Schenefelder Landstr. 14K, 2000 Hamburg 55, W.-Germany

© Berg Publishers Limited 1988

British Library Cataloguing in Publication Data

Dickenson, Donna
  George Sand: a brave man, a womanly woman.
  —(Berg women's series).
  1. Sand, George—Biography   2. Authors,
  French—19th century—Biography
  I. Title
  843'.8   PQ2412

  ISBN 0–85496–536–X
  ISBN 0–85496–537–8 Pbk

Library of Congress Cataloguing-in-Publication Data

Dickenson, Donna.
  George Sand: a brave man, a womanly woman.

  (Berg women's series)
  Bibliography: p.
  Includes index.
  1. Sand, George, 1804–1876.   2. Novelists, French—
19th century—Biography.   3. Women and literature—
France.   I. Title.   II. Series.
PQ2412.D5   1987   843'.7   [B]   87–11782
ISBN 0–85496–536–X
ISBN 0–85496–537–8 (pbk.)

Printed and bound in Great Britain by
Redwood Burn Limited, Trowbridge, Wiltshire

Contents

Illustrations

To the memory of my father,
Donald Moody Dickenson Jr.,
who died when I was four, and he five years younger
than Maurice

What a brave man she was, and what a good woman!

Ivan Turgenev, of George Sand

The most womanly woman.

Alfred de Musset, of George Sand

Introduction

Until now there has been no book-length introductory study in English of Sand and her works. What I have tried to provide in this book is just that — not a straight biography, of which there are many. However, I have also brought in a good deal of Sand's voluminous life, particularly in Chapters 1 and 4, as well as a complete chronology of events and works. I hope that my style is clear and my assumptions about readers' prior knowledge undemanding. (Except for a few French passages included to give a flavour of Sand's much-praised style, all quotations are in English.) But I have also aimed to create a properly scholarly book, footnoted and directed towards further reading.

If my book is interpreted as one more rehash of the old 'truths' about Sand, I shall be frustrated and dismayed. I believe no one else has pointed out that Baudelaire's most-quoted line, 'Mon semblable, mon frère', appears to be borrowed from Sand's *A Winter in Majorca*.[1] Perusing the Georges Lubin edition of Sand's letters at the time she took on her masculine pseudonym has enabled me to make some original deductions about Sand's androgynous sense of herself. To the best of my knowledge no one has discussed Sand in terms of the theories of Carol Gilligan, Michel Foucault, or Sandra Gilbert and Susan Gubar.

But what I hope is most original about this book is that in it I have pulled together all the tired myths about Sand, and given reasons from the primary sources and the novels for challenging them. Even to her advocates, Sand is known as a maternal bosom and the darling of the muses, a writer to whom a vast body of work came painlessly and at will. In Chapters 4 and 5 I take some offence at these backhanded compliments. By way of contrast, in Chapter 3 I surmise that Sand's friends have been too generous in presenting her as a doughty campaigner for women's rights. Sand's legion enemies have often painted her as loose in her morals, wide-eyed in her political radicalism, and pernicious in her effect on the wearing of skirts. Most of all, they have seen her only in terms of her sexuality. I have included a long chapter on this subject, to put the record straight, or at least to wipe clean some of the worst mud. But I have striven to present Sand as a professional writer first, as almost certainly she would still be known if she had been a man. Readers of my earlier *Emily Dickinson*[2] will realise that I remain tiresomely faithful to my conviction that women writers generally have trouble in getting themselves taken seriously *as* writers. Although Sand attained fame as well as notoriety during her lifetime, now only the notoriety remains. Chopin's mistress, who smoked cigars and wore trousers — that is the popular image of her, to the extent that there *is* a popular image at all, even a stereotyped one.

To Christopher Britton I am grateful for his guidance on modern views of Chopin, his dreaming about Chopin when I do, and the infallible support I could almost begin to take for granted. My piano teacher Jack Gibbons, winner of the 1982 Newport International Competition, also deserves a mention for his dream that he ordered from Blackwell's music shop the 28-record boxed set of Chopin's works — all played and recorded by George Sand. To the example of my grandmother, Jane Orton Moore, ninety this year, I owe my admiration for women with many strings to their bows — in her case, tatting lace, mixing concrete, dowsing for water, rooting pachysandra, sprouting mimosa trees, and playing the musical saw. My editor, Miriam Kochan, has been enthusiastic and warm throughout, and my publisher, Marion Berghahn, has been, as usual, as firm a foundation as any author could wish.

Donna Dickenson
Oxford, February 1987

Notes

1. Francine Mallet (*George Sand*, Paris: Grasset, Livre de Poche, 1976, p. 429) mentions that there is a scholarly study of Baudelaire's quotations and paraphrases from Sand, but since she gives no foot-notes, I have been unable to trace this work.
2. *Emily Dickinson* (Leamington Spa: Berg Publishers, 1985).

1 A Thinking Bosom?

> ... a thinking bosom and one who overpowered her
> young lovers, all sybil ... a Romantic ....
>
> V.S. Pritchett

Once upon a time a would-be French man of letters overcame the
handicaps of a traumatic childhood, a patchy education, and a
precipitate marriage to become an instant popular and critical
success on the publication of his first novel. He went on to write
over one hundred further volumes of fiction, travel narrative,
political and literary essays, plays and autobiography. His works
were read and generally praised by audiences from America to
Russia, and his friends and admirers — to whom he wrote 20,000
letters in all — included Turgenev, Flaubert, Mazzini, Heine,
Sarah Bernhardt, Matthew Arnold, Elizabeth Barrett Browning,
Victor Hugo, Dumas *fils*, and Henry James. Always generous
with both his time and his purse, he sponsored a number of
proletarian writers and became unofficial minister of information
in the provisional government following the 1848 Revolution. In
thirty years he gave away over one million pounds in charity to
persecuted republicans, Paris artisans, and needy peasants on his
small estate. In addition he interceded with Napoleon III on
behalf of a number of exiled or imprisoned supporters of the 1848
government and supported their families with his own money.
His early love life was unfortunate: his marriage ended in a legal
separation by which he lost a great deal of his fortune to his
grasping wife. An idyll in Venice with an early mistress ended
badly after she careered naked around the room in hysterics,
before two doctors, and tried to strangle him. Another mistress
with whom he lived for ten years, providing her with a stable
home at his country house and nursing her with an almost
feminine devotion during her illnesses, later turned on him and
supported a vitriolic campaign of vilification by a relative who
was trying to blackmail him. But in middle age he gained a solid
support in a woman who used her own funds to buy him a writing
retreat and who laid out his ink and paper with care for his

3

disciplined daily stint of work. After her death he retired to his estate for the most part, dying much-respected after a lifetime of solid professional work and altruistic concern for progressive causes.

The realistic reader will have little doubt that this is a fairy story. Disillusioning actuality might seem better typified by another French tale: that of a woman whose name has become a byword for loose living and aggressively masculine behaviour, George Sand. Fastening upon men of talent and sucking them dry with her insatiable demands, she ruined the health and threatened the careers of her hapless lovers, among them the poet Alfred de Musset and the composer Frédéric Chopin. Those men whom she did not pursue with a voracious sexuality, she mothered half to death. According to V.S. Pritchett, she was 'a domineering, ruthless woman and very cunning and double-minded with it. . . . Men were consumable. She liked to pilfer their brains'.[1] Her sloppily dashed-off novels are overblown and florid to modern taste, sickly and cloying, although they met with some minor success in the high period of Romanticism. Today she is remembered only as Chopin's mistress, a wearer of trousers, and one of the first women to smoke cigarettes and cigars. 'The name of George Sand has come to mean to most people not an author at all, but a target for labels: transvestite, man-eater, lesbian, nymphomaniac.'[2]

These are actually the two stories which could be told about George Sand — and if she had been a man in fact, not just in pen name, perhaps the first would be the accepted account. Certainly the second would not be, since it could only be used to slander a woman. Nevertheless, the second account is much the better known — although, despite its veneer of worldly wisdom, it is actually much closer to fairy tale than the first. But all the facts I have stated about my imaginary man in the first story are true of Sand. The violent fit I attribute to a hysterical mistress in my fable was actually put on by Musset. My interpretation of Chopin as ungrateful for Sand's support and care — which I qualify to some extent in Chapter 4 — is becoming the more accepted view of a relationship formerly seen in terms of Sand as a tigress and Chopin as her prey.[3] Alexandre Manceau, who lived with and cared for Sand for fourteen years until his death from consumption in 1865, should be recognised as the happiest male influence on Sand's life, I believe — the 'wife' she had needed for a long time. To some extent the 'fairy story' is coming to be recognised as nearer the truth about Sand than the misogynous myths in the second account. Her reputation has resisted these libels in France and the Soviet Union more than in Anglo-Saxon countries. Even in America there have been some twenty new translations of Sand in recent years, and feminists take a growing interest in her life and works. The centenary of her death in 1976 occasioned many tributes and much scholarship on both sides of the Atlantic, although far more in France than in England on this side. It has even been suggested that it is now exaggerated to say that Sand's work has been largely forgotten since her death.[4] Perhaps in American and French academia this may be so, but popular awareness of Sand is still bounded by the film treatment of her life with Chopin. And the old woman-hating stereotypes were alive and thriving in a play at the Gate Theatre in London last year which depicted Sand pursuing poor Musset to Venice, nagging him into an unpoetic frenzy, and then dropping him abruptly so that she could sleep around with myriad Italians.

It seems to me undeniable that the tattling legends about Sand are conditioned by her sex, that they could not be told about a man, that they are arguments *ad feminam*. She is typically defined by her sexuality, as a 'thinking bosom'. No male writer I know of has ever been described as 'cogitating testicles'. But if Sand has been demeaned and forgotten since her death simply because she was a woman, how did she manage to achieve success in her lifetime with this mark against her? Although there may have been some use in the male pen name when she published her first novel, *Indiana*, her female identity was known by the time her later novels appeared. Scandal about her affairs with the writer Jules Sandeau and with Musset was current at the time of all her early novels; yet she was never branded as a camp follower with vague literary pretensions. Did her sexual notoriety actually *help* her to become famous? And what are we to make of the veneration accorded this impenitent Magdalen by the most strait-laced of Victorians?

This is the paradox I want to consider in this book — along with a debunking of the myths, which I hope to administer. Sand was seen primarily — and rightfully — as a professional writer in her time, with a record of successful work in all genres except poetry, which she abandoned after her schooldays, and a reputation as the greatest French stylist of her time. Her personal life was known and frequently condemned, but it seems not to have affected her professional standing. After she died, her fame as a writer sank, and all that remained was the *ill* fame. If this muck-raking went on because she was a woman, why was she largely immune to it during her lifetime? In the 1840s Sand's friends, the singer Pauline Garcia Viardot and her husband, were fêted and acclaimed during their visit to Russia simply because they were acquainted with her. They wrote to Sand that she was the most famous French writer of her generation in a country where French was the universal language of cultured people. By the mid-twentieth century her translations were out of print in English, and my year-long course on the French Romantics at university in the 1960s made no mention of her. What explains this about-face? How have we been persuaded that the 'real' story of Sand centres on her affairs and cigarettes?

These matters will be considered throughout this book, particularly in Chapter 6 which deals with the decline and fall of Sand's reputation. Before I look to her future, however, I need to say something about her past — her family circumstances, in this first chapter, and the influences on her work in the second. Sand's childhood was intensely sad: her father was killed at the age of thirty in a riding accident when she was four, and she received little proper mothering afterwards. (The inadequacy of Sand's preparation for becoming a 'thinking bosom,' for mothering her own children — and supposedly her lovers too — rarely seems to occur to biographers and critics, who treat maternal nature as instinctive to all women and unproblematic.)[5] After her father's death she became the centre of a feud between her paternal grandmother and her mother, a struggle which ended in the grandmother's somewhat pyrrhic victory because the widowed mother had no independent means. This conflict gave Sand an object — or abject — lesson in women's economic dependence, the issue on which she can most properly be called a feminist. The two Madame Dupins — both more sympathetic than I may have made them sound, but neither an adequate mother to Sand — were the twin stars of her early life, with their opposing gravitational pulls. The conflict between them — a sort of opposition between the Virgin and the Magdalen — recurs in much of

Sand's later work, especially her *succès de scandale, Lélia*. It is wrong-headed to assume that all Sand's work can be reduced to autobiography, although it is another common critical error.[6] Sand herself protested against the tendency to deny her professionalism in this way: 'How easy it is to write a novelist's biography: you present her fiction as the truth about her life, with little expenditure of imagination'.[7] Nevertheless her childhood was so extraordinary, and the manner in which she was torn between these two women so traumatic, that her early years need as full a consideration as I can give them in this brief study.

Born Amantine-Lucile-Aurore Dupin, Sand was just saved from illegitimacy by the shotgun marriage a month before of her mother, Antoinette-Sophie-Victoire Delaborde (1773–1837), to Maurice Dupin (1778–1808), aide-de-camp to Joachim Murat, Napoleon's brother-in-law. 'Saved from illegitimacy' may be more an expression of twentieth-century prurience than of early nineteenth-century French conventions. Maurice was the legitimate and only son of Claude Dupin de Francueil — prudently shortened to Dupin during the Terror. But Maurice's mother, born Marie-Aurore de Saxe, was the illegitimate daughter of the field marshal Maurice de Saxe, himself the illegitimate son of King Augustus III of Poland and his mistress, Aurore of Königsmark. Since Maurice de Saxe's niece, Marie de Saxe, had married the eldest son of Louis XV, the Dauphin, George Sand was a second cousin on the wrong side of the blanket to Louis XVI, Louis XVIII and Charles X. What is fascinating about this tangled lineage is that Sand made an unusually conventional marriage for her background when she wed a man of her own age and class, and produced her first child a respectable nine months afterwards. This was a disappointing start for the woman who is often depicted as a sexual Antichrist.

Sand's paternal grandmother, Mme Dupin de Francueil (1748–1821), had been married off at fifteen to the Count of Horn, the bastard son of Louis XV. (That Maurice de Saxe was her father was not acknowledged until the same year.) On her wedding night, a valet interceded to prevent her sleeping with the count, probably because he had venereal disease. (It is small wonder — though again surprising to conventional prejudice — that Sand characterised the morals of the eighteenth century as 'lax'.)[8] Widowed while still in her teens, the young countess returned to the Convent of Saint-Cyr, from which she had been withdrawn in order to be married, until her wedding at twenty-nine to a wealthy man of sixty-two, Louis-Claude Dupin de Francueil. Predictably, this marriage only managed to produce one child — Maurice Dupin, George Sand's father. Claude Dupin de Francueil died when Maurice was nine, and all his wife's affections went into rearing the solitary son. Maurice's early death left Mme Dupin de Francueil with no other legitimate heir than the four-year-old Aurore. (There was also an illegitimate son, Hippolyte Chatiron, Aurore's half-brother, whom Mme Dupin de Francueil raised at the family estate, Nohant in Berry, with his younger half-sister, but it was years before she confessed to Aurore that Hippolyte was actually her blood kin.) Having been a virgin even after her first wedding, and later married to a much older man, Mme Dupin de Francueil 'never had any passion but maternal love', as Sand wrote in her autobiography.[9] This exclusive dedication to mother love — and its sorry outcome in terms of Maurice's death and Mme Dupin de Francueil's desperate determination to keep Aurore at Nohant — appeared unhealthy to Sand. It is another reason for doubting the accepted wisdom that Sand's sexuality was mostly maternal.

But Sand did express a sideways admiration for her grandmother's straightforwardness in sexual matters — even despite the silence over Hippolyte's origins. Later Sand emulated this frankness — to many catcalls — in a famous letter at the start of her relationship with Chopin, discussed in Chapter 4. In her autobiography she makes her grandmother express her views in this fashion: 'We were philosophical; we did not play at austerity, but we were austere, without flaunting it. If we were chaste, it was by inclination, not out of prudery'.[10] Sand rather envied her grandmother's escape from her own sexuality, I think, and from the rumour-mongering which attends women who try to express theirs. 'She made her way through a licentious world without losing a feather from her wing; and condemned by fate never to know love in marriage, she solved the problem of how to escape ill will and calumny.'[11] Sand was also tempted by her grandmother's eighteenth-century style of life, the heritage of a mannered age which is symbolised for Sand's biographer Curtis Cate by the battle of Fontenoy. Before the slaughter — in this engagement presided over by Maurice de Saxe — the British and French graciously bowed to each other. In her autobiography Sand sighs: 'It is certainly seductive, this philosophy of wealth, independence, tolerance and graciousness'. But she quickly adds: 'You needed an income of 6,000 pounds a year to support it, and I don't quite see what it did for the wretched and downtrodden'.[12]

Eighteenth-century *bon ton* finally imprisoned Mme Dupin de Francueil quite literally: years of inactivity, with servants to take care of her every bodily function, left her unable to bend down to retrieve a snuffbox or handkerchief. (That snuff was acceptable for gentlewomen in the eighteenth century, whereas smoking was an even greater stigma than affairs for Sand in the nineteenth, sums up the odd contradictions in the supposedly genteel classical period and the stereotypically free-living Romantic era.) 'Good manners' also hemmed in the young Aurore, who was required to address her elders in the third person, refrain from running or rolling on the ground with Hippolyte, and wear her hair in a Chinese bun pulled back with a chafing ribbon.

> My every natural spurt of energy was curbed — gently, of course, but insistently. . . . Whenever she [Mme Dupin de Francueil] said "Run along now and play quietly," I felt she was shutting me up with her in a shoebox. . . . She, too, had lived too long in a shoebox, and her blood had lost its pulse; whenever she was bled not a drop came out, so dead was it in her veins. I was horribly afraid of becoming like her, and when I was beside her, and she ordered me not to fidget or shout, I felt that she was asking me to be dead.[13]

Mme Dupin de Francueil took a three-hour nap every afternoon requiring absolute silence in all the adjoining main rooms. Except at meal-times and during the evening card game, she had little contact with the child whom she was really too old to raise.

The musical atmosphere at Nohant was equally stultifying — intense but outdated. Aurore was taught singing and keyboard, but not the increasingly popular fortepiano — rather, Gluck, Piccini, Hasse and Durante on the harpsichord. Her writing master forced her into a contraption of his own devising — which she later characterised as producing profits for him, since he held the monopoly on its manufacture, but little benefit for his pupils. This device, worthy of Torquemada, comprised a whalebone corset reaching from head to waist, a wooden bar to keep the

9

elbow aloft, and a brass ring on boxwood rollers for the pen and index finger. (Schumann, who invented himself a similarly agonising gadget to increase the mobility of his fourth finger, was nearly crippled by it and never played the piano properly again. It remains a minor wonder that George Sand ever took up the pen voluntarily after this torture.) Aurore was also taught French and Latin grammar, mathematics, history, geography, and a smattering of science by her father's former tutor, François Deschartres, who epitomised eighteenth-century *sang-froid* so elegantly that he was able to boil, skin and dissect heads from the guillotine, safe in his conviction of the impartiality of science. It is some credit to both Deschartres and scientific rationalism, however, that he was unable to perform this operation on the head of a friend of whose death he had previously been unaware.

Mme Dupin de Francueil also embodied the convictions of the *philosophes* in her anticlericalism. As Sand wrote: 'She was no bigot, her only religion being that of the eighteenth century, the deism of Rousseau and Voltaire'.[14] She had taken *Emile* sufficiently seriously to attempt Rousseau's recommendation and breast-feed the infant Maurice herself. Sand was well aware of the irony in this, contrasting her grandmother's provision for the serving-maid's son Hippolyte with Rousseau's dismissal of his own children to the foundling hospital. As she noted: 'My grandmother had read and cherished Rousseau, and she had profited not only by his truths but also by his errors'.[15] Nevertheless this willingness to challenge both deist philosophy and contemporary mores — which pronounced breast-feeding suitable only for wet-nurses, an attitude still to be found in *Madame Bovary*'s time — co-existed with conventionality and hypocrisy in Mme Dupin de Francueil, particularly as she aged. Although she was willing to have her son's bastard brought up in her household, she forbade Aurore to receive her half-sister on her mother's side, Caroline Delaborde — Sophie's illegitimate daughter from a previous affair. Mme Dupin de Francueil's own childhood had been marred by an order from the paternal aunt who raised her that she was not to see her own, unmarried mother, Mlle de Verrières. Yet this same woman set down as a condition of her daughter-in-law's lifetime pension from the Nohant estate that she was to renounce her rights to little Aurore.

While Aurore was a baby, Mme Dupin de Francueil's jealousy

of rivals for her son's affections had combined with disdain for Sophie's low origins — the daughter of a bird-seller on the Quai d'Orsay — to ban the young couple from Nohant. Indeed, she tried unsuccessfully to have their marriage annulled. Maurice and his wife were only made welcome after his return from the Spanish campaign in 1808, bearing in tow the four-year-old Aurore and a new baby son destined for the heirdom of Nohant. Sophie had come through a progression of Gothic incidents which would appear unbelievable in a novel — and which far outdo Sand's supposedly arch-Romantic plots. To supplement the only available food for herself and her child — raw onions, green lemons and sunflower seeds — she had let foot-soldiers feed Aurore on their soup of candle stubs. In another incident Aurore remembered pulling playfully on the sleeve of a soldier, only to find that there was no longer an arm inside. Maurice had slashed in two an enormous snake which lay across the entire width of the narrow road they were following through the mountains. The wheel of the wagon in which the women and children were travelling had run over a corpse with a crunch, and Sophie, only just recovered from childbirth, had to find a plausible story to divert her little daughter from the truth. Once they had finally reached France, their boat had foundered in the Bay of Biscay; the deck was awash and the ship sinking before they were rescued. Shortly after their arrival at Nohant, Aurore's baby brother Louis — who had been born blind — died. Sophie had now borne five children, of whom she had only one left with her. Her first child, born out of wedlock in 1790 when she was seventeen, had disappeared during the Revolution. Her second, Caroline, also illegitimate, had been left behind when the family went to Spain. Aurore was the third; a boy had been born and died in 1806, and now this last son was dead. Sophie's stunned incomprehension was so great that she pressed Maurice to ex-hume the coffin secretly so that she could make sure her baby had not been buried alive. Eight days later Maurice himself was dead and buried in the same plot — thrown on a gallop over a bridge on a wet September night. What Aurore remembered of his funeral was being made to wear black stockings, which repulsed and terrified her. 'I claimed they were drawing "Death's legs" on me.'[16]

After Maurice's death his mother and wife made efforts to get along, out of decorum, concern for Aurore, and a certain mutual respect which they were surprised to find themselves sharing once they actually met. Sand later speculated that Mme Dupin de Francueil only restrained herself from genuinely liking her daughter-in-law out of concern for what her 'old countess' friends would say. Sophie's practical nature set off Mme Dupin de Francueil's decorous indolence as neatly as her dark colouring and mercurial temperament did her mother-in-law's pale complexion and dignified comportment. Inventive and frugal, Sophie provided all the household clothing at Nohant, as well as restringing and tuning the spinet with an accurate though untaught ear. Aurore was always aware of an undertow of conflict, however, centring on her own upbringing and Sophie's shady past. Sophie was at first an affectionate mother: although she dealt out blows in fits of anger, she was also free with her caresses. Sand later wrote that her first sense was of her mother's immense love for her. Before her father's death, she reckoned: 'Doubtless I was very happy, for I was much loved; we were poor, and I utterly unaware of it'.[17] But Sophie's affection was consciously tempered, Sand wrote, by the realisation that she would have to leave Aurore behind at Nohant one day. Even as a small child Sand claims to have known her mother would be taken from her — as her father and little brother had been just at the age, she said, when she was beginning to emerge from infantile self-absorption. She never loved her grandmother with equal warmth, although the elderly woman was never physically violent with her.

> I was so happy to win back [Sophie's] tenderness that I begged her to forgive herself for the blows she'd given me. . . . If my grandmother had been a fraction so harsh with me, I'd have risen up at once. I was much more afraid of her, and a word from her made me go pale; but I would not have forgiven her the least unfairness, while all my mother's injustices went unnoticed, and even increased my love.[18]

But even though she loved Aurore and had lost her other children from the marriage, Sophie signed a formal contract leaving the little girl with her mother-in-law and retired to Paris. At the time Aurore felt that she had been openly sold: in exchange for a pension of 1,500 francs from Nohant, to be added to the 1,000 to which she was entitled as an army widow, Sophie renounced her rights in the rearing of her daughter as the heiress of the small estate. This arrangement was negotiated in large part by Mme Dupin de Francueil's half-brother, the Abbé Charles Godefroi Marie de Beaumont — indicating that churchmen in those days had few firm feelings on the sanctity of the maternal bond. This financial commitment was honoured by Mme Dupin de Francueil, who also made up the extra 1,000 francs pension to which Sophie lost her claim after the Napoleonic Empire was disbanded. Following a final tiff with her mother-in-law over whether it was 'chaste' for the nine-year-old Aurore to sleep in her mother's bed, Sophie left Nohant. In fairness, she was torn between her two remaining children: Caroline was not allowed to visit. But what Sand was later to find intolerably weak, though sincere, in Sophie's behaviour — and her autobiography is rarely so unforgiving, although it is sometimes sanctimonious — was that she promised to send for Aurore later, so that she and her two daughters could set up a millinery shop in Orléans. Sand was later unsure whether Sophie told this nursery tale as much to convince herself as the little girl. But when Aurore realised that she had been duped, she concocted a plan of walking halfway across France from Berry to Paris — a scheme which she had to abandon when her grandmother suffered the first of the fortnightly cataleptic seizures which marked the rest of her days. Aurore now blamed herself for her grandmother's ill health as well as for her mother's desertion. Her actions were henceforth to be moulded by duty, rather than love. As would happen when she was caught between Chopin and her son Maurice, and as nearly happened when she was trapped between Maurice and Manceau, Sand was pinned in the middle. This pattern of conflicting forces in love was to continue throughout her life: she was more often the victim of two stronger spirits than the domineering initiator of affairs and scandals portrayed by Pritchett.

With Sophie generally absent in Paris except for increasingly brief mutual visits, Mme Dupin de Francueil's prejudices seem to have returned in their full abstract inflexibility — encouraged perhaps by Deschartres, who was also jealous of any rival to his dead master's affections. No doubt Mme Dupin de Francueil was embittered by Aurore's apparent ingratitude and coldness. Sand later recognised ruefully that '[cool] and staid though my grandmother seemed . . . she needed to be loved, and even slight attentions touched her and made her grateful'.[19] Although the girl dutifully called the old woman 'maman', she later admitted that 'I never really loved my grandmother until I could reason. Until then, I confess, I had for her a sort of veneration conjoined with an irresistible physical repulsion'.[20] When Aurore was just entering puberty, this stubborn preference for her mother finally prodded the elderly noblewoman into exposing to the young girl — to whom she had not even confided the facts of life yet — all the grimiest details of her mother's 'fallen' past. This traumatic interview threw Aurore into a paroxysm of hatred for her own femaleness, and indeed, of self-abhorrence. In later life, too, she often found her sexuality burdensome — another respect in which I believe the myths of deliberate and reckless promiscuity to be quite wrong. After her grandmother had accused her mother of being a 'lost woman', Sand wrote in her autobiography: 'I was dead to everything. I no longer knew if I loved or hated anyone; I felt no warmth for anyone, no resentment against a soul; I had a sort of huge internal wound, a searing emptiness in place of my heart. . . . I no longer loved myself. If my mother was contempt-ible, then so was the fruit of her womb'.[21]

Mme Dupin de Francueil had not succeeded in making Aurore love her any better by this tactic: only in making the girl dislike herself, and in reinforcing the considerable doubts she already had about her mother's attachment and character. Ironically, Sophie was even more concerned about propriety by now than her mother-in-law was: a few years later she chastised Aurore by letter for having science lessons in her room at Nohant with her first beau, Stéphane Ajasson de Grandsagne — an arrangement which the older Madame Dupin found perfectly acceptable. But although Aurore still admired her mother's industry, pluck, humour, and pithy Parisian expression, she was also becoming aware that Sophie was 'the most difficult woman who ever lived . . . an *enfant terrible* who was eating herself alive'.[22] The intense suffering inflicted on her had left her bitter, apathetic, migraine-ridden, and as cold in her openly emotional way as Mme Dupin de Francueil in her reserved one. 'My mother had for me, as for all the people she had loved, more passion than tenderness. Large cavities had gradually appeared in her soul, and she was unable to see them herself. Along with her precious love she had abysses of neglect and lassitude. She had suffered too much; she needed not to suffer anymore'.[23] It may be this numbed egocentricity which accounts for Sophie's callous use of her daughter after Mme de Francueil's death — which largely explains Aurore's mistimed and misjudged marriage to Casimir Dudevant, who could at least rescue her from her mother's domination. Sand's marriage — another case which contradicts the stereotype by showing her as passive in the face of more powerful personalities — will be considered in Chapter 4. For now, I need to conclude my account of her formative years with some mention of her convent days and her grandmother's death.

Aurore was sent to the fashionable Couvent des Anglaises, run by British nuns, at the age of thirteen, to learn the usual female accomplishments — Italian, English, drawing and dancing. There she was generally happy, and at least free from the vendetta over her person which had been waged until Sophie became too apathetic to care. Although Aurore had known some enjoyments at Nohant — riding, studying wild flowers, and constructing a grotto for the worship of an imaginary god, Corambé — she preferred to remain at the convent in the holidays. But when she was sixteen her grandmother's increasing weakness forced her to leave the sisters — viewed, in any case, with some suspicion by the rationalist Mme Dupin de Francueil, especially when Aurore showed symptoms of wanting to take the veil. Aurore nursed her grandmother with the diligence which she was later to demonstrate with Chopin on Majorca, sleeping only every other night. Fatigue, loneliness, and an early social awareness soon pushed her into depression, alleviated in its early stages by riding in male attire, learning estate management from Deschartres, and studying anatomy and physiology with Grandsagne, but later deepening into the first of many suicidal impulses. On a ride with Deschartres, she deliberately reined her horse off the safe track across a ford and was almost pleasantly surprised to find herself drowning. With difficulty Deschartres saved her. Sand captured her motives later in the autobiography:

And so it came about that at the age of seventeen I wilfully withdrew from the society of those about me. The laws of property and inheritance, murderous oppression, the provocation of wars; the privileges of fortune and education; the prejudices of rank, and those of moral intolerance; the childish

15

idleness of people of fashion; the brutishness of avarice; whatever remains of pagan institutions or customs in a self-styled Christian society — all these revolted me so deeply that my soul was prompted to protest against the work of the centuries. I hadn't the notion 'progress' — it wasn't popular then, and it hadn't reached me through my reading — so I saw no way out of my anguish, and the idea of working [for progress], even in my obscure and closely bounded social environment, could scarcely occur to me. Thus melancholy turned to sadness, sadness to grief, and thence, from distaste for life to a longing for death was but a step.[24]

Mme Dupin de Francueil died in December 1821, after attempting unsuccessfully to settle her granddaughter in marriage before her death — and warning Aurore on her death-bed that the girl was losing her best friend. On the night before the old woman was to be buried, Deschartres came to Aurore with a proposition whose macabre romanticism again outshines anything Sand was to invent on paper. The hole dug for Mme Dupin de Francueil's coffin was next to Maurice's grave, and the casket laid down thirteen years before had developed a loose lid. This would be the ideal opportunity for Aurore to join him in kissing Maurice's remains as a mark of respect. Encouraging her with such rallying sentiments as '[tomorrow] this ditch will be filled, and doubtless it will not be dug again till it receives your own remains', Deschartres accompanied Aurore to the open grave in the depth of the winter night. Both kissed Maurice's skull, and Sand wrote that she found this apparently ghoulish act more quieting in her grief for her grandmother than all the condolences produced by untoward well-wishers at the funeral the following day. Throughout her life Sand demonstrated a matter-of-fact nonchalance about matters which could have been expected to disgust a nineteenth-century woman of nice upbringing. Yet this acceptance of physical dissolution and decay was not founded on any comforting spirituality. Although she had experienced a direct religious awakening at the convent, she had little belief in the after-life. Kissing her father's remains seems to have helped her to accept death's finality, not to hope for a glorious resurrection. 'It filled me with an absolute despair of being able to communicate directly with the beloved dead.'[25] This impossibility, paradoxically, freed her from any hold the dead had on her.

16

Sand's difficult childhood, which ended with her grandmother's death, was passed in the time of transition from eighteenth- to nineteenth-century values. Indeed, the two Madame Dupins could be said to embody the two centuries: the older woman in her deism and anticlericalism, the younger herself a Napoleonic figure in her sudden rise and decline. The convention is that Sand herself stands for the worst excesses of the Romantic era.[26] Certainly her *life*, from her earliest girlhood, strung together one Gothic incident after another. But there is great confusion between life and *work* in many accounts of Sand — with the solidly professional generally ignored in favour of the titillating personal, the 'thinking' underemphasised in favour of the 'bosom'. Is Sand's *writing* really the heady essence of overripe Romanticism? She was largely raised in the eighteenth century, in spirit if not in time — by an *ancien régime* gentlewoman and an elderly tutor of *philosophe* bent, in a house whose decor had remained unchanged since the time of Louis XVI. Indeed, Chopin and Sand had in common their unusually out-of-step backgrounds. Chopin's father had emigrated from France to Poland before the Revolution, and what the young Frédéric learnt of the country to which he was to return would have been of the older France still embedded in his father's mind. It is now far less usual to view Chopin as a pure musical Romantic, with the term's associations of pictoralism and formlessness. Chopin's veneration for the then unpopular Bach, coupled with his dislike of Liszt, Schumann, and other overtly Romantic musicians, may indicate that he was as much classical as Romantic.[27] Could the same be true of Sand? Is the supposed High Priestess of High Romanticism really classical, too?

Notes

1. V. S. Pritchett, 'George Sand', in *The Myth Makers* (London: Chatto and Windus, 1979), p. 124. In this collection of essays on nineteen writers, Sand is both the only woman and the only author who does not merit some grander chapter heading than name alone.

2. Ellen Moers, quoted in Diane Johnson's chapter on 'Experience and Melodrama: George Sand' in her *Terrorists and Novelists* (New York: Alfred A. Knopf, 1982), p. 46. If Moers is correct, then Pritchett needs no other epithet to describe Sand, whose name is not a name but a symbol.

3. See for example, the preface to *Les Maîtres Sonneurs* (Paris: Editions Gallimard, 1979) by Marie-Claire Bancquart, who calls Chopin 'a selfish and ungrateful child' (p. 11).

4. Germaine Bree, preface to Natalie Datlof et al. (eds.), *George Sand Papers: Conference Proceedings, 1978* (Hofstra University Center for Cultural and Intercultural Studies) (New York: AMS Press, 1982).

5. Even the most competent and scholarly biographers and critics in the forefront of the Sand revival accept this maternal stereotype. See, for example, Curtis Cate, *George Sand: A Biography* (London: Hamish Hamilton, 1975) and Patricia Thomson, *George Sand and the Victorians* (London: Macmillan, 1977).

6. Cate's complete and readable biography, though probably the best available in English, is nevertheless prone to this fallacy, too.

7. George Sand, *My Life* (tr. and ed.) Dan Hofstadter (London: Victor Gollancz, 1979), p. 1.

8. Ibid., p. 4.

9. Ibid., p. 5.

10. Ibid., p. 7.

11. Ibid., p. 5.

12. Ibid., p. 7.

13. Ibid., pp. 81–3.

14. Ibid., p. 5.

15. Ibid., p. 15.

16. Ibid., p. 60.

17. Ibid., p. 34.

18. Ibid., p. 71.

19. Ibid.

20. Ibid., p. 83.

21. Ibid., p. 129.

22. Ibid., p. 68.

23. Ibid., p. 120.

24. Ibid., p. 161.

25. Ibid., p. 166.

26. As well as in Pritchett, this standard line occurs, for example, in Francis Gribbell's prejudiced, pedestrian and factually sloppy *George Sand and her Lovers* (London: Eveleigh, Nash and Grayson, 1927). This abysmal work was reissued in 1976, perhaps to take advantage of the centenary of Sand's death, but I can recommend neither the original nor the rehash.

27. This view is taken by Enid M. Standring in her article 'George Sand, Chopin and the Process of Creation', in Janis Glasgow (ed.), *George Sand: Collected Essays* (Troy, New York: Whitston Publishing Com-

pany, 1985), pp. 2–17; by Marie-Paule Rambeau in *Chopin dans la Vie et l'Oeuvre de George Sand* (Paris: Société d'Edition 'Les Belles Lettres', 1985); and by Ates Orga in *Chopin* (London: Omnibus Press, 1976), which mentions 'that classical allegiance which was one of the secrets of his art and its survival' (p. 65).

2 The French Byron?

> You will live, Madame, and you will be the Lord
> Byron of France.
> Chateaubriand to Sand, after reading *Lélia*

Although Sand has been called a 'latrine' (by Baudelaire), a 'writing cow' (by Nietzsche), and a 'thinking bosom', those who took her work more seriously than her person used more intelligent metaphors. To the Romantic grand old man René de Chateaubriand, who supposedly read all three volumes of *Lélia* at one sitting, Sand was destined to be the Lord Byron of France — not for her love life, Byronic though that has been accused of being, but for her novels. This judgement places her firmly within the Romantic tradition, and that is indeed the prevailing view. But other authors have also likened her to eighteenth-century writers, and even her early novels — written in the 1830s, when Paris was most star-struck by the luminary Victor Hugo — have been said to resemble Jane Austen's in their elegant style,[1] to be spare rather than florid. Now it may simply be true that all the French Romantics were classical in spite of themselves, as Pierre Moreau argued,[2] and it is almost certainly true that labels such as 'classical', 'Romantic', 'pre-Romantic', 'post-Romantic' and 'realist' tend either to become procrustean beds or one-size-fits-all garments. Nevertheless, it is important to consider whether what Sand wrote typifies classicism or Romanticism, if only to evaluate the platitude that she was solely and impulsively Romantic. First, however, it is equally necessary to consider what Sand read.

After her blotchy formal education, Sand was almost entirely self-taught. One of the most attractive aspects of her character is that she was never satisfied with her education — and indeed, she had a good deal to be dissatisfied with. Periodically she would embark on new voyages of learning — beginning a self-improvement course in Latin so that she could read the *Georgics* in the original before she wrote her bucolic set of novels, or teaching herself mineralogy in her old age, with her son Maurice's help. Of course these ventures could be called feminine whims by a sexist critic, or Samuel Smiles-isms by cynical twentieth-century readers. To me they evidence the energy which allowed Sand to produce over sixty novels despite her belated start, and of the professionalism which prodded her to research her facts and locales — another reason for doubting the myth that she was a naïve primitive who churned out one pot-boiler after another.

In her childhood Sand read classical epics and romantic fairy tales with equal delight, both Perrault's stories and the *Iliad*. But it was not until after leaving the convent that the solitary girl began reading with the gravity that was to typify her self-teaching. At sixteen she was reading a good deal of religious material — the lives of the saints, the Gospels, *The Imitation of Christ* — but had also been authorised to read more widely by her 'director of conscience' at the convent, the Abbé de Prémord. As he put it: 'Read the poets, they are all religious. Have no fear of the *philosophes*, they are all powerless'. With this blank cheque in her pocket, Sand read Shakespeare and Tasso, partly in the originals. *Jerusalem Delivered* was a joy to her, as to her heroine Edmée de Mauprat: a blend of epic grandeur and romantic subplots, often featuring valiant women in soldier's guise. At this time she also read Dante, Pope, Milton and Virgil. Of the 'powerless' philosophers, she read Locke, Condillac, Montesquieu, Bacon, Aristotle, Pascal, Montaigne — whose misogyny angered her — , Benjamin Franklin and Rousseau. This impressive list has sometimes been sniffed at by her biographers: Pierre Salomon doubts how much of it she understood.[3] But of course that puts Sand in a double bind: if she had not read serious works, she could be called a flibbertigibbet. That she was no bluestocking, however — another sexist gibe sometimes levelled at her, in odd pairing with the equally common 'slut' taunt — is shown by her lighter reading: *Robinson Crusoe*, *Paul et Virginie*, and *Corinne*.

While her grandmother was still alive, she and the young Aurore read Chateaubriand's *Génie du christianisme* together. Mme Dupin de Francueil was a sceptic, and Aurore had recently undergone an experience of grace in the convent, where she felt she heard a voice speaking the words in St Augustine to her: 'Tolle, lege'. One would expect Aurore to be the one converted to Chateaubriand's highly Romantic form of Christianity — and indeed, Mme Dupin de Francueil disliked the book's style. But so did Aurore dislike Chateaubriand's *René*, which she found affected and self-indulgent in its despair. What she liked in *Le Génie du christianisme* was its social message — fifteen years before she met Michel de Bourges, the radical lawyer generally said to have awakened her social conscience. Aurore was perfectly capable of rousing her own social awareness without masculine aid. Chateaubriand's outward-reaching, doctrinally tolerant variety of Christianity convinced her that holy asceticism, as typified for her by *The Imitation of Christ*, was 'sublime and stupid'. Thomas à Kempis's work was 'mortal to the soul of anyone who has not broken with human society and the duties of human life'.[4] This humanistic interpretation of Christian belief in terms of justification by acts recurs throughout Sand's writing — along with the anticlericalism she may have imbibed from her grandmother, which led her to paint the Church establishment as vicious and self-interested in the second edition of *Lélia*. Sand combined a Romantic variant of Christianity with good eighteenth-century suspicion of the First Estate.

In deference to her grandmother's rather out-of-character request, Sand did not read Voltaire until she was thirty. The eighteenth-century philosopher who most influenced her was, of course, Jean-Jacques Rousseau. As her grandmother had done, Aurore tried to apply Rousseau's tract on education, *Emile*, to the rearing of her own children — with completely disillusioning results. Rousseau's recommendation that children be spared formal learning until the age of ten was impractical, she wrote later. Her son Maurice resisted the discipline of learning to read at the earlier age of six because he had been left untutored for too long. Sand's daughter Solange learnt earlier, before she knew how heady complete liberty could be.[5] Sand also grew exasperated with Rousseau — as Mary Wollstonecraft had done — because he advocated that girls be educated only in the arts of pleasing men. In the end she jettisoned all philosophies of education: 'For a long time education was my hobby horse. I practically memorised *Emile*. But I wound up abjuring all systems and making my plans conform only to the character of the child'.[6] Even this individualistic emphasis, however, left her discouraged. She lacked Condorcet's faith in progress — most poignantly, especially where her own children were concerned. Sand's son and daughter were in many senses the bane of her later existence, and this letter, written when Solange was only four and Sand still less than thirty, previews her future disappointment with sad perspicacity.

> Maternal love instructs me to look for progress and to work for it in my children as if I believed in it, but there are times when, after the least setback, I come back to my sad conviction that man is incorrigible. . . . It was Jean-Jacques, your Jean-Jacques and mine, who said that. . . . At your age I was all Locke, all Condillac, all Montesquieu, all Machiavelli. I was on the trail of truth, which I tracked down with eagerness and thought I'd found. . . . I've grown old, and I'm tired of man, his future, my future, everything.[7]

This pessimism, which Sand identifies with Rousseau, is generally regarded as deeply Romantic. But as always, these classifications can too easily become pigeonholes. Even Rousseau had a great admiration for classical Greece, though more for Sparta than for Athens. And what Sand liked best in Rousseau was the combination of reason *and* sentiment, of the stereotypically classical invocation of rationality and the supposedly Romantic reliance on emotion. This union is a constant theme in Sand.

Among this roster of male authors, Sand also read one woman who impressed her greatly — Madame du Châtelet, translator of Newton and mistress of Voltaire. She was the first female writer whom the young Aurore found on the bookshelves at Nohant, and the girl found her mere existence encouraging. An odd family link may have heightened Aurore's interest: Louis-Claude Dupin de Francueil, her grandfather, had sold his town house in Paris to Mme du Châtelet. It is also worth noting that Mme du Châtelet's liaison with Voltaire was known in her own time but generally tolerated — perhaps because the marquise took appropriate precautions to avoid unnecessary gossip and give cause for scandal, even though she travelled widely with Voltaire. In Chapter 4 I shall return to Sand's sexuality and the thundering invectives against her expression of it. For now, I simply want to raise the possibility that the eighteenth century was more tolerant than the nineteenth — and the equal likelihood that Sand was a child of her Romantic time in holding sincerity and frankness more important virtues than the etiquette whose satisfaction apparently enabled Mme du Châtelet to maintain her good reputation.

Sand was also exposed to the writings of Mme du Genlis, who influenced her early religious beliefs, and whose appointment as *gouverneur* to the Duke of Chartres's sons had angered all the boys' male tutors into resigning. She also read Mme de Sévigné, Mme de Lafayette, and Mme de Staël, whose *Corinne* I have already mentioned. The critic Sainte-Beuve judged that Sand and Mme de Staël had similar temperaments, and a modern critic, Eve Sourian, has noted other similarities.[8] Both married to escape from their mothers, she claims; both were disappointed in marriage, and both took lovers frequently younger than themselves. (Not entirely facetiously, I suggest in Chapter 4 that what annoys many male critics — perhaps including Pritchett — is that younger, handsome men such as Musset and Chopin found Sand attractive, and this threatens the masculine privilege of picking and choosing from nubile young females, which still prevails in the lonely hearts advertisements.) More importantly, Sourian suggests, Sand and de Staël too often confused the Romantic love of the Absolute with love of a man.

> Both women were convinced that love was the essence of life, and it is essential to keep in mind that for both women, real happiness could be found only within the framework of marriage. It was out of the tensions inherent in this paradoxical dilemma as experienced in their personal lives (no happiness within marriage, no happiness outside of marriage) that each woman created her fiction.[9]

Of course this questions the received truth about Sand as an enemy of marriage — an accusation which Sand always denied, although her Russian admirers viewed her as a noble crusader against this moribund institution.

Although Sand — with the self-abasement always omitted from the myths — maintained that Mme de Staël was a much greater genius than she was, Sourian thinks there are other parallels between the writers. Their treatment by the public is the most striking similarity: both suffered somewhat for their sex. De Staël's *De l'Allemagne* was attributed to a man, August Wilhelm Schlegel, and Sand was later scolded by her original sponsor, the editor Hyacinthe de Latouche, for merely echoing her male mentors. Latouche claimed that Sand's (very) mildly feminist

Lettres à Marcie were a pastiche of the social critic Lamennais, that her *Lettres d'un Voyageur* were only readable where Musset's genius had rubbed off on them, and that the enormous success of *Indiana* no doubt reflected its slavish copying of his own ideas. Leaving aside Latouche's modest assertion about his own influence on *Indiana*, I shall merely point out that it was actually Musset who used Sand's idea and research for *Lorenzaccio* — with her selfless permission — and that Lamennais rounded on the *Lettres à Marcie* for being too wildly pro-women. It would be pleasanter for modern feminists to think that Sand was inspired to write and able to succeed because she stood on the shoulders of female titans. But even with the example of Mme de Staël and other women to accustom the public to female writers, Sand chose a male pen name.

Both Mme de Staël and Sand suffered a certain amount of censorship as well, whether or not because of their sex. Indeed, one answer to the question of why Sand's reputation sank after her death has to do with the French Senate's edict against her work. Originally, in the mid-century climate of anti-republican repression, the legislators had planned to ban all her books from public libraries. After a desperate intercession from Sainte-Beuve, two novels were exempted: the short bucolic romances *La Petite Fadette* and *La Mare au diable*. Since only these two novels out of her sixty or seventy were known to several generations of French readers, she was slighted as a writer of rural fantasies for adolescent girls. The irony, of course, is that she was relegated to this scorned obscurity because she was regarded as an immoral and dangerous writer. By no fault of his own, Sainte-Beuve did Sand no favours. Had she been totally proscribed, she might be remembered as the communist who was too subversive to be allowed a free voice.

Sand was herself too shy to keep a salon — another characteristic which the brazen hussy myth overlooks. But she was a frequent attender at the one opened by her friend Marie d'Agoult, Liszt's mistress, though she seems to have been more adept at the traditional female role of listening to great men than at speaking herself. She had a pleasantly low but largely inaudible voice, and a wit which she often described with self-disgust as bovine. However, both she and Mme de Staël — whose connection with the world of the salon is plainer — may have benefitted from the eighteenth-century salon tradition. There were once some forty of these in Paris, and they constituted a female-run counterpart to the male-dominated cafés.[10] The inadequacies of a girl's education, such as the one Sand received, were somewhat offset in France by later cultural opportunities — not true in nineteenth-century England, although American women enjoyed more or less equal education and self-improvement through lectures and organised readings during the 1830s and 1840s.

Another French feminine tradition which has been seen as a possible influence on Sand's work is the *roman intime*. Sand's library included nearly 150 novels, collections of letters, or memoirs by female writers, and biographies of women. The *roman intime* was thought by Sainte-Beuve to be a product of this seventeenth- and eighteenth-century background of female autobiography, biography, and fiction. Sand's own novels are not characterised as *romans intimes* by Sainte-Beuve, but there are nevertheless similarities in her early fiction.[11] The genre generally comprises love stories with a small cast of characters, a great deal of emotion, and offsetting realistic touches from everyday life. Often the form is a series of letters — a borrowing, perhaps, from *La Nouvelle Heloïse* of Rousseau — or a journal found after the death of one of the lovers. The ending is normally tragic — as is broadly true of *Indiana* and *Lélia*, though not of most later Sand novels — and the beauty of nature a frequent theme. None of these traits is particularly and exclusively Sandian, or even unusual, except for the softly feminist slant of the *romans intimes*. The authors of these novels were often critical of arranged marriages for gain, and generally more sympathetic to their female characters than to their male personnages. However, they were hardly revolutionary in their feminism; indeed, this sort of novel could deaden women to their lot, rather than call them to arms. In this there may be a parallel with modern pulp romance, although some feminist literary theory regards romances as actually liberating in that they express a female need for sexual satisfaction. But Sand's portraits are less stereotyped than those of the *roman intime*, and her comments more mordant and Stendhalian. Despite some similarities of plot, there is a major difference in tone between Sand's novels and popular fiction of her time for women.

At best, their women lament their lot in life, but they never question the value system of the prevailing society. Sand's women are generally not passive victims, but agents who act to control or improve their life. This is the reason why Sand's novels were seen as subversive, while the *romans intimes* were calmly accepted by the aristocratic society in which they were written.[12]

By the start of her writing career in the early 1830s, Sand's forced marches in reading had carried her over the German border, beyond the Channel, and into the Celtic hinterlands. She was familiar with the famous forgery *Ossian*, fond of *Tristram Shandy*'s free association, and greatly influenced by the fantastical tales of E.T.A. Hoffmann, first read at the convent but particularly important to her between 1834 and 1837. The German Romantics were highly influential in France from the time of Goethe's *Sorrows of Young Werther*. But so unusually intense was Sand's involvement in Hoffmann that she intended to think herself into one of his novels, to write a conclusion for the life of his character Kreisler from *Kater Murr* — the centre of Schumann's 1838 set of fantasies dedicated to Chopin, *Kreisleriana*. Although this became one of the rare Sandian ideas which was never turned into words and perenially needed cash, Hoffmann remained a major influence on Sand's work. Fantasy occurs even in her late works, such as *Laura*, a little-known but compelling mental journey through a science-fictionalised volcanic hell-hole at the back of the North Pole. Earlier works, such as *Lélia* and *Mauprat*, appear at first to owe even more to Hoffmann, in their Gothic situations, and *Consuelo*, her 1,200-page *magnum opus* of the early 1840s, shares with Hoffmann the use of music as a novel's subject. There are common themes in the two authors: the superiority of the artist to social convention and common mores, the faith in simplicity and distaste for hypocrisy, and the power of imagination.[13]

Hoffmann would seem an arch-Romantic, and his power over Sand might indicate that the conventional interpretation of her as a pure Romantic is quite correct. But Hoffmann also argued that the imagination can work only with the help of the conscious intellect, that reason and inspiration must co-exist. This idea of union between the imaginative and rational faculties influenced

Sand's views on writing and creativity. Her journal entry for 5 June 1837, during the period when she was most immersed in his work, depicts him as more rational than Romantic. Hoffmann *used* fantasy in a conscious, cerebral manner, she thought:

> No human spirit has ever entered more boldly and cleverly into the dream-world, none has ever trod the fantasies of poetic induction with more logic, common sense, and reason. No one has ever surrendered less to his imagination. . . . That he preserved his *sang-froid* in the face of his visions is what gives the greatest charm to his fantastic compositions. . . . Deep down, his feelings never arise from feverish delirium, but may be examined in reason's daylight.[14]

Despite his choice of Gothic locales, Hoffmann demanded realism in characterisation: 'The art of the poet has to consist of having characters appear not only perfectly rounded, poetically true, but also taken from ordinary life, so that one says to himself, "See, that's the neighbour I talk to every day! That's the student who goes to his lecture every day and sighs dreadfully before his cousin's windows"'.[15] Similarly, Sand wrote: 'One wants to find a human being in the depths of every story and every fact', and: 'The novel needs true situations and real characters'.[16] Although she was fond of embodying abstract sentiments in characters, particularly in *Lélia*, she was also very down-to-earth. Sand was one of the first novelists to use lower-class characters — well before Zola — and unsophisticated peasants at that, rural bumpkins rather than city slickers. Her characters are also less black-and-white than Hoffmann's. There is only one real exception to Sand's inability to portray any character as totally evil — the consistently unsympathetic central character in *L'Uscoque*, the novel which bears the Byronic imprint most clearly. It is time to conclude this discussion of the influences Sand encountered through her reading by returning to the question of whether she was indeed a French Byron by conscious imitation.

Byron may be the counter-argument to my proposition that it tends to be women writers whose lives are fastened on with repulsed fascination and hypocritical voyeurism, while their works are overlooked. Sand herself was more impressed by Byron's romantic persona than by his poems in her youth. The difference is that Byron more or less deliberately sought to create his image. By contrast Sand used her male persona to *hide* her sexuality in her novels, and only allowed herself frank and free expression in her personal correspondence. Unlike Sand's, Byron's image was generally viewed as a glamorous one, thanks, too, to the operation of the double standard then as now. Many of the writers of Sand's generation shared this veneration for what Byron represented, as much as for his writing. On their Venice excursion, Musset told Sand that he could hardly consider himself an artist and a man if he did not live up to Lord Byron's amorous standards in this most Byronic of cities. (That he did — and caught venereal disease — tends to be omitted from the accounts which condemn Sand's breaking up with him.) Even if Byron did consciously cultivate a 'media personality', however, confusion between his life and his characters caused the man himself some annoyance. 'I should be glad to have rendered my personages more perfect and amiable, if possible', he wrote, 'inasmuch as I have been sometimes criticised, and considered no less responsible for their deeds and qualities than if all had been personal.'[17]

But Sand thought that Byron probably deserved this treatment by the reader, since he let himself melt into his hero in 'The Corsair'. By implication, she viewed over-close identification of an author with his creation as a lack of professionalism — another reason for doubting the autobiographical line about her novels. Although she acknowledged her copious borrowings from the enormously popular Byron poem — which sold 10,000 copies its first day out — she explicitly drew the reader's attention to 'the distance between the title "corsair" which Byron gives his hero and that of "uscoque" which ours bears'. She went on:

It is roughly the distinction between . . . fantasy and reality. . . . The poet fancied that he would turn his protagonist into a great man at the end; and he could hardly do otherwise because . . . bit by bit he had forgotten his character . . . and could only see himself in Conrad. But we intend to confine ourselves to the historically accurate and the empirically lifelike, and so we shall portray a far less noble pirate.[18]

Again, Sand claims to be more a Realist than a Romantic.

Byron could write marvellously funny lines, such as this verse from the poem 'Growing Old':

What are the hopes of man? Old Egypt's King
Cheops erected the first Pyramid
And largest, thinking it was just the thing
To keep his memory whole, and mummy hid;
But somebody or other rummaging,
Burglariously broke his coffin's lid;
Let not a monument give you or me hopes,
Since not a pinch of dust remains of Cheops.

Judging from this poem, Musset seems to have taken Byron far more seriously than Byron took himself. But there are fewer comic elements in 'The Corsair' than in *L'Uscoque*, a light work which Sand published with the high-serious *Spiridion* to sweeten the pill of the latter's philosophic gravity for her publisher Buloz. Sand's humour is an obvious aspect of her personality which has nevertheless been ignored by both the 'nanny' and the 'whore' stereotypes. After the failure of her affair with Musset, when she was deep in gloom but still quipping, she wrote in her journal that Liszt seemed taken with her. But while every other woman fell paralytic at the fair-hair-haloed virtuoso's feet, she said that she could no more fancy Liszt than spinach. When Chopin developed cold feet before his first concert after a break of several years — a performance into which she prodded him so that he would not be forgotten in Paris, as he was coming to be after a brilliant start — she proposed drily that he could always sell out the house but douse the candles and play on a mute piano. She acceded to her publisher's request for a back-pedalling preface to reassure readers that *Indiana* was not subversive, but warned him that the introduction suited the novel 'about as well as lace cuffs on a cow'. A letter of February 1840 remarks of her eleven-year-old daughter: 'Solange is well, eats like a horse, swears like a teamster, and lies like a dentist'.[19] In the matter of her humour, too, the dead-serious Romantic is a less accurate portrait of Sand than the eighteenth-century wit; or perhaps the stereotype is misleading for many of the Romantics, including Byron.

Although Sand pre-empted Byronic plots and shared Byron's admiration for exotic settings, Chateaubriand probably exaggerated the extent of her resemblance to Byron. However, he was quite accurate if he meant to predict that she would enjoy a similar sweep of success. I˙ mentioned in discussing Hoffmann that Sand wanted to create mainly realistic characters — although she had some tendency to turn her people into symbols, particularly in the early novels. Fantastic settings such as Byron's and Hoffmann's were to act as foils for believable personnages; but Sand rated Byron's characters as less psychologically accurate than her own. In addition she used a greater number of characters in *L'Uscoque* and gave a far more sympathetic treatment to the women, balancing Byron's none-too-covert admiration for the macho corsair. I doubt that Sand's feminism went very far, but critics of her time often slated her for giving women too much attention in her novels. This outrage puts me in mind of a social science experiment in which teachers were told to give boys and girls equal time in class. Many protested that they did this as a matter of course, but the researchers found that boys normally occupied about twice as much of the instructors' time as girls. When the teachers managed to bring this proportion down to somewhere around the 60–40 mark, with the balance still tilted in the boys' favour, the boys complained that the girls were now receiving all the attention. Similarly, Sand replied to criticisms of *L'Uscoque*, *Lélia*, and other novels which feature prominent women but by no means exclusively female casts in a lengthy answer to reviewers 'who still take the author to task for systematically placing women at the front of his compositions, and giving them the best lines. . . . The author has never had any system concerning one sex's priority over another. He has always believed in perfect natural equality'.[20] As Carol Mozet puts it, then: '*L'Uscoque* is the woman's counterpart to what Byron had done on a masculine level'.[21]

What Sand read gave her a self-educated grounding in both classical and Romantic authors, and her feelings about the standard Romantic works of the day were reserved — partly because she was a woman, in her dissatisfaction with Rousseau's and Byron's treatment of 'the second sex'. Was what Sand wrote similarly resistant to easy pigeonholing as High Romantic? Although her earliest prose was the usual juvenile purple, its subjects were classical and its style epic. The personal god she invented and eulogised in her early chants, Corambé, was a composite of qualities from Homer, the Gospels, and Tasso. This androgynous being wore female clothing and possessed the wisdom of Athene, the chastity of Artemis, and the artistic powers of the Muses; but it also enjoyed Apollo's musicality and Christ's charity. Balancing these classical allusions, however, is a school-girl poem with a Romantic subject and diction.

> Prête-moi la lueur de ton pâle flambeau,
> Lune, mélancolique amante du tombeau.
> Combien j'aime le soir et ta clarté douteuse
> Favorable au penchant de mon âme rêveuse.[22]

When she began writing seriously, Sand was as disillusioned with the excesses of the Hugo generation as with the stultifying *bon ton* of the eighteenth century. She was faithful to an earlier Romantic spirit, perhaps, when she wrote in her autobiography:

I suppose that it is to the disgust which this perpetual hectoring [to be elegant, from her grandmother] gave me for all affectation that I owe my faithfulness to my natural thoughts and feelings. I hate the false, the stilted, the mannered, and I spot them even when cleverly lacquered with false simplicity. I see no beauty or goodness except in what is true and simple.[23]

She thought the post-1830 generation just as prone to artifice as her grandmother's 'old countess' friends. It is important to bear in mind just how exaggerated were the plots and characters in vogue at the time Sand began writing; beside them, she looks very moderate indeed. Charles Lassailly had written a novel in which the valiant hero slays a host of rivals, then finishes off his mistress by tickling her feet until she passes away in hysterical giggles. The apparently even more misogynous Xavier Forneret penned a romance in which the protagonist kills himself by swallowing his lady friend's eyeball. The justly forgotten Count Auguste de Kératry — who had the gall to advise the young George Sand that she should make children, not novels — authored another monstrosity, *Les Derniers de Beaumanoir*, in which a priest rapes a dead woman he is meant to bury. (Sand retorted that the 62-year-old novelist should 'keep his motto for himself' and his 25-year-old wife.)

Sand connected the excess triggered by Hugo's *Hernani* with the political disquiet of the early 1830s. She came to know the political climate better than she might have wished when the morgue opposite her Paris attic flat began spilling blood out its doors onto the pavement after the demonstrations of June 1832.

To her friend Laure Decerfz she wrote:

> If we had ten years of political calm, literature would doubtless
> enter a flourishing age, for after the reaction of the false against
> the true, there would follow that of the true against the false,
> that which every reader craves, which every writer dreams
> about, but which cannot flourish in a century of furious clam-
> our and on an earth full of hospitals.[24]

Failing this social deliverance for the arts, she shrugged, she too
would have to produce freaks. 'Everyone wants to dabble in the
new and ends up dabbling in the ridiculous. Balzac is on the crest
of a wave for having depicted a soldier's love for a tigress and an
artist's love for a castrato. What is all this, good heavens! Monsters are in fashion. Let us produce monsters.'[25]

How good was Sand at running this kind of High Romantic
sideshow? An early *Edinburgh Review* article suggests that even in
this first period she failed to achieve her rather half-hearted goal
of producing 'monsters'. After fulminating against the worst
literary debauches of the 1830 generation in France, the author
specifically exempts the novels of 'Monsieur Sand, which are
written in a calmer, truer, better spirit than those with which we
have been occupied'.[26] This article was somewhat atypical in that
its author had not yet tumbled to Sand's sex. A reviewer who had
done painted Sand herself as 'a monster, a Byronic woman' on
the strength of her third novel, *Lélia*.[27] But what shocks the writer
is not the content of Sand's novel, but her sex. Lélia's philosophy
had surfaced before in French literature, but what is freakish
about the book is that 'no woman has heretofore declared herself
as a disciple'. Again there is confusion between Sand's authorial
persona and the content of her work. Now if any one of Sand's
early works *does* epitomise Romanticism, it ought to be *Lélia*
(1833), besprinkled with convents, mountains and palaces,
chock-full of floating pleasure barges and Rousseauesque lakes,
and written in a high tone which the modern reader can only
digest with considerable suspension of disbelief. But even *Lélia* —
despite the female Werther at its centre — is far from being a
purely Romantic work. And Sand's later novels are even less
so.

Sand certainly employs romantic settings in *Lélia*, and telling
exotic touches, of which the deftest is perhaps the barge of

musicians who float past a pavilion for midnight assignations playing entirely on copper instruments. There are ebony, glass, wood, platinum, silver, and gold flutes, but never has there been a copper one, as far as I know. This evocative image may be an example of why Matthew Arnold, Elizabeth Barrett Browning, Charlotte Brontë and George Eliot, among others, thought Sand the greatest French stylist of her time, and some reckoned her the greatest writer of prose in any language. There is no end of stunning description in the novel. Lélia's first sight of the convent of the Camaldules reveals it as more fit for odalisques than nuns.

Cette cour frappa Lélia de surprise et d'admiration: d'abord ce fut une longue galerie, dont la voûte de marbre blanc était soutenue par des colonnes corinthiennes d'un marbre rose veiné de bleu, separées l'une de l'autre par un vase de malachite où l'aloès dressait ses grandes arêtes épineuses; et puis d'immenses cours . . . de riches parterres bigarés des plus belles fleurs. La rosée dont toutes ces plantes étaient fraîchement inondées semblait les revêtir encore d'une gaze d'argent. Au centre des ornements symmétriques que ces parterres dessinaient sur le sol, des fontaines, jaillissant dans des bassins de jaspe, élevaient leurs jets transparents dans l'air bleu du matin, et le premier rayon du soleil qui commencait à dépasser le sommet de l'édifice, tombant sur cette pluie fine et bondissante, couronnait chaque jet d'une aigrette de diamants. De superbes faisans de Chine, qui se dérangeaient à peine sous les pieds de Lélia, promenaient parmi les fleurs leurs panaches de filigrane et leurs flancs de velours. Le paon étalait sur les gazons sa robe de pierreries, et le canard musque, au poitrail d'émeraude, poursuivait, dans les bassins, les mouches d'or qui traçaient sur la surface de l'eau des cercles insaissables.[28]

The Romantic sense of place also remains pronounced throughout all of Sand's work, but rarely are the actual locales she chooses as romantic as those of *Lélia*. Over one-third of her novels are set in Italy or have Italian characters, and this is often cited as proof of High Romanticism. But in the *Lettres d'un Voyageur* a eulogy to Venice as the incarnation of the Romantic dream is cut short rather snidely by an actual Venetian, who retorts that Italy embodies the *classical* ideal and that the fantastic and Romantic belong to the still-barbarous Germans. The novels set in Sand's native Berry make good use of local colour, in ceremonies such as the peasant wedding which occupies the last third of *La Mare au diable* (1845). But there is nothing more inherently 'Romantic' about this than in the 'Realist' Flaubert's detailed description of the wedding meats and Norman ceremonies in *Madame Bovary*. Ruined castles, charcoal-burners' isolated huts, and ghost-ridden swamps bespatter the Berry novels, true; but conversely, Sand deliberately plays down the full Gothicism of the most romantic image of all, the monastery at Valldemosa where she lived with Chopin. *Un Hiver à Majorque* (*A Winter in Majorca*) (1842) may begin by evoking Byron, Rousseau and Chateaubriand, but it also journeys from the Alps in the first paragraph's invocation to the lovers' return voyage from their 'romantic idyll', on a steamer full of pigs, in a February drizzle, with Chopin coughing phlegm and blood.

Indeed, I would maintain that *A Winter in Majorca* should be read as a voyage of disillusionment with the Romantic ideal. Chopin himself is never even referred to as the acme of romantic lovers, only as 'the sick man' — and that with an infrequency which frustrates readers who hope to find all the self-aggrandising detail of a great love story. The ignorance and greed Sand attributes to the Spanish peasants may be exaggerated to us — particularly as their backwardness rests largely in their benighted conviction that tuberculosis is actually contagious. But Sand's disillusionment with the simple life hardly supports the claim that she swallowed Romantic ideology on this score. In this description of the monastery Sand's *style* may still be Romantic, and as enthralling a siren call as ever:

Jamais je n'ai entendu le vent promener des voix lamentables et pousser des hurlements désespérés, comme dans ces galeries creuses et sonores. Le bruit des torrents, la course précipitée des nuages, la grande clameur monotone de la mer interrompue par le sifflement de l'orage, et les plaintes des oiseaux de mer qui passaient tout éffarés et tout déroutés dans les rafales; puis de grands brouillards qui tombaient tout à coup comme un linceul, et qui, pénétrant dans les cloîtres par les arcades brisées, nous rendaient invisibles et faisaient paraître la petite lampe que nous portions pour nous diriger, comme un esprit follet errant sous les galeries . . . tout cela faisait de cette Chartreuse le séjour le plus romantique de la terre.[29]

But now the Romanticism is conscious, a straw man set up to be knocked down. The message of *A Winter in Majorca* is deeply *anti*-Romantic: Sand rejects self-absorption and the cult of solitude, which had characterised Romanticism at least since Rousseau's *Confessions*. With an outwardness which I shall characterise in Chapter 3 as typifying what Carol Gilligan identifies as the female ethic, Sand mounts a head-on assault against what Gilligan might see as the masculine belief that any man — or woman — can be an island. The island of Majorca becomes a symbol for Sand's Donne-like conviction that we must all be a part of the continent.

> Puerile as it might seem, the sincerely felt moral of this story is that man is not made to live with trees, stones, the open sky, the azure sea, flowers and mountains, but with those made in his likeness. In the stormy days of youth, one imagines that solitude is the great refuge from all troubles, the best remedy for wounds; that is a serious error, and experience of life teaches us that if one cannot live in peace with other men, there can be no poetic wonderment or artistic enjoyments that can span the abyss which opens out deep in the soul. I always dreamt of living in the wild, and any frank dreamer like myself will admit to the same fantasy. But believe me, my brethren, we have too much feeling in our hearts to do without each other, and our best course is mutual support; for we are all children of one breast, teasing each other, squabbling, but still unable to separate.[30]

The Romantic *culte du moi* is as absent from Sand's novels — particularly *Valvèdre*, which explicitly rejects it — as from her generally self-disparaging letters. Even another work of her supposedly arch-Romantic early period, *Lettres d'un Voyageur* (1835–7), can at most be seen as tentative in its Romanticism. Sand glorifies childhood in the best Wordsworthian manner, trots out lakes and mountains as symbols, laments her suicidal 'spleen', and confesses to *ennui* in the prescribed Romantic manner. As always her style is full-blown, as in this description of the floating meadows of Venice in April:

> Les pierres même reverdissent; les grands marécages infects, que fuyaient nos gondoles, il y a deux mois, sont des prairies aquatiques couvertes de cressons, d'algue, de joncs, de glaïeuls,

et de mille sortes de mousses marines d'où s'exhale un parfum tout particulier, cher à ceux qui aiment la mer, et où nichent des milliers de goélands, de plongeons et de canepetières. De grands pétrels rasent incessament ces prés flottants. . . .[31]

And it is also true that in the tenth letter Sand appears to state the conventional Romantic claim that the only foreign clime we can fully explore is our own psyche. 'A journey, for me, is only a course of psychology and physiology of which I am the *subject*, put to all the tests and experiences that tempt me.'[32]

But it is a *fictionalised* self that Sand presents in this book: an invisible woman hidden behind the letters' puzzling use of a male narrator. I shall return to this androgyny and secrecy in Sand's presentation of herself in Chapter 4 on her sexuality. For now, I shall simply set in opposition to the previous quotation this self-effacing one from Sand's preface to the *Lettres*:

No one knows, on reading these letters, whether it is a man, an old person, or a child giving his impressions. Why should the reader care about how old I am or the way I walk? . . . What he is entitled to demand of the reader, who opens his soul to pity or his heart to examination, is to let him see this heart's movements *personified*. So if sometimes I speak as a runaway schoolboy, or an old gout-ridden uncle, or a hotheaded young soldier, all I have done is to portray my spirit in the disguise it takes on from one moment to the next. . . . Who isn't both senile and infantile in their emotions? Have I written anything more than everybody's story? No, I have done nothing else, and I wish to do nothing more. I had no desire to make my readers search out the secret of my bizarre or remarkable individuality in the guise of this mysterious traveller.[33]

It is interesting to note that all the costumes in which Sand travels are masculine. For this reason alone, she could hardly be said to peddle her own personality in her novels — or to ignore male characters.

What is often said to be most Romantic about Sand's work is the primacy she supposedly accords to heart over head, and especially to love. Now to begin with, this rests on a rather simple-minded definition of Romanticism as purely emotional and classicism as only cerebral. But if we accept this black-and-white distinction for argument's sake, is it really applicable to

Sand? Or is it a stereotyped classification of women's writing as emotional? The argument that Sand is all feeling but little brain often cites as proof her famous reply to Flaubert's shyness at revealing his feelings in his novels. 'Put nothing of what you feel into what you write?' she exclaims. 'I don't see how you can put in anything else.'[34] It is sometimes said that Sand thought what distinguishes man from apes is the ability to love, not the power of reason. Now this is partly true, and the claim is not always used to put Sand down. Curtis Cate, for example, advances the idea that her universal doctrine was love, of the Teresa of Avila rather than the courtesan variety. Sand was consistently dismissive of nineteenth-century scientific rationalism — not so much of the eighteenth-century deist sort, but of the later positivistic variant which held science to be value-free, metaphysics imprecise and useless, and material progress humanity's highest goal. *Lélia* includes some wry speculations on the danger that the heroine's beloved mountain retreats will sooner or later resound to the factory hooter. And in *La Mare au diable* Sand justifies her elevation of 'ignorant' peasants to quasi-heroism, against Aristotelian and classical rules, on the grounds that the most backward peasant is superior to the arid modern man of science.

> However incomplete and eternally juvenile he may be, he is still more noble than men in whom knowledge and science have smothered sentiment. Don't think yourselves above him, you who are endowed with an inalienable power over him, because this terrifying error of yours proves that your mind has killed off your heart and that you are the most partial and blind of men![35]

If there has to be a choice between heart and head, Sand opts for heart. But the more important theme in her work, particularly in later life, is the unnaturalness of any such split. In this sense, Sand rejects the entire Romantic–classical contest as meaningless. The best illustration of Sand's synthesis of reason and emotion is *Laura* (1863), rarely read but called a masterpiece by Francine Mallet in her 1976 biography of Sand. This odd tale, influenced by Hoffmann, concerns a dream voyage undertaken by Alexis, an unworldly student of mineralogy, after his rejection by his cousin Laura in favour of the prosaic engineer Walter. Alexis believes — and the whole novel makes us believe — that he has been abducted to the polar regions by Laura's self-styled father, Nasias, who returns from commercial chicanery in the Orient to search for the riches of a 'land of crystal' behind the North Pole. There the world which may be seen inside a cracked-open lump of quartz is written full-scale, in petrified but unchanging Platonic beauty. After fantastic adventures combined with hideous deprivation of the senses in tunnels of ice whose crossing takes months of the polar night, Alexis and Nasias arrive at the volcanic land beyond the pole and cross the lake of glass beneath whose fragile crust is to be found the crystal land. Just before they are to make the hazardous descent, Walter appears to enter the scene and wake Alexis from the dream. But Walter himself — the spirit of scientific cynicism — then vanishes, and the malevolent charlatan Nasias appears again in his place.

Nasias ventures down the volcano and is engulfed in a crystal abyss. The next voice is that of Laura, who symbolises the genuine reality that can break the enchantment worked by evil fantasy, in the person of Nasias. In a reversal of the usual damsel-in-distress gender roles, Laura promises to save Alexis from his own imagination, even though his Romantic hallucinations have been proven stronger than Walter's cerebral form of reality by Nasias's displacement of Walter. But she maintains one condition: Alexis must not idealise her, as he had done when he saw her in his dreams, impeccable in her beauty.

> There you always saw me as tall, beautiful, fairylike. But now, in real life, you see me as I am: short, simple, ignorant, rather middle-class, and tone-deaf to boot. Will that be enough to make you happy, and shall I break my engagement to Walter? He may not feel much love for me, but he accepts me for what I am, and doesn't insist on finding an inferior person to protect in his wife. . . . You try to turn me into an angel of light, a pure spirit, but I'm only a nice little person without any pretensions. Think about it: I should be very miserable if I always had to shuttle back and forth from the empyrean to the kitchen. Isn't there some limit between the two extremes?[36]

The phrase 'and tone-deaf to boot' is another nice piece of wry humour from Sand.

Laura, mildly feminist in its abhorrence of pedestals, and concerned with the illusory nature of illusion, is only Romantic on the surface. It uses fantasy and revives Sand's earlier interest in the tales of Hoffmann. But its theme is both anti-Romantic and anti-classical — or more properly, it denies that the conflict between reason and fantasy is important or insoluble. Similarly, *Lucrézia Floriani* (1846) — another acid test like *Lélia*, a novel which ought to be Romantic if anything in Sand is — is at best superficially Romantic. What Sand is trying to do in this work — taken to depict Sand's relationship with Chopin by literal-minded critics, even though both Sand and Chopin maintained it was nothing personal — is to consciously *tone down* Romanticism. By puncturing the characters' most highfalutin speeches with wry asides and spiking the plot with mines laid by the narrator, it has been argued, Sand hoped to create a new genre situated between classical restraint and Romantic surfeit. As Laura urged Alexis towards moderation, a middle way between fantasy and worka-day reality, so in *Lucrézia* Sand deliberately eschewed high feel-ing, and purposely introduced a deflating irony into a High Romantic setting.

> Loving as I do strong emotions in fiction, I have however walked the extreme other way, not out of reasons of taste, but because of my conscience, because I saw the other way was being neglected and abandoned by the fashion. I have made every effort . . . to retain the literature of my time in a practical road between the peaceful lake and the wild torrent. . . . *Lucrézia Floriani*, this book composed entirely of analysis and meditation, is . . . nothing but a protest against the excessive use of old-fashioned techniques, those veritable surprise ma-chines, whose qualities and defects seemed, in my view, to disconcert the undiscerning public.[37]

Thus halfway through the novel the narrator undercuts the reader's suspense over whether Prince Karol will leave Lucrézia by clucking: 'You know perfectly well that my novel isn't far enough along for me to send the hero packing'. The ending, when it does come, is delivered with a mocking ill grace. After sighing that the reader really ought to get over this infantile compulsion to know all the facts, Sand throws up her hands: 'If you absol-utely insist. . . . They loved for a long time and lived very unhap-pily together. Their love was a battle to the death, to see which would absorb the other'.[38] This highly un-romantic conclusion has only one qualifier, even more sarcastic: after Lucrézia dies, Sand refuses to allow the reader the luxury of wallowing in Karol's grief. 'Did he die of it, or did he go mad? It would be too easy to finish him off like that, I'm not saying another word. . . . I have enough to do, killing off the main character.'[39]

It seems that Chateaubriand erred in both his judgements. Sand has not 'lived', but has been largely unread for most of this century, at least in Anglo-Saxon countries; nor is she really the French Byron. My aim in this chapter has not been to show that Sand was unique among the writers of her generation in satirising High Romanticism. Balzac, in particular, often does the same. But Sand is usually taken by her admirers (such as Chateaubriand) and by her detractors to be the essence of excessive, emotional Romanticism, and this is often used to explain why she is no longer read — to solve the paradox about her decline and fall which began this book. This is a simplistic stereotype, as it turns out — perhaps based on the sexist association of women with emotional hysterics. In her style, locales, and some of her plots Sand may appear Romantic, but her Romanticism is skin-deep. Her preference for moderation between high-flown and pedestrian style, reason and emotion, realism and fantasy is actually a classical trait: Pierre Moreau argues that it is *the* classical trait, the advocacy of the middle way in all things. Both 'art for art's sake' and 'art for the people's sake' are Romantic extremes, for example. The classical position — that art should both please and instruct — actually made classicism more democratic than Romanticism, in its insistence that art should be at least potentially popular. Again, both extreme realism and extreme imaginativeness are Romantic, according to this argument. Classicism erased cattle and donkeys from nativity scenes in the cleansing conviction that reality required a little imaginative redemption. Romanticism, by contrast, glories in the eccentric. It is the frequent lack of Cousin Bettes and Old Goriots in Sand which sometimes makes modern readers find her boring. Her peasant heroes and heroines do show a distressing tendency towards consistent nobility of spirit. But critics who dislike this smoothing of reality should not simultaneously accuse Sand of being sloppily Romantic. Her fault in this is not a surfeit of Byronism, but a little too much house-proud classicism. When Lélia calls herself 'a soul from ancient times', we should not doubt her because she is a woman, and therefore barred from antique virtues. Sand was impressed with stoicism; perhaps she, too, really was, as it were, more an antique Roman than a dame.

The classical formula was that the virtuous man should 'surmount his own will, in order to legislate for himself maxims centred firmly on right reason'.[40] Feminists of the same century, such as Mary Wollstonecraft, sought to show that women were fully capable of reasonable action, if properly educated, and therefore potentially equal to men. Sand refused to rely exclusively on rationality as a guide to behaviour. Lacking this belief that reason marked full humanity, and that men and women were equal in reason, could she believe them equal at all? It is time to turn to Sand's feminism, to assess the common statement that both in her life and her writings, she was 'the first modern liberated woman'.[41]

Notes

1. Cate, *George Sand*, p. xiii.
2. Pierre Moreau, *Le Classicisme des romantiques* (Paris: Librairie Plon, 1932).
3. Pierre Salomon, *George Sand* (Paris: Hatier-Boivin, 1953), p. 14.
4. Sand, quoted in Cate, *George Sand*, p. 75.
5. Sand, letter to Emile Poultre, 3 September 1832, *Correspondance* (ed.) Georges Lubin (Paris: Garnier Frères, 1966), vol. II, pp. 155–8. Hereafter cited as *Corr.* All translations from the Lubin edition of the letters are mine.
6. Ibid., p. 156.
7. Ibid., p. 156. Lubin identifies this pessimistic interpretation of human nature as a common theme throughout Rousseau, but as especially prevalent in his *Discours sur l'origine et les fondements de l'inégalité parmi les hommes*. It seems odd to me, however, that Machiavelli should be seen by Sand as an optimist about human nature. Perhaps, in her anticlericalism, she might view the final chapter of *The Prince* as a call to progress — the 'Exhortation to Liberate Italy from the Barbarians', Machiavelli's ironic term for the Pope and his minions.
8. Eve Sourian, 'Mme. de Staël and George Sand', in Datlof et al. (eds.), *George Sand Papers: 1978*, pp. 122–9.
9. Ibid., p. 124.

10. For a further description of eighteenth-century salons and cafés, see Esther Ehrman, *Mme du Châtelet* (Leamington Spa: Berg Publishers, 1986), pp. 10–12.

11. See Lucy McCallum Schwartz, 'George Sand et *le roman intime*: Tradition and Innovation in Women's Literature', in Glasgow (ed.), *Essays*, pp. 220–6.

12. Ibid., p. 225.

13. See Elaine Boney, 'The Influence of E.T.A. Hoffmann on George Sand', in Glasgow (ed.), *Essays*, pp. 42–52.

14. Sand, *Journal Intime* (Paris: Calmann-Lévy, 1926), pp. 51–3. All translations from the *Intimate Journal* are mine.

15. Hoffmann, *Der Serapionsbruder*, quoted in Boney, 'Influence of E.T.A. Hoffmann', p. 45, translation hers.

16. Sand, *Oeuvres autobiographiques* (ed.) Georges Lubin (Paris: Garnier Frères, 1970), vol. II, p. 161, quoted in Boney, 'Influence of E.T.A. Hoffmann' p. 45, translation hers.

17. Byron, *Poetic Works* (Oxford: Oxford University Press, 1945), p. 277, quoted by Carol Mozet in 'Lord Byron and George Sand: "Le Corsaire", "Lara", et *L'Uscoque*', in Glasgow (ed.), *Essays*, p. 54.

18. Sand, *L'Uscoque*, quoted in Mozet, 'Lord Byron and George Sand', p. 57, translation mine.

19. *Corr.* IV, 622, quoted in Cate, *George Sand*, p. 776, footnote.

20. Sand, preface to 1861 coll. edn, p. i, quoted in Mozet, 'Lord Byron and George Sand', p. 61, translation mine. Sand always uses the masculine of herself in her novels and essays — an anomaly I discuss in Chapter 4.

21. Mozet, 'Lord Byron and George Sand', p. 64, translation mine.

22. 'Lend me your torch's pallid gloom,/ Moon, melancholy lover of the tomb./ How I love the dark and your dubious light/ That sits so well with my soul's dreamy plight.'

23. Sand, *My Life*, p. 106.

24. *Corr.*, II, 112–13, quoted in Cate, *George Sand*, p. 205.

25. Letter to Jules Boucoiran, *Corr.*, I, pp. 825–6, quoted in Cate, *George Sand*, p. 179. The two Balzac stories were 'Une Passion dans le désert' and 'Sarrasine'.

26. *Edinburgh Review*, July 1833, quoted in Patricia Thomson, *George Sand and the Victorians: Her Influence and Reputation in 19th-Century England* (London: Macmillan, 1977), p. 14.

27. *Atheneum*, September 1833, quoted in Thomson, *George Sand and the Victorians*, p. 12.

28. Sand, *Lélia*, 1839 edn (Paris: Calmann-Lévy), 2 vols, I, p. 277. 'This courtyard struck Lelia dumb with surprise and wonderment: first there was a long gallery, whose white marble vault was supported by Corinthian columns of a pink marble veined with blue, separated from each other by malachite vases in which aloe plants raised up their huge thorny spines; and then enormous courts . . . sumptuous flower-beds mottled with the finest flowers. The dew which had just swept over these plants seemed to bedeck them with silver

gauze. In the middle of the symmetrical decorations which these beds formed on the ground, fountains surging in jasper basins lifted their transparent arcs into the blue morning air, and the first ray of the sun which was just beginning to clear the top of the building fell on this fine, throbbing rain and crowned each spray with a crest of diamonds. Handsome Chinese pheasants, hardly bothering to move away from Lélia's feet, strolled among the flowers displaying their filigree plumes and their velvet flanks. The peacock spread out his jeweled robe on the lawn, and the Muscovy duck with its emerald breast chased little golden flies in the basins, marked with the insects' spreading circles on the water's surface.'

29. Sand, *Un Hiver à Majorque* (Paris: Livre de Poche, 1984), pp. 137–8. 'I never heard the wind give off such a lamenting voice or such desperate shrieks as in those hollow, echoing galleries. The waterfalls' roar, the hasty passing of the clouds, the huge monotonous grumbling of the sea, broken only by the storm's hiss, and the cries of the sea-birds who flew by, completely disoriented in the squalls; then great fogs that fell suddenly, like a shroud, and that made their way into the cloisters through the broken archways, made us invisible and gave the little lamp we carried as a guide the look of a will o' the wisp flitting through the galleries. . . . All this made the Charterhouse the most romantic stopping-place on earth.'

30. Ibid., pp. 204–5, translation mine.

31. Sand, *Lettres d'un voyageur* (Paris: Garnier-Flammarion, 1971), p. 72. 'Even the rocks grew green: the broad disease-ridden marshes that our gondolas fled two months ago are now watery prairies covered with cress, algae, reeds, sword-flags, and a thousand kinds of marine mosses which give off a strange odour, dear to those who love the sea, and in which thousands of gulls, loons and bustards have made their nests. Large petrels skim continually over these floating meadows . . . '

32. Ibid., quoted in preface by Henri Bonnet, p. 20, translation mine.

33. Ibid., pp. 38–9, translation mine, italics original.

34. *Corr.*, XX, p. 217, 7 December 1866, translation mine.

35. Sand, *La Mare au diable* (Paris: Livre de Poche, 1973), p. 18, translation mine.

36. Sand, *Laura: Voyage dans le cristal* (Paris: Librairie A.G. Nizet, 1977), p. 152, translation mine.

37. Sand, preface to 1857 edition of *Lucrézia Floriani* (Paris: Michel Lévy Frères), quoted by Alex Szogyi (translation his) in 'High Analytical Romanticism: The Narrative Voice in George Sand's *Lucrézia Floriani*', in Natalie Datlof et al. (eds.), *The George Sand Papers: Conference Proceedings, 1976* (New York: AMS Press, 1980), p. 192.

38. Ibid., pp. 196–7.

39. Ibid., p. 197.

40. Foret, *L'honnête homme* (1749), quoted in Moreau, *Le Classicisme des romantiques*, p. 20, translation mine.

41. The title of Noel Gerson's 1973 biography of Sand.

3 The First Liberated Woman?
Feminism in Sand

> They [women] are mistreated, reproached for the stupidity imposed on them, scorned as ignorant, their wisdom mocked. In love they are treated like courtesans, in conjugal friendship like servants. They are not loved, they are used, they are exploited.
>
> Sand, *Intimate Journal*, 25 June 1837

> Too proud of their recently acquired education, certain women have shown signs of personal ambition. . . . The smug daydreams of modern philosophies have encouraged them, and these women have given sad proof of the powerlessness of their reasoning. . . . In vain do they gather into clubs, in vain do they engage in polemics, if the expression of their discontent proves that they are incapable of properly managing their affairs and of governing their affections.
>
> Sand, *Third Letter to Marcie*, March 1837

Sand wrote this apparently contradictory pair of quotations in the same year; the second mocking women's rationality and wisdom in exactly the manner the first one detests. Although 1837 was difficult for Sand, with her mother's death, the public humiliation of her court case for separation and the dissolution of her affair with the radical lawyer Michel de Bourges, there is no reason to think that Sand's confusion over feminism was confined to one bad year. At many other times in her life she gave voice to the crusading fellow-feeling for women which characterises the first excerpt. In 1838, for example, she wrote to Chopin's friend Albert Grzymala that she always took the part of wronged or violated women, and that she was rightfully thought to be the advocate of her sex.[1] In *La Comtesse de Rudolstadt* (1843–4) she battled against the double standard: 'Virtue, imposed on women, you will never be more than a name until men take up their half of the task'.[2] Adultery in women was punishable by solitary confinement in prison, she noted bitterly, but congratulated in men. In the 1842 preface to *Indiana* — in which the publisher had requested that she restrain herself — she stuck to her guns about 'the injustice and barbarity of the laws which govern women's existence in marriage, the family, and society'.[3] Is it any wonder that in her lifetime Sand was reputed an opponent of marriage and of what modern feminists have called 'the anti-social family'?[4]

But Sand always denied that she was a partisan of 'free love': she once answered a critic of her supposedly earth-shattering views with the untranslatable aphorism that she was indeed an enemy of *maris* but not of *mariage*,[5] of husbands but not of marriage. Nor was she by any means a 'man-hater': *husbands* (as the law defined their duties and powers) were her enemy, but *men* she often venerated above women. The second quotation in the chapter heading is woman-hating, not man-hating. Without any apparent awareness that she was condemning herself out of her own mouth, she wrote: 'We must ask the ladies' pardon if, judging from current examples, we plump for the intellectual superiority of men. . . . The greatest women in science and litera- ture — with no exceptions — have never been and are not at present anything more than second-rate men'.[6] She could be very patronising towards her female acquaintances. To the spinster Marie de Rozières she sent this rather hypocritical explanation of why she had decided her daughter Solange should not come on a visit:

In the old days you were not a coquette, but now, my love, your eyes have become terribly voluptuous. . . . All the men have noticed it, though of course if you do not mind, why should I?. . . All the same, I have decided that Solange had better not see quite so much of you — until this little nervous trouble of yours is over, and you have taken either a lover or a husband *ad libitum*.[7]

Rejecting the chivalry of a minority of male Académie Française members who proposed her candidature to that female-exclud- ing body in 1863, Sand wrote that women were not worthy of the honour: 'The majority of women in this generation fall into one of two camps: the religious and the worldly. The non- entities don't count and never have done. . . . Everything of spark and fire in women tends to be joined to something excessive, either religious intolerance or infatuation with luxury and flirtatiousness'.[8] This lack of identification with her own sex is borne out by her admission that:

> With very few exceptions, I do not long endure the company of women. Not that I feel them inferior to me in intelligence: I consume so few of them in the habitual commerce of my life that everyone has more of them around than I. But women, generally speaking, are nervous, anxious beings who, my resistance notwithstanding, communicate their eternal disquiet to me apropos of everything. I begin by listening to them with regret, then I let myself be caught up in a natural interest for what they are saying, only to perceive that there was really nothing to get worked up about in their puerile agitations. . . . I thus like men better than women, and I say so without malice.[9]

A 'lack of malice' like this would be interpreted as rabid malevolence in a man, and rightly so. At best, Sand emerges from this second set of quotations as a woman of the self-made sort who has little sympathy for females who have *not* succeeded against the odds of poor education for girls, rigid marriage laws for wives, and a male-centred literary world. At the strangest, she appears to have no inkling that she *is* a woman at all. In the next chapter I suggest that Sand's pen name may indeed have created some confusion in her mind over her own gender identity. By this I do not mean to suggest that she had a 'masculinity complex', as has been argued.[10] I doubt there is any such thing: it is not neurotic but perfectly rational to want to be a man in a world of male privilege. For the moment, however, I want to consider whether Sand was a feminist in her *works*, not whether she was liberated in her *life* — Chapter 4's concern. To do this I shall need to separate her works of non-fiction — her twenty volumes of political pamphlets and literary essays, her twelve-volume autobiography — from her sixty or seventy novels. I argue that the latter are more obviously feminist than the former, but that both are rooted in Sand's unchanging and not necessarily feminist conviction that women and men possess separate identities and roles. In the essays, this dogma of 'separate but equal' often degenerates into 'certainly separate, and not so equal as all that'. In the novels, paradoxically, women are often presented as different and *superior*.

Sand never argued that biology was destiny in the simple-minded reductionist way, but she did offer a conventional basis for distinguishing between male and female 'natures'. Very roughly speaking, she equated man with head and woman with heart. This is a very loose categorisation, and Sand always denied that there was any real opposition between heart and head — as in *Laura*. She viewed the division between 'the masculine' and 'the feminine' as created by Providence and intractable to change, but she did *not* equate it with her society's standard gender roles. In this passage she sounds quite modern in her refusal to take her contemporaries' prejudices about male and female *roles* as timeless truths about male and female *natures*:

> *There is only one sex.* Men and women are exactly the same, so much so that I can make no sense of the welter of distinctions and subtle arguments raised on this score by society. I watched my son and daughter develop. My son was like me, and therefore a woman — more so than my daughter, who was a failed man.[11]

But the modern feminism this resembles is an Eighties variant, not a Sixties version. Sand was sure that women were more sensitive than men, due largely to their mothering role. She doubted that better education would entirely dissolve women's tendency to set more store — perhaps too much — by the affairs of the heart. Therefore she would not have accepted Wollstonecraft's argument that male and female minds would reason identically if male and female education were identical. Nevertheless, she certainly proposed a far less limited schooling for women than was current in her own youth. Her novel *Gabriel* (1840) concerns a princess who is given a boy's education by mistake, and turns out a perfectly capable 'prince'. She complained that women were scorned if they remained in squalid ignorance and mocked as 'femmes savantes' if they tried to acquire any learning. And she castigated Rousseau for his unimaginativeness towards girls' education — just as Wollstonecraft had done. Particularly degrading, she argued, was Rousseau's scornful granting of *carte blanche* for women to continue their irrational faith in organised religion. The educated man, he asserted, would have no need of such shibboleths.

In these aspects Sand thought women just as rational as men — or to be more precise, she reckoned that women were as capable of arriving at truth and justice through sensibility as men were through reason. Since the division between heart and head was artificial to her, it would be surprising to find her making it airtight in her theory of gender. It was the union of the two she valued, and she urged society to honour both natures equally. When she browbeat feminists — as in the second quotation at the start of the chapter — it was usually for neglecting their crucial feminine sensibilities. As a Christian humanist she hoped that pacifistic 'female' values would come to carry more weight, and she often speculated that women were the better devotees of St Paul, despite his aversion to them. Society's claim to value Christian love and to esteem women as guardians of a higher ethic was hypocritical, in her mind. Although women were placed on pedestals — recall this argument in *Laura* — and motherhood officially venerated, in fact most women were their husband's slaves, and most mothers glorified wet-nurses.

However, Sand made frequent tactical retreats from these reasonably advanced positions. Not all the male writers and critics of her day were as comparatively enlightened as Jules Sandeau, Alfred de Vigny, and Prosper Mérimée, the triumvirate plotting Sand's election to the Académie Française. Sand wrote three *Letters to Marcie* — advice to a putative young woman on female roles and male rights — for the Abbé Félicité Robert de Lamennais, an egalitarian priest, editor of *Le Monde*. Lamennais's anarchistic *Paroles d'un croyant* has been called 'a lyrical version of the *Communist Manifesto*'.[12] Sand met him through Liszt, at a dinner party also attended by the poet Heinrich Heine. (The glamour of Sand's life lies in her treasure trove of famous and intellectually challenging acquaintances, I think, not in the roster of her often unsatisfactory lovers.) Although she was favourably struck by Lamennais's socialism and his defiance of the papal establishment, and though she came to view him as her spiritual advisor, she was to find that his progressivism stopped short of equal rights for women. This troubled Sand, particularly when Lamennais later brought out a misogynous pamphlet, *Discussions pratiques et pensées diverses sur la religion et la philosophie*. Sand confided her doubts to her journal:

I would attribute this inferiority [of women, which Lamennais had laid down as a natural law], which is a real fact, in general, to the inferiority which society would like to consecrate in perpetuity as a principle, in order to prey on women's weakness, ignorance, and vanity, in a word, on all the failings produced by education. This is not to say that the evil is part of our nature, but rather . . . that it arises from the way in which your sex has governed us.[13]

Although Sand was little bolder than this in the *Letters to Marcie* — condemning contemporary feminists and apostrophising an angelic ideal of motherhood — she was still not reactionary enough for Lamennais, who excised the most progressive bits of the *Letters*, on divorce.

It is only fair to Lamennais to point out that Sand's consciousness was only raised on issues which had affected her personally, such as divorce and separation. Elsewhere her delineation of male and female roles is quite conventional, as is the stereotype at the root of them: that women are creatures of emotion, whether noble or trivial, and that men are blessed with all the brainpower. Her elaborate division of the human psyche into these two components often sounds very platitudinous when applied to particulars. For example, in her autobiography she speculates that men's honour centres on business affairs and women's on marriage. It is unsurprising that most women, even the ostensibly pious, cheat at cards: there is no question of honour in it for them. Men can cheat on their wives with no risk to their reputation; indeed, they may gain honour as casanovas. Both men and women would be better advised, she thinks, to practice a little more honesty in their respective spheres; but she does not challenge the basis of the spheres themselves. In another excerpt she describes how she learned to ride by hanging onto her unschooled filly's mane. But rather than making a feminist point about women's equal courage, she shrugs off her achievement by putting it down to 'woman's nervous will'.[14]

At worst, Sand allows female superiority in understanding, tact and commitment to become an apologia for female submission. In a letter written during the early days of her marriage, she enthuses about the joys of obeying her husband:

What an unquenchable source, obeying the one you love. Each privation is a new pleasure. One sacrifices to God and to conjugal love at the same time, doing one's duty and ensuring one's happiness. The only question remaining is whether the man or the woman ought to remould themselves so, and since all power is on the side of the beard, and men aren't capable of such an attachment, we are perforce the ones who must bend in obedience.[15]

Sand was only eighteen when she wrote this protesting-too-much letter, and she could have been expected to echo pietistic homilies — particularly if she was trying to convince herself as much as her friend. Later in life she was more hard-headed — and much more assertively feminist — about marriage. When her foster-daughter's suitor , the artist Théodore Rousseau, insisted that his intended had to have a clean bill of virginity and a promissory note for her dowry, Sand cut him down: 'We are *women*, and for this reason we are not weak, and we do not reply as we could do to men who believe themselves strong. You have doubts about the frankness of the mother and the purity of the daughter. . . . They will not humble themselves further'.[16] Sand *could* see sisterhood as powerful, but most often in her own particular strong-minded case. In the abstract she continued to have mixed and often hackneyed views of women. While writing her first novel, she described its heroine Indiana as

a typical woman, weak as well as strong, at once weary of the air she breathes and capable of shouldering the heavens, timid in everyday life and yet bold in days of battle. . . . Such, I believe, is woman in general, an incredible mixture of weakness and energy, greatness and pettiness, a being forever composed of two opposed natures, now sublime, now wretched, skilled in deceiving, yet easily deceived.[17]

Most to the point, Sand always regarded woman as the Other, to use de Beauvoir's formulation — as the negative end of a scale whose middle and positive pole are both occupied by 'man'. 'Woman' was an entity which could be compassed in such generalisations as that about Indiana, a paradox which needed explanation. No one would make such speculations about 'man' in general; that would be read as 'the human species' — which is certainly not what Sand meant.

But in her novels Sand does not distance herself from her women in this way; perhaps that explains why her female figures are rounded, compelling personnages — so much so that male

critics complained. The women in Sand make Madame Bovary
— usually regarded as a sympathetic and tragic figure — appear
stupid and tiresome. One of the most robust women in Sand's
novels is Lélia, and it was on her account that the novel was
variously slammed as 'stinking of mud and prostitution' and
admired as liberating for women. Lélia is such a powerful character that she has had to be contained by sexual boxing-in, then as
now. The modern convention is that *Lélia* is a book about a frigid
woman. Now of course this is a bit of post-Freudian anachronism,
although Sand seems to have had a premonition that her heroine
would be slurred like this — perhaps because her own professionalism was so often taken for granted and her sexual peccadilloes magnified. Men call women frigid when they are frightened
of their rightful demands, she says. 'Now a self-respecting woman
cannot experience pleasure without love; that is why she will
never find either one in the arms of most men. As for the male sex,
it is far more difficult for them to respond to our noble instincts
and to nourish our generous desires than to accuse us of coldness.'[18]
   It is not too extreme to say that Lélia has been slandered as
frigid for the same reason that Sand herself has been insulted:
because she terrifies men — and perhaps more conventional
women — with her capability. Lélia is a superior logician and
supremely skilled orator who defeats her would-be seducer Sténio
in a debate on nineteenth-century permissive society, as embodied in Don Juan — whom Sand abominates, interestingly enough.
Lélia considers taking the sexual initiative — rather than settling
for the more decorous occupation of being pursued — and defines
the male sex in relation to the female, not the orthodox reverse.
She refuses to pray, preferring to rely 'on a columnar Self', as
Emily Dickinson put it. More broadly, she always remains sym-
bolically standing, never bends the knee, never lowers the eye.
She is allowed some scathing lines about masculine vanity, as
when, describing her previous lover, she remarks to her sister:
'He reproached me with the sin of being less childish than he was,
he who enjoyed treating me like a child. And then at last he
turned his anger against my race, because he was furious at
feeling smaller than me, and cursed my entire sex so as to have
the right to curse me'.[19] She and her sister, the courtesan Pulchérie,
tell each other hen-party-raunchy stories about men, bemoaning
premature ejaculation and satirising male hypocrisy towards prosti-

52

tutes. Lélia accuses her demanding admirer, the poet Sténio, of wanting her only for her admittedly superb body — primarily so that he can boast about it afterwards to his mates. She pronounces men and women equal before God, and challenges the religious and social ethic which restricts women's lives: 'Is woman's role necessarily bounded by the transports of love?'[20] She regrets the limited opportunities in her own life which have turned her into a female Werther, a useless dreamer, when she was cut out for crusades and cannon-fire.

> If I were a man, I should have gloried in combat, the smell of blood, the strictures of danger; perhaps my youth would have been blessed by the dream of ruling through my intelligence, of dominating other men through my powerful words. As a woman, I had only one noble destiny on earth, that is, loving. So I loved *valiantly*. . . . [21]

Men, she scolds Sténio, have no excuse for Romantic *ennui*:

> You have a goal in life; if I were a man, I should have one too, and however perilous it was, I should advance towards it calmly. But you fail to remember that I am a woman and that my career is limited by uncrossable bounds. I was supposed to content myself with that which is the pride and joy of other women [conventional romantic love]; I could have done so, were I not cursed with a serious mind and a yearning for affections which I have not found.[22]

This last quotation raises another ground for doubting that Lélia is frigid: she wants more love, not less. In particular, she demands a more genuine and high-minded love than the shallow society of her time offers her in the person of the self-centred, pestering Sténio. Sand did exemplify the Romantic in so far as she longed for this ideal of love. By it she measured the mean-minded Napoleonic Code on women's property rights, the double standard, and the legalised prostitution which she identified as contemporary marriage. (The law appears to have reflected and ensured the truth of Napoleon's famous remark: 'Nature has made women our slaves'.) This search for the ideal was to occupy the female sensibility, in Sand's thought, and this is what Lélia teaches her novices when she becomes abbess of the convent of

53

the Camaldules.

> Lélia knew how to escort them towards her ideas without
> shocking their prejudices or putting their piety on guard. She
> found some aid in Christian ethics for teaching her most
> heartfelt beliefs: purity of thought, elevation of sentiment,
> disdain for the little vanities that destroy women, aspiration
> towards an infinite love of a sort they knew and understood but
> poorly.[23]

It is almost as inappropriate to charge Lélia with frigidity as it
would be the Virgin Mary. Indeed, Sand makes the parallel
herself: Lélia's raiment is always spotless, 'without stain or fold,
with something fantastical about it, as if she were an immaterial
existence, a serenity out of reach of the laws of the possible'.[24]
Sténio is afraid to look into the face of a marble Virgin he passes
because he knows he will see Lélia's features there. He invokes
her support for the ex-convict Trenmor in these Marian terms:
'You voluntarily became his friend, his consolation, his good
angel; you went to him, you said, "Come unto me, you who are
accursed, I shall return to you the heaven you have lost! Come to
me, who am without spot or blame, I shall make clean your sins
with my hands!"'[25] When Lélia becomes a nun, the Church gives
her the name of Annunziata — either she unto whom the Annun-
ciation is made, or even, perhaps, a female Messiah. In a pairing
of two characters which is a frequent device in Sand,[26] she is
doubled with her long-lost sister Pulchérie, who represents Mary
Magdalen. This is ironically limited if Sand really is a feminist,
since, as Marina Warner points out in her excellent *Alone of All
Her Sex*, the Virgin and the Magdalen have compassed and
restricted the gamut of female roles for two millenia.[27]

But Lélia is not translated heavenwards at the end of the novel.
In both editions of the book, she ends badly — in the first,
strangled by a monk with a rosary in the worst traditions of 1830s
'frenetic literature', in the second hounded by the Church establishment, vilified with sexual rumours from which her chastity
cannot protect her, and left to die of pneumonia in a remote and
cold convent to which she is exiled. Cold is a recurring theme in
the book, and if Lélia cannot be accused of frigidity, Sand does
portray her will as glacial. (Interestingly, Sand called Lélia
impotent, not frigid, in her journal, but then rebutted that charge

too.) Lélia is ultimately incomplete because she represents the masculine, reasoning side of human nature too narrowly. By presenting a chilly, over-cerebral nature in a *woman*, Sand highlights its inadequacy in a *man* when it is unmatched by 'feminine' sensibility. She keeps to her Platonic theme, drawn from the myth in *The Symposium* (*The Banquet*) which relates that all human creatures were originally hermaphroditic until the two sexes were split, and that the halves have been searching for each other since then. This necessary union of the rational and the spiritual may appear trite and platitudinous in Sand's essays and autobiography, but the device Sand uses in the novel *Lélia* gives it sudden force. Lélia's lack of fellow-feeling with humankind evokes the young Raskolnikov, but it is even more terrifying in her — because it knocks our expectations of women into a cocked hat — than in *Crime and Punishment*, where it terminates in a blood-soaked axe.

Sand denied that *Lélia* was any sort of manifesto for women. In 1834, the year after its publication, she wrote to a friend:

> *Lélia* is not a book: it is a scream of pain, or a bad dream, or a splenetic digression full of both truth and paradox, injustice and warning. It has everything except calm. And without calm there can be no acceptable conclusion. One should no more ask Lélia to enunciate a moral code than require witty remarks of a dying man. If a few women of spirit thought they should try to be either exactly like or perfectly unlike her, they were mistaken. You understood her better . . . because you saw in her nothing but a woman to be pitied.[28]

Sand refused to accept that Lélia *was* a superior character, despite her tragic stature. This appears to contradict my earlier point: that female nature is depicted as different from men's nature in the novels, but superior, whereas it is usually piddling and inferior in her non-fiction. But of course Lélia is not the embodiment of *ideal* female nature: this is exactly the tragedy of the novel. She does enjoy the higher masculine attributes and lacks male violence — which kills her in the first edition. If she could wed to the better male qualities a greater sense of feminine compassion, then she would be a whole creature.

Sand often made this common philosophical error in discussing women's questions: confusing the descriptive with the normative, mixing up how women are with how they ought to be. It is a failing to which modern feminists are not immune when they idealise female nature, it has been argued. Nevertheless, if Lélia as she *is* cannot be termed a morally enlightened being, she is certainly the book's fulcrum. She and Pulchérie have all the best lines, some very outrageous indeed. One critic of the time warned readers to lock the book away from their daughters, and another thought it so licentious and cynical that it had certainly put paid to the rumours that George Sand was really a woman. But of course *Lélia* could only have been written by a woman: it puts the 'female question' centre stage. As Pulchérie remarks to Lélia: 'You have had a problematic existence, being a woman'.[29]

Tillie Olsen claims that George Sand was the only nineteenth-century woman writer who viewed her sex's position as problematic.[30] I am not sure this is true, particularly not of American writers: Harriet Beecher Stowe tends more and more to be read as a feminist as well as an abolitionist; Margaret Fuller wrote a bestseller on 'the woman question'. Elizabeth Barrett Browning also presented the creative woman's dilemma in *Aurora Leigh*. But whether or not what Sand *said* was feminist — and I doubt that it was — the fact of her *concern* for women is feminist. Lélia is the incarnation of this interest, the Daughter rather than the Son of Man, a female Job, Hamlet or Werther. It was the casting of a woman in these plum roles which was revolutionary — and which has had to be minimised by scaling Lélia down to the comfortably low level of a sexually maladjusted female. The same tactic has often been used against Sand herself. Indeed, Sand is often equated with Lélia even by her sympathetic biographers, such as André Maurois, who actually calls his account of Sand's life *Lélia*. But Sand denied that she was Lélia any more than she was one of the book's other characters. Some critics have reproached her for letting her own personality dominate Pulchérie's — and Pulchérie is presented as Lélia's opposite. Sand wrote in her autobiography that she had never appeared on her own stage in female guise — though her acknowledgement that if she was anyone, it was the monk Spiridion, did not exclude the possibility of a bit of literary transvestism. Why not, when Flaubert used to say that he was Madame Bovary? But in general the tendency to read Sand's novels as purely autobiographical leads to ridiculous contradictions and denigrates her professionalism.

La Petite Fadette, though written fifteen years after *Lélia* and demonstrating a master craftsman's unity of themes and delicacy of expression, is also stereotypically read as autobiographical. (Never mind that this makes Sand a tall Italian countess who was also a diminutive French provincial ragamuffin.) Fadette, the tomboy who mends her hoydenish ways and gets her man, is thought by proponents of the 'masculinity complex' view to represent Sand, the betrousered cigar-smoking virago. According to this thesis, Sand's myriad maladjustments — ranging in contradictory plenitude from frigidity to nymphomania — stemmed from her grandmother's harrowing revelations about her mother's scarlet past.

'Masculinity complex' adherents see in *Fadette* the tale of a girl awakened to proper feminine mental health by the love of a good man. If this were the course of the story, it would be hard to regard Sand's message as feminist, even though a female character stars in the title. But the novel is much more to do with the reform of a *man* — indeed, of two men — by a woman. This theme of woman as moral educator is very common in Sand. *Mauprat* (1837) concerns a Heathcliff-like wolf boy who is taught to control his temper and libido by his cousin, herself equally prone to the family fiery spirits but saved by feminine sensibility — as he is, too, in the end, by hers. *Laura* likewise uses a woman to symbolise the just middle way between extremes and to save the narrator from the excesses of his own fantasies. In *La Mare au diable* the chirpy peasant girl Marie inspires the virtuous but bovine Germain with her stoicism and cheer when they are lost together at night in an evil marsh. Unlike Dickens's women, Sandian heroines are not legless angels. They have faults, and it is these minor wrinkles which Fadette has to iron out of her character. But they are not sufficient vices to brand her as neurotic, or to threaten the superiority of female nature, as she typifies it.

La Petite Fadette actually begins with the heroine well off-stage: a year before her birth, when the twin boys Sylvinet and Landry are born to a wealthy peasant family, the Barbeaus. The identical twins develop a profound affinity which the family encourages despite the midwife's warning that treating two twins as one person can only bring grief. (The theme of the wise woman recurs in this novel: Fadette herself is a sort of good witch, having been tutored in taming will o' the wisps and discerning medicinal virtues in plants by her grandmother.) When the farm can no longer support both sons, one has to go 'away' — to work on the neighbouring farm, which Sand correctly portrays as an immense distance to the country mind. The twin left behind, Sylvinet, develops an insatiable jealousy of his brother, whose life no longer revolves solely around him. Described by his mother as having 'the heart of a girl, tender and gentle', Sylvinet is also prey to unreasonable possessiveness, usually depicted as feminine. (Recall the cartoons in *Mad* magazine: a man stands with his arm tightly clasped around a woman, and in the background a spectator whispers admiringly: 'Isn't he protective?' In the next frame a woman assumes the same posture with a man, and the onlooker clucks: 'Isn't she possessive?') Here once again Sand reverses the stereotypes of masculine and feminine. Landry tries to reason with his brother but makes no headway, although he warns Sylvinet that '[love,] through being too great, can sometimes become a sickness'.[31]

Though stoical and devoted, Landry has his own failings: he is superstitious, rather condescending, materialistic, and ungrateful to Fadette, who overturns the usual knightly myth by saving the boys twice — once when Sylvinet goes missing and she locates him for Landry, once when Landry has been deluded off the safe track through a ford at night by a will o' the wisp. (Fadette's name is a diminutive for fairy or will o' the wisp, and it is clear that she possesses considerable powers, though Sand leaves open the question of whether their 'otherworldliness' is only a figment of peasant imagination.) When Fadette encounters Landry at the dangerous ford, she pulls him through the dark night and the water that he cannot swim with a force she looks too slight to possess. Later, Sand remarks that 'she taught him reason';[32] she is learned in country lore and has a scientific enquiring mind.

Thus most of the story concerns the men's awakening: they are the sleeping beauties, and Fadette the prince. Her own transformation from an ugly duckling she effects without any help from Landry other than a bit of frank advice, and all in the space of a week. All she has to do is reform her appearance, which is ill-kempt because she has no mother to teach her basic cleanliness and no money to buy herself girlish gewgaws. She could obtain work as a servant if she were concerned to buy such fripperies.

But this she refuses to do because she will not leave her lame younger brother, who has been likewise deprived of his mother. Although the villagers judge the daughter by the sins of the mother, who has run off to follow the soldiers, in fact she has the best of feminine virtues under her tomboy appearance. It is maternal concern for her brother which has kept her in tatters. She washes and irons a little more frequently, puts a stop to the swearing at which she was proficient, and learns to curb her over-hasty wit; this is the extent of her 'taming'. Another local girl, Madelon — contrasted with Fadette in a typical Sandian doubling, as indeed is the device of twins — conceals a selfish and perfidious nature under her belle's looks. Even in her gaucherie Fadette is the superior character: coquetterie is selfish, and unconcern over a proper feminine appearance at least has the merit of humility.

By the end of the novel, Fadette, initially better endowed with spirit than with charity, has expanded in kindliness without shrinking in wit — much the same progression that Elizabeth Bennett undergoes in *Pride and Prejudice*. She is still devilish, playing pranks on her mercenary prospective father-in-law. Old Barbeau forbids Landry to see Fadette because he does not know that her grandmother has left her wealthy — until she brings him the coffers to tally up, with the demure fib that she is not adept at counting over 100. Actually her head for business is better than anyone's, and her 'heart and blood' stronger than Landry's. Most tellingly, at the climax of the book she alone can cure Sylvinet of his jealousy, which has provoked a psychosomatic fever after Sylvinet learns that Fadette and Landry are to be married. Although she is skilled in herbal cures, she uses no drugs with him: only touching, in both a literal and a symbolic sense. This casting out of devils, this touching Sylvinet deep down in his heart, has been called a proto-Freudian analysis session.[33] It is treated with the psychological acuity and sympathy for both characters which mark most of Sand's novels. The female nature is certainly superior here — an ideal female nature now, though a believable one. But Sylvinet is made credible and likeable in both his weakness and his willingness to be cured of it.

He felt that she was right, deep down, and that she was not over-strict except on one point: she seemed to think that he had never fought his sickness and that he was perfectly aware of his own egotism; whereas he had been selfish without knowing or wishing it. That pained and shamed him a good deal, and he wished he could give her a better opinion of his good conscience. As for her, she knew perfectly well that she was exaggerating, and she did it deliberately, to plague his spirit and soften him up for kindness and consolation. She forced herself to talk harshly to him and to seem angry with him, whilst in her heart she felt so much pity and sympathy for him that she was quite sick with her own deception, and she was more exhausted than he when she left.[34]

The two boys grow up through achieving separateness from each other; Fadette, through establishing her connection with ordinary femaleness by renouncing her superficial oddities of dress and manner. (Sand herself was a self-sacrificing, good-listening, 'womanly woman', despite her aberrant costume in her youth — though as I have said, the autobiographical parallels with Fadette should not be exaggerated.) In *La Petite Fadette* male and female sentimental educations are separate but only unequal in that the men have much more work to do. This distinction fits Sand's emphasis on different natures, which will remain even after education and maturation. It also suits a modern feminist analysis — that of Carol Gilligan in her enormously influential *In a Different Voice*. Gilligan represents a strain of modern women's studies which argues that men and women are indeed separate but equal — a chimera to earlier feminists. Could Sand be a feminist of the Gilligan sort?

Carol Gilligan suggests that psychological scales of maturity have measured only one judgement of what it is to be an adult human being — a male version which sets most store by independence and self-assertion. This is not what being grown up means to most women, if only — Sand would agree — because 90 per cent of them are mothers. Gilligan found that even eleven-year-old boys and girls had differing opinions, by sex, of how much they owed to themselves and how much to others. One boy had a precise mathematical quantification of his rights as against his duties: he owed three-quarters to himself, he announced, and one-quarter to the rest of humankind. Girls typically saw moral conundrums as less black-and-white because they sympathised with all parties. Because they perceived more complexity in ethical problems, their opinions of the right thing to do looked less well-formed and definite — whereas arguably they were actually more sophisticated than the boys. Adult women were found to regard selfishness as the prime sin — the opposite of the supposed virtue of self-assertion. Developmental psychology, Gilligan argues, has put women in a double bind. They cannot be both mature women, locked in relationships, and mature human beings, meant to be independent first and foremost.

Now, Gilligan never says that the female ethic is superior, and she also avoids pronouncing on whether these differences are innate or learned: 'No claims are made about the origins of the differences described or their distribution in a wider population, across cultures, or through time. Clearly, these differences arise in a social context where factors of social status and power combine with reproductive biology to shape the experience of males and females and the relations between the sexes'.[35] This slightly bet-hedging formulation is elaborated in terms of the unquestionably greater amount of mothering which women do in our culture. Both boys and girls are mostly brought up by women. Boys have to separate from their mothers in order to grow up, whereas girls have to fathom their connection with this other female more fully. This is the parallel with *La Petite Fadette* — although the link is not exact, since Sylvinet's closest bond is with his male twin, not his mother.

It is still a common charge against feminists that they only want to be second-rate imitations of men. (Let us leave aside the contradictory accusation which often proceeds from the same critics — that feminists hate men and everything they stand for.) Gilligan's impact has been the empirical proof she suggests for a separate female ethic: women need not imitate masculine behaviour in order to liberate themselves. If it is ridiculous for misogynists to assert both that feminists hate men and that they want to ape them, it is nevertheless true that many women want male rights but not male self-absorption, deadness to emotion, and fear of threats to precious self-esteem. 'Separate but equal' is therefore an attractive formulation. Many recent feminists have certainly found it so: Brownmiller, Daly, Dworkin and Rich have posited a separate — though generally *irrational* and *inferior* — male nature, rooted in the urge to rape or the insecurity of being marginal to reproduction. Adrienne Rich (*Of Woman Born*) seems particularly close to Sand in her celebration of motherhood, which Sixties feminists were often thought to scorn. Even though patriarchal society has used mothers and motherhood for its own ends, Rich asserts, maternity is a bubbling spring of compensations and virtues for women. Women are more in touch with reality than men, too, because of the physicality of motherhood. Thus Rich takes the old equation of 'women' with 'body' and turns it around, to women's benefit.

In Sand's formulation of the 'separate but equal' argument, the variations between male and female natures should not count towards moral worth or human rights.

> I am very far from thinking that woman is inferior to man. She is his equal in the sight of God, and nothing in the designs of Providence destines her to slavery. But she is not like man, and her nature and temperament assign her to another role, no less fine, no less noble, and of which I do not think she can complain unless mentally depraved.[36]

However, she also remarked: 'Should this difference, essential to the harmony of life and the highest charms of love, necessarily constitute grounds for moral inferiority?'[37] Now logically this is a perfectly valid distinction, even a rather fine one. But it never works in practice. The United States Supreme Court overruled exactly this formula in the 1954 *Brown v. Board of Education* ruling because supposedly 'separate but equal' schools for Blacks were certainly segregated, but nothing like as good as those for Whites. Sand's separatist code plays into the hands of opponents of feminism who want to restrict women to the home, on the time-sanctified and hypocritical grounds that family duties are just as important as paid work. In real terms, the 'naturalness' of women's love for their families has been used to deny married women the right to benefit paid to single women and married men who care for elderly relatives, to bar them from pension schemes, and, of course, to make 'wages for housework' sound like a utopian demand. Unwaged work at home is meant to be holy; yet maintaining a home does not count as an equal con-tribution to accumulation of family wealth in the English divorce courts, which only recognise the wife's contribution as being enough to merit a share in disposal of proceeds if she has also worked outside the home. And of course the argument that women's moral sense is different from men's will justify both placing them on a pedestal — which Sand hated — and treating them as irrational slaves of instinct. A typical anti-suffragist tract of Sand's time illustrates how separatist arguments can be used to deny women their rights.

> Men assumed the direction of government and war, women of the domestic and family affairs and training of the child. . . . It has been so from the beginning, and it will continue to be so to the end, because it is in conformity to nature and its laws, and is sustained and confirmed by the experience and reason of six thousand years. . . . The domestic altar is a sacred flame where women is the high and officiating priestess. . . . To keep her in that condition of purity, it is necessary that she should be separated from the exercise of the suffrage.[38]

Sand herself — quite consistently — always opposed the vote for women. How can this be called feminist?

There are philosophical as well as practical problems with the 'separate but equal' argument, as should already be clear from the contradictions to which it leads. The claim for equal rights traditionally proceeded from a view that women were just as rational as men — because that is how the argument for rights arose in men's case, from rationality. The earliest liberal thinkers, Hobbes and Locke, presupposed a social contract in which individuals — men, in fact — surrender some power to a governing body in order to better protect their property and their lives. They retain as many rights as possible because they are clever enough to see what is in their self-interest. Total lawlessness — what Hobbes called 'the war of all against all' — is not, but neither is dictatorship.[39] Rights such as freedom of speech and religion are kept, both in order to enhance men's ability to reason (to provide debate) and as an expression of that rationality. Thus there is a connection between rationality (or self-interest) and rights of political expression (such as voting). There is no such bond in the history of ideas between feeling (or sensibility) and rights.

Rationality is also more universal than sensibility. Logical debates follow laws on which most of us can agree — even though modern mathematics has played with the idea that a proposition and its opposite can both be included in a perfectly logical argument.[40] But the dictates of the heart vary across time and space. Good mothering is thought by the Ik of East Africa to consist in laughing at a child who burns herself in the fire, so as to accustom her to the truth that life is hard and people callous. The idea that there is some mystic body of mothering lore known — instinctively? — to all women is a far cry from most women's uncertainties and quandaries as they grope their way towards trying to produce decent offspring. Jean Grimshaw points out that much of the current ethic about good mothering has been prescribed for women by male experts, whose opinion has varied from the injunction never to pick up a crying baby lest it become a spoiled brat — the prevalent orthodoxy thirty or forty years ago — to the modern insistence that nursing mothers feed on demand, even every hour — whatever happens to the mother's sleep. Grimshaw also warns that the maternal model should not be extended to all relationships: feminists who do so are making a cross for women's backs. The modern view of mothering — not the Puritan, which enforced filial obedience — exempts the child from any responsibility for the relationship's success. Do women really want their affairs with men to fall into that pattern?

Sand's own often did, and she later regretted her too-easy willingness to go along with a man's urge to be mothered. Perfectly rationally, Chopin and Musset both pressed her to mother them. Why not, when it excused them if they behaved childishly? In the next chapter I question the stereotype about Sand's maternal feelings towards her lovers. *They* wanted to be children with her, but that is another matter altogether. However, Sand did idealise motherhood, and this opens her to a final attack. The seraphic mother is the oldest and least realistic stereotype of women in existence. How can it be feminist to define women solely in terms of this caricature?

By now it should be clear that I have pressing doubts about Sand's qualifications as a feminist, although I grant that the women in her novels are sometimes more gripping than and often morally superior to the men. I also recognise that she parallels a strain in modern feminism which resists the over-easy equation of a 'liberated' woman with a 'career' woman, a woman who has no personal ties and wants none. To the separatist insistence that 'male' values are not the same as 'human' values I am sympathetic. But I think the mistake lies in the equation of 'male' with 'rational' — a blurring which Sand generally accepts. I also admire Sand's exhausting concern to exemplify an outward-reaching feminine selflessness in her own life. Despite her own frequent ill health and suicidal bouts, she could write in 1845: 'Life is a long ache which rarely sleeps and can never be cured. I am very sad, very gloomy, but, for that reason, love those who deserve my love more than ever'.[41]

Still, the clinching argument against regarding Sand as a feminist lies in her own inconsistency. She repudiates the attempt to turn psychological variations between men and women into moral or political prescriptions for female inferiority. 'Should this difference . . . necessarily constitute a grounds for moral inferiority?' And yet in practical politics she always let it do exactly that. She opposed the vote for women; rejected a move by French feminists to elect her to the National Assembly; spoke in disparaging terms of advanced women such as Flora Tristan (though she charitably supported Tristan's daughter); replied rudely to a proposal that she be elected to the French Academy; and reserved for suffragists a cattiness which she rarely demonstrated in her normally fair-minded reviews and essays. Only in matters concerning marriage and divorce did she put women first. Here, of course, she spoke from her own experience. She had not been barred from a role in the events of 1848 because she was a woman — although her position as propaganda minister was left purely informal. Perhaps she had little sympathy with the exclusion of other women from politics. But she had suffered the loss of her Paris properties in the separation settlement, the humiliation of her husband's right to administer (badly) the estates that were hers by birth, and smutty charges about her affairs — none about Casimir's — during the proceedings.

Now there is nothing unfeminist about being radicalised by divorce, or, conversely, marriage. If modern feminism were said to have contributed only one crucial idea, it would be that the personal is political. Nevertheless, Sand was highly traditional in restricting her demands for women's rights to the *private* sphere, that of marriage and the family. She never challenged the old assumption -– dating at least from the Athenians' exclusion of women from voting and jury service — that *public* life was not the place for the female sex. Other women of her time did, and Wollstonecraft had proposed women's suffrage sixty years before.

A gauntlet had been thrown down to male dominance in the public domain, but Sand was quite happy to see men leave it on the ground in the hope that it would eventually melt camouflaged into the mud.

As the sole heir to Nohant, Sand was considerably wealthier on her marriage than her husband Casimir Dudevant, the bastard son of a minor Gascon noble who was not to come into his limited estate until his stepmother died. But the Napoleonic Code — which erased many of the French Revolution's gains for women — dictated that she should surrender all control of her property to her husband, although she retained its technical title. This diminution in women's property rights was typical in the nineteenth century. English common law had provided widows with a right of dower, a lifetime share of roughly a third of the husband's estate. By the Dower Act of 1833, husbands were allowed to bar this right by disposing differently of their property either in life or through their wills. Nothing was left to counteract the common law provision that a married woman lost all her existing property and her right to any income she earned during the marriage. 'Oddly enough, this was the property regime which the bridegroom brought into being by pronouncing the words, "With all my worldly goods I thee endow"'.[42] The last restriction on married women's property rights was not removed until 1935 in England — and it still lingers in the primitive tribal customs of the Inland Revenue, which treats wives' income as their husbands'. In France married women still enjoyed the 'protection' of inegalitarian property laws until 1970.

Property was potentially a feminist issue in Sand's time, then, and very much to the point in her own unsatisfactory dealings with Casimir. Not until she had been married eight years did Sand manage to retrieve some control over Nohant's administration, and then only after Casimir lost 10,000 francs speculating on a Bordeaux cargo vessel. He was shamefaced enough to 'concede' her an 'allowance' of 1,000 francs a month so that she could begin to run her own estate — though she overran that amount — and later to 'grant' her a much smaller sum so that she could set up as a writer in Paris. Even though Casimir retained some rights over her wealth well after their separation, Sand always maintained that it was her very relative financial independence which enabled her to begin an independent life, and her writing earnings which allowed her to go on living it. Women with no independent means could not have independent minds, she asserted, and economic liberation would have to precede the vote. Wives would merely vote according to their husbands' orders until they had the economic wherewithal to defy male authority. (Sometimes Sand also argued that women would vote even more conservatively than their menfolk — an unacceptable possibility for her, as a socialist, and generally true of women's voting in England at least until the 1980s, when the pendulum swung the other way.) 'Should women participate one day in politics?' she wrote in a letter to the provisional government central committee in April 1848, the Revolution's salad days. 'Yes, one day, I believe as do you, but is this day near? No, I do not believe so, and for the condition of women to be thus transformed, it is necessary that society be radically transformed.'[43]

Here Sand was an accurate Jeremiah, but whereas his soothsaying was self-denying when Jerusalem repented and evaded the wrath of God, Sand's prophecy was of the self-fulfilling sort. It is perfectly true that the 'one day' when women got the vote was a long time coming in France. Frenchwomen lacked political rights until after the Second World War, whereas universal male suffrage began in 1884 — making France one of the first countries to give the vote to men and among the last to grant it to women. The gap is only greater in Switzerland — one of the only three European countries to institute universal male suffrage before 1900 (Norway was the third). Swiss women, however, remained political minors until 1971. But was this shilly-shallying historically inevitable? Arguments such as Sand's 'wait and be patient' thesis could certainly have helped to *produce* the delay in women's equal rights. After all, one can wait forever for society to be radically transformed. 'Women cry out against slavery; let them wait until man is free', she wrote in the Third Letter to Marcie. It hardly needs saying that this might be a lengthy interruption.

Sand was a socialist first, and a feminist way afterwards. Now Marxist feminists would not claim that their Marxism prevents them from being feminists, and socialism and women's rights co-existed happily in the halcyon early days.[44] But no socialist feminist who was genuine about feminism would adopt the high tone Sand took towards suffragists.

As for you women who pretend to begin by the exercise of your rights, permit me to tell you again that you are amusing yourselves with childishness. Your house is on fire, your home is in peril, and you want to go expose yourself to railleries and public affronts when you should be defending your home and setting up again your outraged household gods. . . . To what ridiculous attacks, to what possible vile scandals, would such an innovation [votes for women] give rise? Good sense thrusts it aside, and the pride that your sex ought to have makes it nearly a crime for you to think of braving such outrages.[45]

Sand demonstrates her old failure to identify with other women — 'your sex', not 'our sex' — and an ironic concern for suffragists' pure reputations. Of course she suffered from vile smears on her own good name, but the women's moral lily-whiteness was surely their own concern. Again, what would we make of this letter if a man had written it? Is there *any* way it could be considered feminist?

The vote was certainly no cure-all, and the campaigners for it have been attacked even by other, later feminists for their naïve assumption that it would be. Nevertheless, Sand's feminism must be considered half-baked, at best, if it reserves the entire public sphere for patriarchy. She was prepared to be quite radical in the private sphere, true, although the thoroughness of her demands even there is sometimes masked by her mealy-mouthed apotheosis of marriage. Even the gutsy heroines of her novels generally live happily ever after in wedded bliss — with the prominent exceptions of Lélia and Lucrézia. To the central committee of the 1848 government she wrote less a clarion call than a piccolo trill: 'Civil equality, equality in marriage, equality in the family, that is what you ought to demand. But do it with a deep sense of the sanctity of marriage, conjugal fidelity, and family love'.[46]

Indeed, Sand attacked contemporary feminists as promiscuous threats to the holy marriage vows — in the best continuing traditions of the modern tabloid press. Although she berated the Napoleonic Code for stipulating that women should be jailed in solitary confinement for adultery — which Casimir was fortunately too lazy and too timid of scandal to invoke against her — she blamed the law only because it was likely to increase adultery through publicity. A women's rights argument would not consider the likely consequences of this legislation, but its essential injustice — the discrepancy between treatment of women and of men, who could only be divorced if they actually brought their mistresses into the matrimonial home. Sand thought divorce was essentially wrong, but the sole remedy for the economic pressures which forced women into marriage. If the female sex had equal property rights and marriage were thus truly voluntary, she hoped there would be no separations or divorces. Husbands' authority over their wives was the bastion against which she launched her most sustained fusillades.

> People ask what will happen to the principle of authority which the family requires if fathers and mothers share power equally. We say that this authority won't be left unchanged in the hands of a man who can do wrong without getting caught out, but rather that it will pass back and forth continuously between husband and wife, according to the arbitration of sentiment or reason. [Note Sand's unshaken conviction that sentiment and reason are not at odds.] . . . When people ask how a conjugal association can survive if the husband isn't the unchallenged head, the judge and party both, with no appeal, it makes no more sense than when they ask how a free man can get along without a master or a republican without a king. The principle of uncontrolled authority in one individual went out with the divine right of kings.[47]

But she was hardly Jacobin in her plans for actually achieving these revolutionary goals.

> Let women set themselves right and cling to the purest example, let them suffer and pray while waiting until marriage, without ceasing to be a sacred bond, at least stops being a degrading tyranny. What will they accomplish through revolt? When the male world has been converted, woman will be converted without anyone having had any need to bother about her.[48]

This Uncle Tom-ism spilled over into high-and-mighty rebukes to women who were less sanguine that equality could be magicked into existence with any such sleight-of-hand: 'We believe that the rude protests which have arisen in our day have done more harm than good to women's emancipation. They have rushed to gain rights which they have not proved themselves worthy to enjoy, although perhaps after considerable progress they may be'.[49]

But what were these outrageous demands? They were very moderate indeed — and far more even-tempered than Sand's haughty reply — in the case of an article in *La Voix des femmes* which proposed Sand for the National Assembly. The Club of Paris, a woman's group behind this proposal, was actively working for practical socialist aims that would benefit working-class females directly: government-sponsored workshops for both sexes, national canteens for proletarian families, and reading-rooms where both men and women could further their education. As a socialist, if not as a feminist, Sand could have been expected to sympathise with this platform. And since she had blotted her copybook with the revolutionary government by writing a pamphlet calling the workers back to the barricades when she was meant to be serving as a moderate-minded minister, she might have been glad of the Club's suggestion that she return to politics as a candidate for the National Assembly. Nor was the proposal extreme in its wording:

> The first woman called to the Constituent Assembly must be acceptable to men. Sand is not masculine, but men are stunned by her genius; glorious dreamers that they are, they do her the great honour of calling her spirit masculine. She has become a man through her courage, but remained a woman in her maternal nature. Sand is powerful but frightens no one; she is the one who should be called *by the wish of all women to the vote of all men* [*par le voeu de toutes au vote de tous*].[50]

Sand's quite atypically bitchy reply called the proposal a joke, whined that it had wounded her *amour-propre*, snubbed the women involved as none of her own circle, denounced the Club as over-zealous, and disavowed any sympathy with their aims. Even a commentator who believes that Sand is 'incontestably' a feminist thinks she overstepped the bounds with this reply.[51]

The existence of more advanced feminists than Sand, and the fact that Sand knew of their ideas, puts paid to any claim that Sand was as progressive on women's issues as could have been expected in her day. Of course it is wrong to demand that she evince a sense of sisterhood, since that is very much a twentieth-century feminist concern. Perhaps we should allow her some cattiness on that account — though not much, particularly in light of her far more typical kindly, generous tone in reviews and letters. However, her childhood had been rent in twain by a war between two women. She could hardly have been expected to think of the female sex as naturally pacific or united. But she was just as dismissive of *male* advocates of women's rights.

In 1863 Sainte-Beuve proposed Sand for the Prix Gobert of 20,000 francs, and she was seconded in this submission to the awarding body, the Académie Française, by Alfred de Vigny, backed by Prosper Mérimée. This was a moderately noble about-face by the latter two men, of whom one had once denounced Sand as a lesbian because she was taking up his mistress's time with her friendship, and the second had bodged a one-night stand with Sand. The cabal argued that Sand was as great as Victor Hugo — the general opinion in her day, except among those who, like Walt Whitman, maintained that she was a great deal better than Hugo. Certainly she was a more prolific and successful writer than her one-time collaborator Jules Sandeau, another ancient *amour* who had been elected to the Academy in 1859. The motion for Sand was defeated 18–6; although the delicate question of her sex was not mentioned openly as the reason for refusing her the prize, the pro-Sand faction knew perfectly well that it wouldn't have been. To denounce the decision as sexist, Sandeau and the others prepared an anonymous pamphlet, *Les Femmes à l'Académie*. In this document the coven of feminist men describes the reception of a great female author into the Academy by unanimous election at some unspecified future time. The booklet's language is quite radical: it speaks of 'a long injustice' of barring women from the Academy and its prizes — 'an absurd prejudice' for which the imaginary authoress's success is merely 'tardy reparation'.[52]

In her reply, *Pourquoi les Femmes à l'Académie?*, Sand was equally radical — radical conservative, or reactionary — in denouncing the idea. She rarely confronts the men's arguments head-on; when she does, she contradicts her own creed. For example, the first pamphlet's authors surmise quite modestly that feminine influence in the Academy would be no bad thing. Now Sand could be expected to approve of this, since her constant theme is the need for union of the male and female virtues. But she thinks real live women could only have an evil effect: 'It is quite true that if women could . . . make themselves angels in order to purify and ennoble society, that would be a fine thing, but . . .'[53] Of course Sand is entitled to point out the chasm between an idealised picture of female nature and real women, but she was never immune from confusing the two herself — particularly with mothers. Certainly her non-fiction and novels both suggest that there is a separate and generally superior female sphere, and that the presence of women refines and educates men — exactly the point she shrugs off here. At the end of her pamphlet, after some misogynous ramblings such as those I quoted at the start of this chapter, she returns to her theme. Women have no part in public life — not even in a rather slimline public body composed of a mere forty 'immortals'. 'In our time women's place is no more in the Academy than in the Senate, the legislative body, or the army.'[54] Few of the points raised by the men's pamphlet receive a direct answer; Sand's reply — which even a critic who thinks her a feminist calls virulent — merely rehashes her old prejudices. There can be fewer neater illustrations of the ever-applicable line from the American comic strip 'Pogo': 'We have met the enemy and he' — or she — 'is us'.

In practical politics Sand was actually an enemy of feminism, except in relation to property rights — an ironic distinction for a socialist. In her essays and autobiography she took a separatist stand which is consonant with some modern feminism, but also consistent with anti-feminist arguments confining women to the sacred hearth. Particularly traditional is her strict delineation of a divide between 'public man, private woman'.[55] It is quite true that she wanted massive changes in the private relations between the sexes, and to some slight extent her insistence that women must be given economic independence implies that she envisions roles outside of marriage for them — although it is not clear exactly *what* roles. In her novels Sand certainly gave women good lines, but there are also juicy male parts — such as M. Bricolin or Old Cadoche in *Le Meunier d'Angibault*, whose female characters are rather boring except for a terrifying Miss Haversham-like madwoman. Because Sand is a good craftswoman and a fine painter of the human psyche, men are not treated any less sympathetically than women in her novels. If women are treated as sympathetically as men, it may be as much for professional as for feminist reasons. A woman-murderer is actually presented as a wise old sage in the supposedly feminist *Lélia*, after serving a suitable sentence — five years, exactly the term which occasioned an outcry from women when a brutal rape in a vicarage recently came to trial.

Although the stereotype that Sand was a 'liberated woman' in her espousal of women's rights has generally been corroborated by academics,[56] I do not think that active opposition to feminism in one sphere, an ambivalent doctrine in another, and a few sympathetic female characters in the third add up to 'putting women first'. If feminism is defined as any doctrine which advances women's position,[57] Sand might be seen as feminist. But so might John Maynard Keynes, whose concern for near-full employment helped to provide jobs and some economic independence for women in the post-war era when Keynesian policies dominated the Western economies. With a little more juggling, Marx could be seen as feminist because the Marxist 'reserve army of labour' thesis has been used by feminists to explain why women were booted out of production jobs to make way for returning soldiers after the two wars. But the 'reserve army' idea was originally used to describe black migrants' position, and only borrowed to deal with women's. Marxism maintains that class is the great divide, not sex. Sand's socialism — which she loosely identified as communist, and which we might even more loosely term Marxist — actually led her to tell women *not* to press for their rights. Come the revolution, all would be made equal. In the meantime, women should put up and shut up.

The question is not whether a particular doctrine such as Marxism or Keynesianism does women some good, as an afterthought, but whether it deliberately sets out to put their interests first. Sand was so far from taking this line, which is what I define as feminism, that she reckoned the 'woman problem' would go away quietly. 'When the male world has been converted, woman will be converted without anyone having had to bother about her.' In her works and political activity, on balance, it is incorrect to call Sand 'the first modern liberated woman'. I have deliberately put her works before her life in discussing this stereotype, in order to delineate more clearly the portrait of a professional writer and committed political campaigner — which tends to be obscured behind the trousers and cigar smoke. Now, however, it is time to think about whether Sand was liberated in her life —

primarily in her sexuality, but also in her economic independence, masculine dress, choice of pen name, and, yes, nicotine addiction.

Notes

1. *Corr.*, IV, p. 433.
2. Sand, *La Comtesse de Rudolstadt* (Paris: Editions Garnier, 1959), p. 342.
3. Sand, preface to 1842 edition of *Indiana*, quoted in Pierre Vermeylen, *Les Idées politiques et sociales de George Sand* (Brussels: Editions de l'Université, 1984), p. 24.
4. M. Barrett and M. McIntosh, *The Anti-Social Family* (London: Verso/New Left Books, 1982).
5. Sand, *Lettres d'un Voyageur*, XII, p. 315.
6. Sand, *Questions d'Art et de littérature* (Paris: Calmann-Lévy, 1878), p. 54.
7. Quoted in André Maurois, *Lélia: The Life of George Sand* (tr.) Gerard Hopkins (London: Jonathan Cape, 1953), p. 302.
8. Sand, 'Pourquoi les Femmes à l'Académie?', in *Les Femmes et l'Académie Française* (Paris: Editions de l'Opale, 1980), pp. 87–8.
9. Quoted in Cate, *George Sand*, p. 223. Though sharing Sand's distaste for what he calls 'militant women's liberationists', Cate rightly draws attention to the nastily 'gynaecophagic' expression, 'I *consume* so few of them'.
10. For the 'masculinity complex' thesis, see Helene Deutsch, *The Psychology of Women* (New York: Grune and Stratton, 1944). A rebuttal of the claim that *La Petite Fadette* exemplifies this complex has been made by Naomi Schor, 'Reading Double: Sand's Difference', in Nancy K. Miller (ed.), *The Poetics of Gender* (New York: Columbia University Press, 1986), pp. 248–69.
11. *Corr.* XX, pp. 285–87 (9 January 1867). This theme was also taken up, Lubin points out, in an article of 1872 in *Le Temps* and in her *Impressions et souvenirs*.
12. Harold Laski, quoted in Cate, *George Sand*, p. 364.
13. Quoted in Vermeylen, *Idées politiques*, p. 25.
14. Sand, *My Life*, p. 154.
15. *Corr.*, I, p. 104, 30 January 1823.
16. Quoted in Cate, *George Sand*, p. 561.
17. Quoted ibid., p. 199.
18. Sand, *Lélia*, I, p. 272.

19. Ibid., I, p. 195.
20. Ibid., I, p. 249.
21. Ibid., I, p. 184.
22. Ibid., I, p. 285.
23. Ibid., II, p. 92.
24. Ibid., II, p. 112.
25. Ibid., I, p. 39.
26. Marilyn Yalom, '*Dédoublement* in the Fiction of George Sand', in Datlof et al. (eds), *George Sand Papers: 1978*, pp. 21–31. Yalom suggests that the Virgin–Magdalen split reflects the division in Sand's childish affections between her grandmother and mother.
27. Marina Warner, *Alone of All Her Sex: The Myth and The Cult of the Virgin Mary* (London: Weidenfeld and Nicolson, 1976).
28. Letter to Marie Talon, 1834, quoted in Pierre Reboul (ed.), *Lélia* (1833 edn) (Paris: Editions Garnier Frères, 1960), pp. 595–6. Reboul is the author of the phrase 'frenetic literature', applied to the post-*Hernani* excesses of the 1830s.
29. *Lélia* (1839 edn), I, p. 172.
30. Tillie Olsen, *Silences* (New York: Dell, 1979).
31. Sand, *La Petite Fadette* (Paris: Livre de Poche, 1973), p. 58.
32. Ibid., p. 166.
33. Schor, 'Reading Double'.
34. *Fadette*, p. 237.
35. Carol Gilligan, *In a Different Voice* (Cambridge, Massachusetts: Harvard University Press, 1982), p. 2.
36. Quoted in Noel B. Gerson, *George Sand: A Biography of the First Modern, Liberated Woman* (London: Robert Hale and Company, 1973), p. 2.
37. Quoted in Vermeylen, *Idées politiques*, p. 19.
38. Quoted in Jean Grimshaw, *Feminist Philosophers: Women's Perspectives on Philosophical Traditions* (Brighton, Sussex: Harvester Press, Wheatsheaf Books, 1986), p. 199. On other ways in which Gilligan's arguments can be directed against feminists, see J. Auerbach et al., 'Commentary on Gilligan's *In a Different Voice*', *Feminist Studies*, XI, no. 1, spring 1985.
39. This is a very rough summary, more accurate on Locke than on Hobbes — whose idea of rights is fuzzy.
40. This is the controversy over the Aristotelian 'law of the excluded middle', that a thing cannot both be and not be.
41. Quoted in Maurois, *Lélia*, p. 292.
42. *Report of the Committee on One-Parent Families* (The Finer Report) (London: HMSO, 1974), vol. 2, appendices, sect. 2, par. 20.
43. Quoted in Dennis O'Brien, 'George Sand and Feminism', *George Sand Papers: 1976*, p. 85.
44. On the relation between early nineteenth-century socialism and feminism, see Barbara Taylor, *Eve and the New Jerusalem* (London: Virago, 1984).

45. Letter of April 1848, quoted in Cate, *George Sand*, p. 419.
46. *Corr.*, VIII, 406, quoted in Vermeylen, *Idées politiques*, p. 40.
47. *Corr.*, II, 741, quoted in O'Brien, 'George Sand and Feminism', p. 78.
48. Sand, *Questions d'Art et de littérature*, p. 54.
49. Ibid., p. 56.
50. *La Voix des femmes*, quoted in Vermeylen, *Idées politiques*, p. 32, original emphasis.
51. Vermeylen, *Idées politiques*, p. 33.
52. *Les Femmes et l'Académie Française*, p. 40.
53. Ibid., p. 89.
54. Ibid., p. 95.
55. The title of a book by Jean Elshtain.
56. Both Vermeylen and O'Brien are sure that Sand was a feminist. Mallet agrees, but under some duress, finding Sand's feminism moderate but genuine.
57. Vermeylen's definition, taken from the *Petit Robert*.

4 The First Liberated Woman?
Sand's Sexuality

> In effect, what is the liberty that a woman can
> seize?. . . Adultery.
>> Sand, Letter to Central Committee, 1848

Did Sand's adultery really emancipate her? Balzac surmised that
she was essentially chaste, and would have remained so had she
not had a point to make. Or did her sexuality expose her to abuse
in life and oblivion after death? The tags for which Sand has
become a dart-board are all to do with female sexuality: 'transvestite, man-eater, lesbian, nymphomaniac', as Ellen Moers has
catalogued them. To be more exact, they are all insults, fancifully
based on contradictory stereotypes of her sexuality. She is most
widely known as Chopin's mistress, defined solely by her love life.
In this book I have set out to avenge this insult to her honour as a
successful, influential, and skilful writer, and it may seem out of
place for me to devote a long chapter to her sexuality. Now it is
mistaken to overstate the extent of Sand's dalliance: she had no
more than a dozen lovers — small beer compared to the 2,000
women whom the official old sage Victor Hugo supposedly boasted
he had 'conquered' in his red-blooded youth.

But there is a job to be done in rehabilitating Sand's sexual
image, as much as in rubbing the tarnish off her professional one.
To the woman-hating slurs listed by Moers is often added the less
obviously misogynous claim that Sand's feeling for her lovers was
exclusively maternal. This is nevertheless a sexist idea — though
accepted by all Sand's biographers — because it takes as right
and natural 'the purely conventional age gap between older,
masterful, wiser man and younger, childish, helpless woman.
Sand had three long-term lovers who were between five- and
six-and-a-half years younger than herself: the novelist Jules Sandeau, the poet Alfred de Musset, and the composer Frédéric
Chopin. This appears to have been normal enough to her: after
all, her mother had been five years older than her father. The
mere fact of a 'wrong-way' age difference does not necessarily
make Sand's feelings for her lovers motherly. Indeed, her letters

and journal yield plenty of evidence of passions unknown to Whistler's Mother. Sand's last lover, the engraver Alexandre Manceau, was thirteen years younger than she, but it is perfectly evident that *he* took care of *her* — and did it well. Manceau is either ignored in analyses of Sand's *amours* — not being quite up to snuff in the glory and renown line — or dismissed with the statement that she could not possibly have loved him very much, since he mothered *her*. This is a backwards logic which takes as given the proposition it sets out to prove, that Sand's kind of loving was limited to the motherly. It also ignores the grief-ridden reclusion which Sand imposed on herself after Manceau died in her arms. Beneath the maternal stereotype lies a shocked conformism, I think, and perhaps even a little jealousy in both male and some female critics of this rather plain double-chinned woman who consistently attracted artistic young men of a delicate handsomeness. (Although that is a speculation, there are so many personal, back-biting remarks about Sand's affairs that some such speculation seems justified.) Rather than accept that Sandeau, Musset, and, to a lesser extent, Chopin felt good honest libido for Sand, these commentators scurry to pronounce the passion safely bounded by filial devotion.

My strong position — that Sand's lovers were not her sons — will have to be defended against the motherly comments which do seem to crop up in her letters, autobiography and journal. Much of this chapter will be devoted to examining that evidence. I believe it indicates that Sand used maternal metaphors mainly when her affections were *asexual* — with her women friends, with Sandeau, Chopin and Musset after the affairs ended, and with Chopin before she slept with him. I also want to consider another interesting piece of iconoclasm, surpassing my own: Michel Foucault's idea that the nineteenth century — usually seen as the period that put piano legs into skirts — was actually the age that brought sex out into the open.[1] This absorbing thesis could apply to Sand in one of two opposing ways. It may be that Sand was slammed for her improper conduct because she carried an older, freer morality into the increasingly repressive nineteenth century. This view would rest on the received idea which Foucault rejects, that the nineteenth century was more sexually hidebound than the eighteenth. But it would be consistent with Sand's *ancien régime* upbringing, itself out of step with the time. It would also fit the suggestion I made in Chapter 2 — that she was equally out of tune with the Romantic era, rather than being its most hysterical representative. And it might be supported by the comparative ease with which the respectably wedded Mme du Châtelet had been able to carry on her liaison with Voltaire in the 'looser' early eighteenth century. The quick waning of Sand's fame after her death might be explained by the century's increasing unwillingness to tolerate even the memory of a brazen hussy. But a reading of Foucault, and an application of his ideas to Sand, could suggest the opposite. Perhaps Sand's sexuality has been allowed to monopolise her literary reputation because we are obsessed with sex, and because Sand had the misfortune to begin her career just as our collective mania began. A Foucault-style claim would have to be qualified by a feminist analysis: we are only obsessed by *female* sexuality, it seems, since Victor Hugo is not known merely by his theoretical 2,000 mistresses, nor Alexandre Dumas *père* by his refusal to recognise his illegitimate son by Catherine Labay as Dumas *fils* for the first part of the boy's life. With this addition, however, Foucault's broad argument — though not applied to Sand in his work — offers a promising solution to the problem with which I began: how has the once-lionised Sand come to be so largely forgotten?

These two prongs of attack will constitute my treatment of whether Sand was 'liberated' in her sexuality. First, however, I need to sweep away some chaff. There are a number of silly arguments about why Sand was or was not a 'free woman' — for example, that she was unliberated because she took pleasure in needlework, jam-making, and tailoring dolls' clothes for her granddaughters. I should have thought women had enough difficulty in liberating themselves without being blamed for such minor slips, if slips they be. The correspondingly inane argument on the other side is that Sand *was* a liberated lady because she rolled her own cigarettes — and puffed the odd cigar as well. This 'Virginia Slims' style of discourse assumes that Sand had 'come a long way, baby' because she was addicted to tobacco. It is hardly worth discussing this proposition, except to note that Sand was indeed eccentric and bold in smoking *publicly*, and that her cigarettes were censured even more than her trousers. They were only smoked by aristocrats and working-class men in 1830s France, not by middle-class men, and emphatically not by women, even 'fallen' ones. By 1848 the male bourgeois, the actress and the street-walker could light up in public, but Sand fitted none of these categories — despite Baudelaire's depiction of her as a 'kept woman'. (In Chapter 6 I surmise that Baudelaire was free with his insults — think of the 'latrine' term of endearment — because he actually pinched his most famous line from Sand: 'mon semblable, mon frère'.) Sand may have needed a raised consciousness to display her habit in public, but if so, smoking would be the *outcome* of *already* liberated attitudes in her. More likely, with her minor-aristocratic eccentricity, she was simply not aware of how wild her behaviour appeared. There is a droll passage in *Un Hiver à Majorque* in which she offers a cigar to her driver as he sweats to get the mules up the stiff hill to Valldemosa in heavy rain. The Spanish were already discomfited by Sand's lack of a marriage certificate and the trousers she dressed Solange in. (She was tactful enough to abandon them herself.) Waving cigars would have done little to improve the driver's opinion of her, but Sand seems to have been careless of the effect she had, lolling in the back of the wagon with her cheroot.

The view that Sand was the 'first liberated woman' because she wore male attire deserves somewhat deeper consideration. Certainly it was uncommon for women to wear trousers, boots, top hat and riding jacket in 1831, when Sand first adopted them — although she had discarded masculine costume by 1840. (Sand was a short woman and was perfectly aware that the weight she put on by middle age made male garb unflattering. She had a respectably 'feminine' concern for her good appearance.) It has been said that male dress of the period was rather androgynous, or at least that there was more diversity of acceptable clothing for men than later in the century. Sand might not have got away with her poor-student attire in the 1860s.[2] Be that as it may, women who shared Sand's bohemian life style, such as Marie d'Agoult, Liszt's mistress, stayed in skirts. Male attire *is* genuinely emancipating in the greater freedom it gives its wearer, and so it is not as ridiculous to say that Sand was liberated because she wore trousers as that she was a free spirit because she smoked cigarettes, a case in which she was more a slave to addiction. But did she adopt male costume in deliberate defiance of convention, as an ideological protest?

Whatever the liberating *effects* of Sand's choice of garb, the *motives* behind it were purely practical. When Sand pulled up stakes for Paris, Casimir made her an 'allowance' — from her own estate — of 250 francs per month, later supplemented very meagrely by the small amounts she earned as a journeyman writer. Balzac said that it was impossible to be a woman in Paris on less than 25,000 francs a year. In her autobiography Sand recounted:

And this paradox, that a woman was not really a woman unless she was smartly dressed, became a reality for a woman who would be an artist. My delicate shoes cracked open in two days, my pattens sent me spilling, and I always forgot to lift my dress. I was muddy, tired and runny-nosed, and I watched my shoes and my clothes — not to forget my little velvet hats, which the drainpipes watered — go to rack and ruin with alarming rapidity.[3]

Sand had resented the tight Chinese bun into which her hair was pulled in her childhood, and the restrictive garments and injunctions which impeded her 'boyish' galloping about. Deschartres had allowed her to hunt with him in knee breeches and a shirt, and she had been taught to ride astride, which precluded the tight skirts then in vogue. Stéphane Ajasson de Grandsagne, a scion of the Berry shabby gentility who taught Aurore medicine and physiology, also tutored her in firing a pistol and encouraged her to wear male riding clothes. Her acquaintances, the du Plessis family, dressed their four eldest daughters in boys' attire, as Sand was later to do with Solange — much to the conventional Balzac's disgust.

Nothing could have been less deliberately shocking and more down-to-earth sensible than for Sand to protect herself against Paris mud with trousers and boots. The clincher was the prohibition against women in the lower stalls of the theatre, where tickets were half the price of the balcony. Sophie mentioned to her daughter that she had adopted student garb in the early days of her marriage to get round this barrier — and Sand did the same. Sand is usually accused of flaunting her sexuality — and sometimes also her asexuality, a contradictory claim — in this choice of androgynous clothing. This she denied:

My manner of being so natural came out of the exceptional position in which I found myself, so that it appeared quite simple to me not to live like the majority of other girls. They judged me very bizarre, and yet I was infinitely less so than I could have been if I had had the taste for affectation and eccentricity.[4]

The same pragmatic factors underlay Sand's choice of a man's pen name. In December 1831 she and her lover Jules Sandeau co-authored a romantic narrative, *Rose et Blanche*. To quiet her mother-in-law's fears that the Dudevants' solidly and deservedly anti-intellectual good name might be sullied by this foray into literature, Aurore and Jules had the book published over the signature of one 'J. Sand'. This abbreviated form of Sandeau was suggested by the editor de Latouche as a mutual pseudonym, but of course it implied that Sandeau had produced most or all of the book — whereas the opposite was actually the case. But Aurore was not particularly proud of this apprentice work. 'I've written a wretched novel of no consequence which I haven't signed', she wrote to a friend.[5] In any case, she was as generous with fame as she was later to prove with her purse. She offered Sandeau the chance to publish *Indiana* — all her own work — under the 'J. Sand' pseudonym, but he had the professional decency to refuse. By now, however, the name 'Sand' had acquired some small acquaintanceship, on which the publisher was eager to capitalise. Aurore added a different Christian pseudonym to it, still a male one — Georges, from the Greek for 'farmer', which, she said, equalled 'native of Berry' to her. It has been suggested that Sand chose 'George' from the start — rather than 'Georges', the proper French equivalent — because she wanted a deliberately androgynous name[6] or because she admired George Gordon, Lord Byron.[7] Neither surmise is borne out by the hard facts: Sand *did* originally call herself 'Georges', and from the publication of *Indiana* in May 1832 she signed her letters that way. In early 1833 she began to use 'George', without the 's', for *professional* rather than ideological reasons. De Latouche disliked the two 's's' following hard upon each other in George*s S*and, and he felt that the Anglo-Saxon Christian name fitted the English-sounding surname.

We are so accustomed now to the convention of male pen names among nineteenth-century women novelists that Sand's pseudonym does not seem problematic. But I think it *should* make us stop short: it was *not* a common tactic then in France, where a long line of literary ladies had retained their feminine monickers. And the stratagem had yet to be used in England by the Brontës and George Eliot. Aurore could easily have retained the name 'Sand' to avoid mother-in-law troubles, but tacked on her own Christian name, or announced that 'J. Sand' was really 'Jeanne Sand'. Why choose a masculine identity? Why stick to this fiction in all her later references to herself with masculine adjectives or pronouns? By then no one supposed that George Sand was anything but the small woman in modest grey dresses which Sand had indeed become by the time Elizabeth Barrett Browning recorded her meetings with her. Why did Sand earlier cast herself firmly in the masculine in the supposedly autobiographical *Lettres d'un Voyageur*? We cannot easily answer these queries without tumbling into the 'masculinity complex' quagmire. One way of tackling them in a less emotive and hackneyed fashion is to look not at the *grounds* for Sand's choice, but at its *effects* on her self-image.

Although the myth-makers have gone over Sand's sexuality with a fine-toothed if not terribly clean comb, no one has considered the effect which posing as a man in her public persona must have had on her inner sense of her sexual self. How could she help being confused, when Musset addressed her simultaneously in the masculine and the feminine? ('Sois fière, mon grand and brave George, tu as fait un homme d'un enfant.') I find this question far more compelling and problematic than the judicial matters of the cigars, the jam, or the top hat. Any woman who has changed her name on marriage, or reverted to her own name after divorce, knows that a formal change of identity is awkward and sometimes painful: we are our names. At the very least it must have been muddling for Sand to be called 'Aurore' by Casimir and Chopin, 'Monsieur Sand' by the reviewers, 'George' by Solange and Musset, 'Madame Dudevant' in her contracts, and 'Madame Sand' by Manceau. (Lest anyone think that Manceau was merely Sand's servant because he called her 'Madame', let me adduce the case of Mrs Micawber, who called her beloved 'Mr. Micawber' or even plain 'Micawber' with normal nineteenth-century formality.) Now the French have at least retained the usage which prevailed in English until the start of the nineteenth century — reserving 'Miss' ('Mademoiselle') for girls and called both married and unmarried older women 'Mrs' ('Madame').[8] Nevertheless, Sand had to live with gender confusion engendered by name for longer than Eliot or the Brontës, who all published their first novels later in life and died younger than Sand. For nearly forty-five years Sand was a private woman and a public man. What did this do to her sense of her own sexual identity? Perhaps it has some bearing on the anomaly in Chapter 3, Sand's paradigmatic reference to 'your sex' rather than 'our sex' when addressing women.

To suggest tentative answers for these enquiries into a new area, I have studied Sand's letters between May 1832 (*Indiana*) and January 1834 — the period just after her 'sex-change'. In addition I have used the *Lettres d'un Voyageur* — the first few of which were written just after this time — and Sand's *Intimate Journal* of 1834–7. My overall impression is that Sand *was* disoriented about her gender identity in this period, sometimes even referring to herself in the masculine in the completely private *Intimate Journal*. Now in her prefaces it was consistent enough for Sand to use masculine adjectival forms and pronouns, if the introduction was to be signed with the male pseudonym 'George Sand'. That she retained this practice until her death is perfectly good grammar and style, even though she was known to be a woman. But even in an incoherent and unpublishable fragment from 1836 which Sand shoved into a drawer, and which her granddaughter edited into part of the *Intimate Journal*, the writer refers to herself as 'he'. Sand never wanted her diary jottings published during her lifetime. She was reticent about baring her emotional breast in public — although she is generally accused of conducting her affairs in print.[9] (Her taciturnity on this score would support the second position at the start of this chapter, based on Foucault: that the prurient nineteenth century wanted to know more than Sand would reveal, and called her a slut in revenge.) Because the journal is a purely personal document, intended to impress or deceive no one, it is most revealing to find Sand calling herself 'poor boy' in it, or addressing herself as 'George'.

The great irony is that much of this journal was written in the aftermath of a very heterosexual affair indeed — her time with Musset, which still inspired her to one or two blue passages in the diary. The journal's masculine self-references are interspersed with traditionally 'feminine' concerns: 'I am thirty, still beautiful, or at least I shall be in a few days' time, as soon as I can stop crying'.[10] Traditionally female, too, is her lack of self-confidence — this in a woman whose decision to leave provincial married life for a very uncertain literary career had been undeniably gutsy, and whose first three novels had by now all become best-sellers. 'All around me I find men of more worth than me, who still take me as they find me.'[11] The once-defiant anticlerical sceptic prays God to give her back her lover, 'and I shall be devout, and my knees will wear out the church flagstones'.[12]

This self-flagellating journal makes compelling reading for many reasons. It puts paid to the 'known truth' that Sand picked up and dropped her lovers — the myth of her callousness, which Pritchett clearly believes. It contrasts instructively with the collected calm of Sand's mature prose. Like Emily Dickinson, who reserved her emotionalism for her private correspondence, Sand kept her professional work in a separate, emotionally spick and span container. But the most paradoxical aspect of the journal is its odd pairing of the 'feminine' urge to be loved, above all else, with masculine self-references. The neatest example of this occurs in an entry for 3 June 1837, at the end of her affair with Michel de Bourges: 'Ah, si j'étais aimé, moi!' — 'Oh, if only I were loved!', with 'aimé' unshakably in the masculine. Already there is strong evidence of the proposition that far from flaunting her sexuality, or being sexually liberated, Sand found her sexuality a burden.

The correspondence of the early 1830s shows a parallel though less pronounced befuddlement over gender sense. After the success of *Indiana* Sand wrote to her friend Laure Decerfz: 'In Paris Madame Dudevant has passed on. But Georges Sand is reputed a sprightly young fellow'.[13] Nevertheless the defunct Madame Dudevant was resurrected in the feminine modifiers which Sand applied to herself in an androgynous letter to an editor, signed with the presumably masculine 'G. Sand'.[14] Her old Berry friends were now expected to recognise her signature of 'Georges', although they had some hints as to the sender's identity in the feminine adjectives and pronouns she coupled with the male Christian name. But a letter to the editor of the *Revue de Paris* two months later is signed with the male pen name and the masculine form of the closing, 'Votre dévoué'.[15] Now a slipped 'e' may not betoken great things. Sand had tacked an extra one onto the adjective 'sûr' as applied to Jules Sandeau in a letter, making him feminine. Sand was not reversing gender roles in this epistle, or regarding Sandeau as her trollop, whatever extremists of the 'masculinity complex' school might read into it. She signed herself suitably and modestly feminine, as 'ton amie Aurore'.

By 1833 Sand was over the worst of this confusion, settling into a steady pattern of referring to herself in the feminine in her correspondence, though signing herself in the masculine. But oddities still occur: a note to Sainte-Beuve uses the feminine of herself but requests two theatre tickets for 'my pseudonym and myself'. The pseudonym she means is Sandeau; yet the letter is signed 'Georges Sand', as if that were *not* her pseudonym, but her real identity. Her business contracts were made out to 'Madame Dudevant', with 'George Sand' in parentheses. Not even professionally was she ever entirely the one or the other.

In her private journal, and to a lesser extent in her letters, Sand revealed some uncertainty over her gender. In her professional writing she showed none: she was a man through and through. Perhaps this may help to explain the male chauvinism with which she treated feminists: in her public life, she was a marginal man who had to assert her 'masculinity' with greater vigour than those cut out by physiology for the job.[16] But this disguise, like Viola's in *Twelfth Night*, led to some embarrassment. Sand was a great exponent of frankness: André Maurois suggests that what shocked the public about her affairs was not their existence, but the 'masculine' honesty with which she admitted them. Discussing her letter to Grzymala in which she admits her frustration at Chopin's coyness about consummating the relationship, he observes:

> What the hypocritical reader, 'mon semblable, mon frère,' will never find it possible to endure patiently in this letter of Sand's, is the note of unperturbed frankness, and above all, the fact that it was written by a *woman*. Change the sex, and it will be generally agreed that it expressed the feelings not of one man only, but of *all men*. Now Sand lived as a man. In that lay her originality, her weakness, and, as she thought, her honour.[17]

But Sand's masculine persona — adopted largely for *professional* reasons — prevented her from expressing her *personal* sexuality with the same candour in her public works. The clearest example of this important point is the *Lettres d'un Voyageur*.

Published in May 1834 and written a fortnight earlier, the first 'letter from a traveller' — with 'voyageur' solidly in the masculine — was subtitled 'To a Poet' and addressed to Musset. After ignoring her persistent fever and migraines when they first arrived in Venice and leaving her to nurse herself while he went gallivanting, Musset had come down with a serious condition himself, through which Sand tended him steadily. Once he was cured, however, she packed him off to France — with plenty of her own cash in his pocket — and embarked on an Alpine rest cure with his doctor, Pietro Pagello. Sand later wrote that Pagello pressed his affections with a Mediterranean machismo for which she was unprepared, and it is undeniable that she owed Musset little. Her version of the story may be less disingenuous than it seems: she was often caught between two domineering spirits — Chopin and her son Maurice, Maurice and the less bossy but more essential Manceau, and of course her mother and grandmother. Whatever the equities of the Pagello flirtation — discussed later in this chapter — it is less than frank of Sand to pretend in the *Lettres* that it never existed.

But the masculine public persona forces this hypocrisy on her. In the *Lettres* she casts herself in the familiar 'poor student' role, even describing 'his' short but dashing appearance in some detail. Now I have criticised the tendency to read Sand's novels as autobiographical, but this is not a novel, though of course it need not be gospel truth. Sand might be allowed to adopt a fictional speaking voice even in this non-fiction work, but this persona is uncomfortably self-serving. Pagello plays a supporting role with plenty of chummy, matey good lines, all applying the masculine to the Sand figure. At one point the Pagello character muses admiringly of the little student: 'I have observed that little men are generally endowed with considerable moral force' — 'or', as Sand wheels out her more typical self-mocking artillery, 'that they are terribly stubborn'.[18] Musset appears as the absent third musketeer, their mutual best friend, by whose holy name they swear — of all things — faith. In the book's prevailing first person — which reinforces the male impersonation — Sand even claims that she 'wept like a woman' at the blissful memory of that sterling friendship.

Although all this is most uncomfortable for the reader, Sand may be excused by her desire to rehabilitate Musset. With a pitiful *naïveté* she imagined that society would blame him, not her, for the *débâcle* in which the dream ended — merely because he was the one most at fault. Sand is better known for the unattractive picture of the character usually taken to be Musset in *Elle et Lui* (1858). But her view of him in the *Lettres* is starry-eyed, particularly in light of the syphilis he contracted in the Venetian bordellos while she was home writing and recovering from her illness. 'You were bound to be a poet, you have been one in spite of yourself. In vain did you abjure the cult of virtue; you will be known as the most handsome of its young Levites . . . [in] the white garment of your purity.'[19]

Anyone with an appetite for smutty revelations about great men will put a Sand book down still famished. *Lettres d'un Voyageur* is consistent with her general reticence. It tends to support the second hypothesis I mentioned earlier: that Sand was a lone voice for modesty — in her professional works, though not in her private letters — during a Bowdlerising, Grundyish age whose surface prudishness actually masked an obsession with sex. But mixing the public and the private as they do, the *Lettres* make contradictory reading. Sand's masculine speaking voice may be a professional necessity, but it is also so terribly convenient. Her private image had been besmirched by the Venetian adventure. The male mask in the *Lettres* does not actually prove that Sand regarded her sexuality as a burden: the pseudonym 'George Sand' required an authorial *man* behind it in this first work of non-fiction which she had produced under that name. But the male figure could have been made considerably more anonymous. Indeed, the first person makes that easier: the narrator does not actually *need* to describe 'himself'. If *Lettres d'un Voyageur* is not actual proof that Sand's sexuality was a handicap to her — not a source of liberation — it is certainly consistent with evidence in that direction from the journal. It also chimes with what Sand described in her autobiography as the androgynous freedom of her obscurity when she first arrived in Paris. 'I was neither a "lady" nor a "gentleman". No one knew me, no one looked at me; I was an atom, lost in the vast crowds.'[20] Similarly she remembered with pleasure the anonymous days before *Lélia*'s *succès de scandale*: the best part was that all the newspapers called her 'Monsieur'. Female sexuality was somewhat of a curse: a professional career could partly free Sand from it, but adultery could not.

There are certainly indications that Sand's marriage was as much a flight from sexuality as from her mother's mercenary domination. After her grandmother's death, Aurore was hastily reclaimed by her mother. Her half-sister Caroline, now married, no longer required Sophie's concern, but the under-age heiress's fortune did. Now Cate's explanation of Sophie's capricious callousness towards Aurore requires to be taken with a pinch of salt, if not fairy dust: 'She had entered the age of menopause, and lacking a man to assuage her passionate feelings, she sought an outlet in tempestuous "scenes"'.[21] It is actually less patronising to think — as I do — that Sophie was after Aurore's money. She had some reason to be panicky, since Mme Dupin de Francueil's will consigned Aurore to the care of her wealthy cousin René de Villeneuve, whose family owned the glorious castle of Chenonceaux.

Sophie fought the will and was rewarded by a local magistrate's decision that de Villeneuve could act only as a surrogate guardian, with no formal powers. This verdict left Sophie free to remove Aurore to Paris, away from Deschartres — Sophie's ancient foe — and thus away from further wee-hour pilgrimages to the Dupin graves, but also away from the library and quiet of Nohant. Still exhausted by her nightly vigils with her dying grandmother, and with her four-year-old's desolation at her father's death renewed by the skull-kissing expedition, Aurore was now almost imprisoned with her increasingly bitter and mean-minded mother. The aristocratic half of her family was forced to abandon Aurore when Sophie refused to condescend to their visits, and the girl lost the hope of a match with one of the Villeneuve sons, which had been her grandmother's aim.

Allowed a visit to her friends, the du Plessis family, Aurore was propositioned by a thirty-year-old officer, Prosper Tessier. She had felt some attraction towards this would-be seducer, but was thrown into a hasty and shamed confusion when she learned that he was only after her body, not even her money. This early quickening of sexuality had ended badly, and it is little wonder that Aurore, still only seventeen, decided she could do without the physical when her next admirer presented himself. Casimir

Dudevant, whose father was the colonel of James Roëttiers du Plessis's regiment of horses, made no bones of being a passionate lover. He treated Aurore like the child she had never been allowed to be, playing games with her and the younger du Plessis girls. When the make-believe came to an end, Casimir still eschewed a conventional suitor's winning ways. He called Aurore 'a capital fellow' — perhaps appealing to her androgynous sense of herself. He had not been impressed by her beauty or even her prettiness, he confessed with an oddly supercilious modesty, but by her quiet and reasonable nature. Casimir's own appearance was unprepossessing, and his nose of Rabelaisian proportions — so much so that Sophie complained she *had* been hoping for a handsome son-in-law. (Perhaps her own nose was out of joint because Casimir asked Aurore for her hand directly, rather than requesting Sophie's permission first — a short-lived burst of egalitarianism which also won Aurore over.) If physical attraction was not the basis of the match, neither was wealth, at least not on Aurore's part. Casimir's father was a newly created baron whose money came mainly from his marriage; Casimir was only his illegitimate son. Aurore could not be accused of chasing the young man for his money any more than for his looks. She had seen enough of snobbery and class division in the war between her grandmother and mother. In a roundabout way she was drawn by Casimir's obvious negatives — the modesty of his means and position, and the sexually neuter nature of his wooing. 'He never mentioned love, and confessed himself little inclined to sudden passion or enthusiasm, and in any case ill fitted to express it seductively. He spoke of never-failing friendship.'[22]

It is hardly surprising, given this start, that the Dudevants' married life appears to have been less than torrid — for which Cate blames Aurore's 'basic frigidity', of course, and sympathises that poor Casimir's manly pride must have been stung. With her grandmother's guilt-inducing revelations to her at the start of her adolescence, the convent prescription that girls were never to walk in pairs for fear of lesbianism, and the near-rape she later implied she had endured on her wedding night, it is surprising that Sand ever saw anything in sex. When her half-brother Hippolyte announced his son's engagement years later, she warned him to make sure his son did not brutalise the bride. There was no worse desolation for a girl than this violation, she wrote. Aurore's first, wounding sexual experiences quickly resulted in pregnancy, followed by literal confinement — to the ground-floor room at Nohant where old age and finally death had trapped her grandmother. She gave birth to her first child, Maurice, at not quite nineteen, with no drugs and no trusted female attendants.

Casimir was soon indulging in modest bouts of wife-slapping, coupled with his other hobbies: hunting, shooting and drinking. Certainly he was not altogether a monster: no better or worse than other minor squires. He did take her on visits to the du Plessis home and on expeditions to the Pyrenees to revive her flagging health. At his father's home in Gascony he spirited her off on picnics to help her avoid her mother-in-law's detested company. Nor was Aurore heroically determined to be free of his tyranny. As the letter to her convent friend shows, she generally accepted that 'all power was on the side of the beard'. When she attracted an admirer in the elegant and witty young Bordeaux magistrate Aurélien de Sèze, she also accepted the double standard. Casimir had probably begun seducing the maids by then; if not, he was soon to pick up the knack. But Aurore is generally accounted to have kept her friendship with de Sèze platonic, though the man himself left the responsibility for its chastity with her. 'Continue to resist me', he enjoined her. 'Fear not that I should take offense. I would hold myself in horror were I to sully the purity of an angel.'[23] What most shocked nineteenth-century society about Sand's later affairs was not that she behaved immorally, but that she refused to behave morally enough for two.

By 1828 it appears that Sand had got over such scruples. Her daughter Solange, born in September of that year, is generally considered the natural child of her childhood companion Stéphane Ajasson de Grandsagne, whom Sand saw during a visit to Paris the winter previous. Solange is universally calumnied in all biographies of Sand for her supposed part in breaking up the Chopin relationship. Indeed, Sand herself wrote in later life that she regarded Maurice's wife Lina as her true daughter, not 'the other'. It may not be too much of a diversion at this point, however, to note that Solange herself had a rough introduction to female sexuality, being constantly harangued as a 'harlot's daughter' by Casimir. There is a story in Gerson that Casimir made love to a maid in an adjoining room while Aurore was in labour with her daughter, as a fitting punishment. Although Cate does not deny Casimir's proclivity for the denizens of the downstairs, he makes no mention of this story, which may be apocryphal. At any rate, it is clear that by this time Casimir and Aurore were no longer sleeping together. Sand wrote in her autobiography that this abstinence began even earlier: 'a complete separation of bodies from the day I conceived the hope of having a second child'.[24] Did Sand deliberately sleep with Grandsagne because she wanted a second baby, which Casimir refused to give her? Certainly her feelings about her first child were strong, tender, and maternal. (I have no wish to deny that Sand was motherly towards her *children*; I simply deny that her lovers were really her sons.)

In any case, if Sand's claim in the autobiography was not justification after the fact — though she rarely stooped to excuse herself against slander — it is consistent with her surprisingly strong belief in serial monogamy. What most shamed her in the Venetian 'idyll', she once wrote, was that she allowed herself to 'belong' to two men at once. If Hugo really enjoyed the favours of 2,000 ladies, he could hardly have been a serial monogamist. Indeed, his marriage to Adèle Foucher co-existed for thirty-five years with his liaison to Juliette Drouet. (It is worth noting that Adèle was required by Victor to keep her own infatuation with the critic Sainte-Beuve firmly under her bonnet.) Bigamy was not usually Sand's style, even when the relationship had lost its sexual component — as in her last years with Chopin. In that case, she insisted that she had remained free of other attachments despite the sexual frustration of their celibacy. It was Chopin's jealous suspicions that she had *not* which most angered her. With Casimir, Aurore was still bound by the very substantial chains of the Napoleonic civil code on marriage. But if the sexual side of the relationship was finished, she seems not to have felt herself bound in any other way.

This is a strange paradox in Sand. She has a twentieth-century cynicism about unconsummated relationships between men and women, along with our modern dogma that sex is natural and celibacy sick-minded. Yet coupled with this belief — and a healthy libido whose demands are made plain in the *Intimate Journal* and some of her letters — is a continual disillusionment with sex. Women are shackled by their sexuality, not freed by expressing it. She was frank enough to acknowledge that the sex drive is at least as great in women as in men; indeed, in her relations with Chopin, it was probably greater. Yet she thought men incapable of egalitarian lasting relationships, and women incapable of brief encounters. Women cannot live with or without long-term lovers or husbands, in Sand's rather tragic view.

Why not live with other women, then? Despite Sand's habitual pooh-poohing of women, she had a good number of female friends and one alleged lesbian lover, the actress Marie Dorval. With one of her friends, Laure Decerfz, she had a standing joke about a maternal relationship, but no one has ever suggested that this was anything but an all-girls-together friendship. If Sand's sexuality supposedly expressed itself by maternal metaphors, so did her *lack* of sexuality. It is a basic premise in logic that a cause cannot be genuine if it produces both an effect and the effect's absence. Sand was quick to bandy about terms like 'my child', but generally only when the relationship had stopped being sexual, when it had never been sexual, or when it might become sexual but had not yet done so.

The leading counsel for the lesbian thesis about Sand and Dorval is Noel Gerson, who also applies the epithet 'first modern liberated woman' to Sand. In Chapter 3 I concluded that Sand was quite *un*liberated as far as her feminism went — which was no distance at all. By now it should be clear that this chapter is written in the same key. Sand was more weighed down by her sexuality than liberated by it, and more confused about her gender identity than firm in a modern pride in womanhood. But of course even if Gerson is wrong about how radically 'free' Sand was, he might still be right about Dorval — except that he plainly intends this case to prove how liberated Sand was. That is, he seems to regard lesbianism as an indicator of feminism. Since Sand was definitely a feminist, in his opinion, she *had* to be a lesbian. Of course this defines women by their sexuality in the most chauvinist manner. Nevertheless, it is worth a look at the question of whether Sand was really bisexual.

Marie Dorval was the illegitimate daughter of two touring players. Her father ran off with another actress when she was five, and her mother died of tuberculosis while Marie was still a child. She married at fifteen — to avoid starvation, it seems — and had

had several husbands and lovers by the time she met Sand at the height of her acting career in 1833. Her current lover was the poet Alfred de Vigny, later to support Sand's candidature for the Academy prize, but at this point patently unimpressed by her person. He remarked in his journal that despite Sand's eyes — 'large and black, like the exemplary eyes of mystics' — and hair — 'black and curled and tumbling down over her collar in the manner of Raphael's angels' — she was far too mannish to be attractive. 'No grace in her bearing, rough in speech. A man in turn of phrase, language, sound of voice, and boldness of expression.'[25]

From this dismissal of Sand as overly masculine — based on the frankness of expression which, Maurois implies, irritates the sex which complains simultaneously that women are deceitful — it was a short step to the surmise that Sand was a lesbian. De Vigny was irritated by the burgeoning closeness between the two women, although he himself devoted little time to his mistress. Perhaps he was also suspicious because the friends' chats tended to occur in the small hours of the morning. But this was a professional necessity on both their parts. Dorval was playing the Countess in *The Marriage of Figaro*, and Sand required friends and lovers alike to call no earlier than nine in the evening, so that she could write. (Her first assignation with Musset stipulated this time clause in a highly unromantic but thoroughly disciplined manner.) Whatever the grounds for de Vigny's displeasure, his expletive about Sand — 'that damned lesbian' — says more about him than her.

Gerson's evidence for the affair is hardly more convincing than his motives in producing it. He makes a great deal of a long excerpt from Sand's sketchbook, published as part of the *Intimate Journal*, claiming it portrays an ardent dawn visit by Marie to George's bed. The bed would have been a bit crowded, still being occupied, if fitfully, by Jules Sandeau, and perhaps by little Solange as well. In any case, Sand always maintained that it was promiscuous to have two lovers at once, and this presumably applied to male or female paramours. The description in the sketchbook concerns an angel with long black hair — more like Sand than the blue-eyed, fair Dorval — or even more likely, a sketch for *Lèlia*, on which Sand had begun work. In any case, the excerpt has since been dated to 1832 by Georges Lubin, the

(*above*) Aurore de Saxe,
Sand's grandmother
(*left*) Louis-Claude
Dupin de Franceuil,
Sand's grandfather

(*above*) Aurore Dupin (Sand) as a child
(*left*) Stephane Ajasson de Grandsagne, who was probably the father of Sand's daughter Solange

(*above*) The house at Nohant
where Sand was born and to
which she returned in 1837
(*left*) Sand's study at Nohant

(*above*) Chopin playing to a group of friends
(*below*) A sketch of Chopin by Sand

(*above*) 'l'Artiste', a
portrait of Marie
[Do]rval
(*right*) Franz Liszt

Alfred de Musset

Gustave Flaubert

George Sand in 1834

foremost Sand textual scholar; Dorval only met Sand in 1833. Gerson's final bit of 'proof' is the undeniable truth that Sand supported and educated Marie Dorval's children after the actress's death in 1849 — the year in which Sand was also to have Chopin to mourn. But Sand was also the monetary mainstay of her half-sister and nephew, sixty Nohant peasant families after the famine of 1845, the plebeian writers Agricole Perdiguier and Charles Poncy, a distant cousin whom she took on as a foster daughter, and even Aline Chazel, daughter of the feminist writer Flora Tristan and mother of Gauguin. (Sand scorned Tristan's beliefs as 'childishness', but nevertheless she supported her old foe's daughter after the feminist's death at forty-two on a tour to recruit partisans for trade unions.) No one suggests that even Sand's supposedly voracious sexuality extended to all these beneficiaries of her kindness.

At just under thirty, in 1833, Sand had not yet been mothered properly. Marie Dorval was an effusive, confident, warm-hearted woman who was simply good for Sand. Anything more complicated in their relationship has been read in by later gossips such as the novelist Arsène Houssaye, whose pen was as poisonous as his Christian name. In his *Confessions*, distillations of *salon* tittle-tattle, Houssaye depicts Dorval returning from the theatre to find 'the strange woman [Sand] waiting for her prey while smoking cigarettes' — that old bogeyman emerging once more out of the gloom. 'A singularly amourous duo followed. The brunette loosened the blonde one's hair. The blonde loosened the dark hair of the other. And these locks of hair were mingled amid the kisses and bites. . . . '[26] Foucault may well be right: under the story of Sand's lesbianism lurks an insatiable smutty-mindedness, perhaps typical of the late nineteenth century, when Houssaye was writing. At least Sand had the grace to confine her excesses to her letters and diaries.

Indeed, there is no lack of libido in Sand's entries about Jules Sandeau, the first of the fair, slight dandies — like Musset and Chopin — for whom she appears to have had a predilection. Born at Aubusson in February 1811, the year after Musset and Chopin, Sandeau grew up at La Châtre near Nohant and won awards for his writing and drawing at the college in Bourges. He met Aurore Dudevant in July 1830, when he was nineteen and she just turned twenty-six — hardly over the hill, and not even approaching the requisite years for a *femme d'un certain âge*. (We should bear in mind that this type has always enjoyed an attractive reputation in France, and that sexual parity is more likely to be achieved when the conventional age differences are reversed. Since male virility peaks at eighteen, and female sexuality around thirty-five, biology dictates the exact opposite of the socially accepted age pattern.)

Jules and Aurore had mildly Jacobin sympathies in common, just dashed by the repression of the July Revolution. Despite Casimir's conviction — held in common with Dorothea's uncle in *Middlemarch* — that 'young ladies don't understand political economy', Aurore was much caught up in the events of the 'glorious July'. She said that the consummation of her feeling for the equally radical-minded Jules occurred spontaneously several weeks later, and there are records of trysts in the park at Nohant, in the nearby woods, and in the house itself on a flying visit by Jules, with Casimir in another wing. After this risky escapade Aurore wrote to her friend Emile Regnault that she was 'covered with tooth marks and bruises' — not generally viewed as the stuff of filial devotion.

It is perfectly true that Sand later wrote that nothing could keep her from regarding herself as Jules's mother — *after* their affair ended in early 1833. Indeed, the whole point of her remark was that because Sandeau was no longer her lover, he could be her surrogate son. This rather mushy remark is nothing more than the usual pious hope of remaining 'just good friends', but it has been seized on as proof that Sand's sexuality was exclusively maternal. Now Sand also called Sandeau her *brother* with equal blitheness, in one of the gender-diffuse 1833 letters in which she refers to herself in the feminine but signs in the masculine.[27] This fraternal simile referred, of course, to the professional partnership. Pragmatic reasons like this explain both the beginning and the end of the Sandeau romance better than 'maternal instinct'.

Sandeau was the catalyst — or more accurately, the excuse — for Aurore's decision to gamble on a writing career. After discovering in Casimir's possession a 'will' chock-a-block with innuendoes against her, she had decided that her self-respect demanded that she leave her husband. With little money of her own and few acquaintances in Paris, she relied on Sandeau's company there, where he was now studying and writing — though as it turned out, *she* wound up supporting *him*. (This pattern was common: she also supported Musset and, to a lesser extent, Chopin. It is one more reason why Baudelaire's slur on Sand as having the 'morals of a kept woman' is twaddle.) Sandeau's inability to keep to a disciplined writing routine — always Sand's professional strong point — combined with his lackadaisical attitude towards earning a living to break up the romance once Sand had found her feet. Like all her ex-lovers — with the embittering exception of Chopin — Sandeau did actually remain 'good friends' with Sand. So did Musset, who described his former mistress with honest love — though with irony in view of her modern reputation — as 'la femme la plus femme', the most womanly woman.

The most telling comment Sand made on her maternal feelings was a complaint that her lovers had exploited them: 'Women's friendship is, generally speaking, very maternal, and this feeling has ruled my life more than I wished it to'.[28] This quotation does show that Sand had a motherly streak, but the first half of the passage is always emphasised at the expense of the second, in which Sand clearly expresses annoyance at the abuse of her caring nature. Whatever Pritchett claims, Sand was more often used by her lovers than the reverse. Of course the Musset liaison has also occasioned the usual accusations that Sand drew the life-blood out of her man and then left him for half-dead. The story of the winter in Venice makes unpleasant reading, but certainly at least as much for Musset partisans as for Sand advocates. Sand always admitted quite openly that she had made mistakes in her love life, and Venice was probably the foremost. But with all her affairs, she typically gave more than she received. It is hard to see what Sand got out of the relationship with Chopin, for example — though he obtained from it the only steady emotional experience of which he ever showed himself capable. She ensured he had the right number of blankets on his bed, got him his needed milk even on top of a cliff in Majorca, and wrote his sympathy notes — to his mother, when his father died. In return he played the piano, which he would have done anyway, albeit brilliantly. 'What was in it for her?' needs to be asked more often of Sand's *amours*. It is generally assumed that the company of great men was all the reward any lucky woman could ask for — though Musset and Chopin were both less successful in their time than Sand.

It is wrong to exaggerate the misery and depravity of the Musset relationship, at least in its early days. Even Alfred's brother Paul — later to engage in a slanging match with Sand over her *Elle et Lui*, to which he wrote a rejoinder, *Lui et Elle* — admitted that he had never experienced as carefree an atmosphere as that in Sand's Paris flat when Musset lived there with her. (The pattern in Sand's affairs was usually that her lovers moved in with her — becoming 'kept men' — or that she paid for, located, and/or furnished flats for them.) Passing the winter in Venice appeared an equally light-hearted romantic lark, and it was also intended to benefit Sand's work. Her motives for the trip were as much professional as personal: her most recent novel, *Le Secrétaire intime*, dissatisfied her because its Dalmatian and Italian settings were not realistic enough. She intended to start a book about her father's army service in Lombardy. How better to combine business with pleasure than to winter in Italy?

Leaving Solange with a nurse at Nohant, and Maurice at his boarding school, Sand and Musset set off cross-country for the south in the autumn of 1833. She had first had to persuade Musset's mother — a job Musset was apparently unwilling to do for himself — that she would take good care of dear Alfred, in the maternal role others were always happy to thrust upon her. There had also been skirmishing sallies from the quarter of Musset's male friends, one of whom condemned the lovers' plans even though he was plotting a similar spree with an actress. When Musset indicted his hypocrisy, he replied piously that lady novelists were more degraded than actresses.

When the lovers arrived in Venice, Sand was already ill with fever and migraines. Musset was unsympathetic, although Sand had nursed him through schizophrenic attacks in France — such as a fit in which he heard an echo trumpeting obscene phrases and saw a dishevelled, raging spectre whose face matched his own. In her untended illness, she was also beset by financial fears. The trip was being financed by a large advance on her next novel, and she was unable to get on with writing it. The couple's money quandaries were worsened by the opulent hotel Musset preferred and the gambling debts he had left behind in Paris, settled by Sand out of her advance. Musset's pride, no doubt piqued by his financial dependence and stung by the repute which his idol Byron had achieved as a womaniser in Venice, was further threatened by Sand's superior knowledge of Italian. The outcome was a public scene in which he told her loudly that he had been mistaken in thinking that he loved her.

Now Sand had plenty of reason to doubt that anyone had ever loved her, and Musset must have known this sore to be very tender. So far the blame, if blame there must be, appears to be almost entirely his. That will be perfectly clear if we imagine *him* arriving in a foreign city in a fever, and *her* announcing that he is a bore who is keeping her from the local gigolos. The idyll would have been cut short at this point if Sand had been well enough to return home; perhaps Musset knew that she was not. With an imperturbable charity, she also feared that he would be unable to manage in Italy on his own. She had little option but to recover and work, which she did with her usual steadiness. Even in their halcyon days Sand's greater output had annoyed Musset. He would write ten lines and down an entire bottle of alcohol while she managed half a volume on no more inspirational substance than a litre of milk, he noted sarcastically. This engendered more quarrels: Musset resented her writing, and her reminders that he ought to be working too. These he dismissed airily with the *bon mot* that he was an artist, not an automaton like her.

Next Sand came down with dysentery, Musset with typhoid and bronchitis. The two doctors called in to examine him witnessed him careering around the hotel room in a six-hour naked screaming fit, during which he tried to rape and strangle Sand; later he also attempted to stab her, and Pagello for good measure. Even Cate, whose remarks about Sand's frigidity reveal mixed sympathies, pronounces Musset 'nothing less than a sadist'.[29] With a double standard from which even bohemians are not exempt, Musset shouted that Sand was a whore, and that he only regretted not having left twenty francs on her mantelpiece the first time he slept with her. Sand's stoicism against these insults only provoked him to more, he later admitted with some generosity in his *Confession d'un Enfant du Siècle*. ('Enfant du siècle' is no more Musset's phrase than 'mon semblable, mon frère' is Baudelaire's, as it turns out: Sand uses the epithet in her earlier *Lettres d'un Voyageur*.)

When Musset had recovered, after a seventeen-day vigil in which Sand slept no more than seventeen hours in all, he left for France with her money in his pocket — along with her research and notes for what was to become his play *Lorenzaccio*. (If any-one's brain was pilfered in this instance, it was Sand's, although she gave him the material. She also gave Balzac the subject for his novel *Béatrix*; Balzac enjoined his mistress to keep that secret.) What now looks culpable in Sand — or at least misguided — is the vehemence with which she entered almost instantly into a new affair with Doctor Pagello. In this relationship she exhibited her old wavering between worshipping her lover and fearing his domination. The search for the ideal always underlay both her fiction and her life, and in this, if in little else, she was a romantic in both the academic and the pulp-fiction senses. 'Love, for me, is a veneration, a cult. And if my god lets himself suddenly sink into the dung' — admittedly, she had just watched Musset vanish into a whole farmyard muck-heap — 'it is impossible for me to lift him up again and adore him. . . . Is it you, is it you at last, my Pietro, who will realise my dream? I think so, and so for this reason I see you as great as God.'[30]

Yet Sand also wanted to keep the freedom for which she may have realised she would have to pay — quite literally — if she separated formally from Casimir, and which she felt Musset had nearly cost her. And she doubted whether Pagello, as an Italian, would allow her a loose rein. 'The ardour of your gaze, the violent hug of your arms, the audacity of your desires tempt and frighten me. . . . You have perhaps been brought up in the conviction that women have no souls. . . . Shall I be your companion or your slave?'[31] Pagello's journal records that he was frightened by this letter, with some reason. Perhaps Sand was relying on him to solve the conundrum of her sexuality, for which she had not yet found any ready answers — although she was liberated to the extent that she acknowledged it openly as a problem.

In his farewell note, Musset called *her* his child — although he also begged her for the fare to Paris in a rather unpaternal manner. On his way home, he wrote another letter: 'You were wrong: you thought you were my mistress, you were only my mother . . . we were committing incest'.[32] In the same note, however, he again calls *her* 'poor dear child'. She replied with a letter addressing him in like vein as 'mon enfant' and 'mon cher petit'. Perhaps both parties slung these terms about as we might use 'baby' now. This inconclusive evidence as to who mothered whom is made even murkier by the fact that Musset's letter *en route* may have been motivated by the urge to hurt, and informed by his usual perspicacity in picking out the sore place, Sand's doubt about whether she could inspire love. Perhaps Musset's missive was only high-falutin sour grapes, with its imagery of mountain eagles and its assertion that he and Sand had once been destined for each other by heaven — which does rather contradict his denial that he ever loved her.

Sand's reply casts herself in every role *but* mother: 'Think of your George, of your true comrade, your nurse, your friend, and something better than all that'.[33] If by 'something better' she does mean 'mother', she never says so, although Musset had given her ample chance. But in a subsequent letter Sand does appear to indulge maternal feelings, though again, only when the relationship with Musset seemed to be over:

> I have next to me a friend [Pagello], my mainstay; he does not suffer; he is not weak, he is not suspicious. . . . He doesn't need my strength. . . he is happy without my having to work for his happiness. Well, I have to suffer for somebody. I have to use up this excess of energy and sensuality that are within me. I have to nourish this maternal solicitude which has grown accustomed to watching over a suffering and tired soul. Oh, why couldn't I have lived between the two of you, and made you happy without belonging to one or the other? I could easily have lived ten years like that, for I truly needed a father, but why couldn't I keep my child near me?[34]

This much-quoted letter has yielded a rich vein of gold, fool's and otherwise. Cate views it as proof that Sand's sexuality was informed by 'sentimental masochism'. Certainly Sand was often abused, by which I include physical battering by Casimir and Musset, but I am always unwilling to blame the victim. The myth of women's masochism[35] is merely another all-too-convenient stereotype about female sexuality, used by the 'M4 rapist' in his trial as an attempted defence.

But it is true that Sand dramatised her suffering after her affairs with Musset and Pagello ended — although the *Intimate Journal* gives certain proof that the torment was also genuine. For the first time she was too depressed to work. Even at the melancholy end of her time with Musset she had managed to complete *Léone Léoni* in fourteen days, and two novels (*André* and *Jacques*) date from the

Venetian six months. Yet despite this fecundity she saw herself as 'sterile' when neither Musset nor Pagello loved her. After the definitive break with Alfred — the romance flared up briefly again when she returned from Italy in the summer of 1834 — she wrote nothing for some time. 'I can't work', the *Intimate Journal* records in November 1834. 'Oh, the isolation, the isolation!'[36] She cut off her hair and sent it to the unsuspecting Musset in a skull which she actually purchased for the purpose. She penned self-debasing diary entries:

> If I could occasionally have a few lines from you [Musset], a word, a picture, permission to send you a little four-sous picture bought on the quai, just once in a while, some cigarettes I've rolled, a bird, a toy, some little thing to lull my misery and boredom, to make me imagine that you think of me when you receive these trifles! Oh, there's no calculation in me, no prudence, no thought of the world's opinion! . . . Everyone knows, everyone talks about me, laughs at me. I don't care.[37]

But to write this and the letter to Musset off as 'masochistic' implies that Sand secretly adored her suffering. If so, then she might have been expected to write about it at excruciating length, not to plummet into a chasm of atypical professional silence. Pity is the only appropriate reaction to these excerpts, I think. Accusing Sand of masochism is a way of forestalling sympathy. The woman simply wanted to be loved, and feared as she entered her thirties that she had already passed the age at which handsome princes were likely to find her worth rescuing. And the letter to Musset makes it plain that Sand wanted to be 'fathered' as much as she wanted to do a bit of 'mothering'.

In any case, this letter is counterbalanced by a plethora of candid references which make it clear that Sand's love for Musset was as physical and un-maternal as her affair with Sandeau. The *Intimate Journal* can be very intimate indeed.

> Lovely head, I shall no longer see you bend over me and wrap me in a soft languor! Never again will you stretch yourself out on my little warm supple body. . . . Farewell, my blond hair, farewell, my white shoulders, farewell to everything I loved, to everything that was mine. Now in my ardent nights, I shall embrace the trunks of pine trees and the rocks in the woods

whilst shouting your name, and after dreaming of pleasure, I shall fall fainting on the damp earth.[38]

If this is mother love, it is Jocasta's for Oedipus. No doubt a strict proponent of the 'maternal' thesis would say it is just that, that Sand's sexuality was not only maternal but incestuous. Occam's razor suggests that it is simpler to view Sand as plain ordinary heterosexual.

If so, how can we explain Sand's contention that she and Chopin lived in mutual chastity for their final six or seven years together? There seems to be an unbridgeable gulf between the letter of May 1838 to Grzymala in which Sand asks for advice on bringing Frédéric to consummate the relationship, and another letter to Gryzmala nine years later which justifies her refusal to sleep with Chopin despite his demands.[39] If the stereotypes about Sand's sexuality are contradictory — frigid and nymphomaniac, mother and sexpot — so does her behaviour seem to have been. Yet the 'maternal' myth is not much help here, either: it might explain the second letter, but not the first. I shall try to explain the two apparently incompatible letters in terms of my contention that Sand had a normal healthy female libido, heterosexual variant. The first letter is easily treated this way: the second requires a little more work.

Needless to say, Sand has been condemned for both letters. The first has been variously summed up as demonstrating 'an almost repulsive sincerity and an incredible frigidity' — Chopin's frigidity, if anyone's, I should think — or as a 'monument of duplicity and hypocrisy'.[40] The weary old spider-spinning-her-net simile has also been trotted out, even though Chopin was less worth 'catching' than Sand herself. Chopin's initial vogue in Paris had passed by the time he met Sand in 1838. His first concert in February 1832 was a critical success, but in a second recital the same year he was drowned by the orchestra. Two well-received concerts with Liszt in 1833 had been followed by a year of no recitals, and then two failed concerts in 1835, after which Chopin played no more in public until the 1840s, when Sand prodded him into it. (She thus revived his career, rather than ruined it.) Sand, on the other hand, was at the acme of her considerable fame at home and abroad in the late 1830s and 1840s. Indeed, Paris wondered what the literary lioness saw in a 'nonentity' like Chopin.

In any case, the first letter shows that Sand was actually very tentative about 'chasing' Chopin. She remarked warily to his friend Grzymala that so far she had only seen the side of Chopin's face which the sun struck. Here she was unwittingly prescient: Chopin was an impeccably mannered would-be gentleman, a witty mimic, an amusing caricaturist, and of course a flowing improviser who could spin out two hours at an informal salon appearance without recourse to printed music. But he was also prone to volcanic eruptions and fits of minor pique. The German poet Heine described him this way in the couple's early days together:

> *She* — beautiful auburn hair falling to her shoulders; eyes rather lustreless and sleepy, but calm and gentle; a smile of great good nature; a somewhat dead, somewhat husky voice, difficult to hear, for George is far from talkative, and takes in a great deal more than she gives out. *He* — endowed with abnormal sensitiveness which the least contact can wound, on which the tiniest sound will strike like thunder; a man made for intimacies, withdrawn into a mysterious world of his own, from which he sometimes emerges in a sudden spate of violent, charming and fantastic speech.

Of course he was also victim to justified depression over his health — although there is reason to think that neither he nor Sand knew officially that he was tubercular until three months before he died. Sand's doctor — and several others — all denied that Chopin was consumptive, and perhaps neither wanted to suspect the truth — though Chopin's youngest sister, Emilia, had died of the disease at fourteen.

In any case, for whatever reason, Chopin was very demanding in his sensitivity — a tactic which has sometimes been referred to jokingly but accurately as 'negotiating from weakness'. He was the archetype of the artistic soul too lofty for everyday reality — a dodge rarely permitted to women artists, and certainly not a luxury allowed Sand until Manceau took over the day-to-day running of her life. Chopin was able to impose on both his male and female acquaintances to do his work for him, and impose he did, in very peremptory and pernickety terms. To his unofficial and unfortunate factotum Julian Fontana he wrote from Nohant in 1839:

I forgot to ask you to order a hat for me from Dupont in your street. He has my measurements, and knows how light I need them. Let him give me this year's fashion. . . . Also go in, as you pass, to Dautremont, my tailor on the boulevard, and tell him to make me a pair of grey trousers at once. You can choose a shade of dark grey; winter trousers, good quality, without belt, smooth and stretchy. . . . He will be pleased to hear that I am coming. Also a plain black velvet waistcoat, but with a tiny inconspicuous pattern — something very quiet and elegant.[41]

One might think that Chopin had simply swapped gender roles with Sand, slipping easily into the 'female' role — stereotypically fussy about appearance, passive, helpless and indolent. Indeed, the composer has been called a feminine archangel. But there are many clues that Chopin was very much the domineering male in his relations with Sand. It was he who insisted on accompanying her to Majorca, where she was travelling for Maurice's health and the rheumatism which had seized up her hand so completely the previous winter that she was unable to write. His inability to tolerate the boredom of Nohant in the 'off' season required them to move back to Paris almost every year, at some expense. His requirement of a Pleyel piano in the monastery at Valldemosa had her chasing customs men up and down the docks at Palma and supervising the lifting of the instrument on a crane over the cliffs. He refused to eat olive oil or pork, the two principal foodstuffs on the island. She had to order milk brought up the hillside for him — not for her children — and eventually to buy and tend her own goat when it turned out that the milk consignment was being liberally watered down at a fountain on the way. Chopin dictated the guest list at Nohant, barring the proletarian poets in Sand's patronage and 'disinviting' even her half-brother Hippolyte. The composer's compatriot and friend, the poet Adam Mickiewicz, later said: 'Chopin is her evil genius, her moral vampire, her cross'.[42]

If I dwell on Chopin's vices, it is only to redress the balance, still largely tilted in Chopin's favour in the popular mind, though less and less so in the biographies.[43] For my own part, I cannot sit through the slow section of Chopin's E Major Scherzo dry-eyed. The same affliction troubles me when I hear the Mozart *Requiem* and think that it was sung at Chopin's funeral, with the same bass singing the *Tuba Mirum* who had done that office for Beethoven twenty years before. That Sand was also profoundly devoted to Chopin is clear from the first letter to Grzymala, although her affection was less histrionic than her folly about Musset. (For that reason it has been labelled a less sincere love by some biographers, such as Francine Mallet.) Far from pursuing Chopin, Sand reiterates her willingness to abandon him if he is vowed to a fiancée in Poland. It is most peculiar that Chopin refused to level with Sand on this score. He had been betrothed to Maria Wodzinska, but her family had already disqualified him on grounds of his poor health. Perhaps Chopin still entertained false hopes — though he had bundled up his letters from Maria and written on the outside the resigned comment, 'My miseries'. Or else he used this dead engagement as an excuse for his own ambiguity about sex.

Perhaps this second explanation — which I find more credible — may seem harsh; but everyone always takes Chopin's sexuality to be unproblematically macho. This is so far from being obvious to me that I wonder if it was not Chopin who had the homosexual leanings, rather than Sand. Perhaps this explains why the Parisian aristocracy was happy to trust him with their daughters, among whom he had a lucrative teaching practice. It may also be consonant with his extreme concern about his appearance; at his first concert, as a boy in Poland, he was less worried about his playing than about whether everyone admired his velvet collar. However, perhaps I am only slipping into stereotype about homosexuality. Nevertheless, there is no indication that Chopin had ever had a heterosexual relationship before he met Sand, though there is also no proof of any homosexual encounters. There is some speculation that he contracted a brief bout of syphilis from a prostitute in Vienna, but it is certain that he had had no mistresses before Sand, whom he met at the ripe age of twenty-eight. If the syphilis story is true, Chopin might well be chary of the flesh — and of course his own flesh gave him much reason for disquiet. When the couple returned from Majorca, Chopin weighed in at ninety-eight pounds. If Sand was initially drawn to him as to any other heterosexual male, her sense and sensibility might well have led her to impose a ban on normal relations after the Spanish trauma.

In the first letter to Grzymala, Sand complains that Chopin is hypocritical about sex — for whatever reason — a function which she regards as natural. She finds his delicacy oddly obscene — which supports Foucault — and his prudishness prurient. Sand writes — in italics, for emphasis — that she was actually '*shocked*' by his dawdling excuse that 'certain matters might spoil the memory'. To call love-making an act of 'soiling', as she relates that he did, shows a morbid scorn for the flesh. (It must be remembered, however, that it may be because his flesh was morbid that he scorned it.) '*Disdaining the body* is neither virtuous nor helpful except with creatures who are only body; with someone you love, you shouldn't use the word "disdain" but "respect" when you abstain.'[44] Chopin is only afraid of incurring the world's bad opinion: 'Chopin is scared of society, I can't think why. But I respect what I fail to understand in those I love'.[45]

In fairness, Chopin had spent a good deal of time and trouble convincing the world that he was something other than the grandson of a Lorraine peasant — with some success, judging from the number of biographies which assume his aristocratic disguise was his true colour. On this masquerade depended his living as piano tutor to the daughters of the rich, who sent carriages to fetch him and paid the sky-high fee of twenty francs a lesson. (Remember that Sand and her daughter tried to live on 250 francs *per month* at this time.) Chopin was rather conventional and timid, especially for an artist of the period which also produced the more bohemian Liszt. Sand later remarked of his dislike of modern painting: 'Everything that seems eccentric scandalises him'.[46] How could he take up openly with this least ordinary of women, who already had three novels on the Vatican Index?

What sounds like hypocrisy in Sand's first letter to Grzymala is actually rationalisation of Chopin's nervousness. She constantly tries to persuade herself that their love could and perhaps should remain on an empyrean level. Indeed, Sand is partly to blame for the halo around Chopin's head. When they returned from Majorca, she wrote to her friend Mme Marliani:

This Chopin is an angel. His kindness, his tenderness, his patience sometimes make me anxious. I imagine that his is too delicate, exquisite and perfect a nature to live for long off our fat, heavy, terrestrial existence. In Majorca while deathly ill he wrote music that reeked of paradise. . . . He doesn't know himself in what planet he is living. He is not at all aware of life as we conceive and feel it —

except, perhaps, as regards the fashion in hats. If Sand had swallowed Chopin's noble soul hook, line and sinker by this point — though her letters during his illness, rather than afterwards, complain that he was a very impatient patient — she was already tempted by the bait in her letter to Grzymala. With arduous heroism she asserted: 'I certainly don't want to abandon myself to passion, even though deep down inside me its fires still lick menacingly. My children will give me the moral strength to abandon anything that distances me from them'. Her children — then younger and more in need of her care — had done nothing of the kind when she eloped to Italy with Musset, and Sand was unable to maintain this maternal tone for long. She sighs wistfully that the odd chaste cuddle would be nice: love can't exist without kisses, nor kisses without a bit of spark.

Later in the first letter Sand offers a more sincere presentation of her own perfectly normal sexuality and of the converse unimportance of sexual matters. This passage again supports a Foucault-style view that Sand's letter has been calumnied for lacking the spreading nineteenth-century obsession, for treating sex heretically as natural and less than vital.

I shall tell you quite straightforwardly — you being my brother — this great mystery, on which everyone who pronounces my name makes some outlandish comment. I have no secrets, no theories, no doctrines, no hasty opinions, no political platforms, no pretensions, no philosophical monkey-tricks, in short, nothing thought out or calculated, and no fixed habits [about sexual matters] — and, I believe, no false principles of either complete licence or total repression. . . . I have known several kinds of love. Artistic love, womanly love, sisterly love, maternal love, spiritual love, poetic love, what shall I say? . . . Everything I have done has been sincere. Anyone who followed my actions would have thought them mad or hypocritical on the surface; but someone who knew me deeply would read me as I am: taken with beauty, hungry for truth, very sensitive of heart, very weak of judgment, often ridiculous, always open and loyal, never small-minded or bitter, angry a great deal, and, thank God, completely oblivious to evil sayings and nasty people.[47]

Sand does not deny that she has experienced 'maternal love'; but she carefully distinguishes it from 'womanly love'. In her heterogeneous experience her only fixed idea has been sincerity, and she admits that even that may be too rigid. She is afraid that Grzymala will think her two-faced: she was living with Maurice's tutor, Félicien Mallefille, at the time she realised she was beginning to be attracted to Chopin.

> I am not of an inconstant nature. On the contrary, I am so accustomed to single-minded loving, and so resistant to infatuation, *so used to living with men without thinking for a moment that I am a woman*, that I was really taken aback and confused by this little creature's effect on me [Chopin's]. I'm still not over my surprise, and if I were proud, I should feel quite humiliated . . . It saddens me to say farewell to my fine sincerity . . .[48]

These are Sand's own pronouncements about her sexuality. They should probably be believed, because they are simultaneously more comprehensive and simpler than the 'nymphomaniac', 'lesbian', 'maternal', or 'man-eater' myths. They explain more, and do it with fewer contortions. Indeed, Sand makes me feel a bit humble: how can I be sure that I am not simply another critic with more 'outlandish comments'?

My defence is that I have tried to take Sand at her own word. This works reasonably well for the first letter, but what of the second? In May 1847 Solange was about to marry the sculptor Jean-Baptiste-Auguste Clésinger, at the same age when her mother had made an equally ill-omened match. As often occurred, Sand was caught between other, more forceful personalities. Solange herself was a decisive girl, even headstrong. Although her mother is seen by Cate as having rushed her into the marriage, she was perfectly capable of doing her own rushing. There are also indications that Clésinger had already seduced Solange, and Sand was oddly solicitous of society's good opinion on the part of other women. (Remember her injunctions to feminists to preserve their honour by retreating from the fray over the vote.) For whatever reason, in the second letter to Grzymala Sand is quite lukewarm about the wedding.

> My friend, I'm reasonably content, as much as I can be, about my daughter's marriage, since she is carried away with love

and joy, and Clésinger seems to deserve it, to love her passionately, and to be able to give her the kind of life she wants. But all the same, a decision like this entails a great deal of suffering! I realise that Chopin must also have suffered, not knowing what was going on and not being able to offer any useful advice.[49]

This probably refers to nothing more than Chopin's usual head-in-the-clouds posture. It is sometimes suggested that Chopin entertained more than stepfatherly feelings towards Solange, which she encouraged, but I regard this charge as not proven. Perhaps Frédéric was a bit put out at not having been consulted, but Sand doubtless felt that she had enough strong opinions to contest with. Clésinger was a bulldozer of a man, and she also had to deal with Maurice, whose censorship of his mother's relations with the composer had already produced some distance between Sand and Chopin. Earlier Sand wrote to Mme Marliani that she was trapped between her son and lover on the Paris-versus-Nohant issue: 'I would gladly sacrifice my love of the country for him [Chopin], but Maurice is not of this opinion, and if I listened to Chopin more than to Maurice, there would be an uproar'.[50] The supposed virago Sand actually spent a great deal of her time trying to separate two scrapping dogs.

Maurice slept directly across from his mother's room at Nohant, and clearly felt entitled to supervise her night-time conduct. He later tried the same tactic with Manceau and nearly succeeded in driving him from the house. But Chopin was still officially *persona grata* at Nohant, and three days after Sand's letter to Grzymala, the pianist wrote to her in perfectly cordial terms about Solange's marriage.

Allow me to tell you how much pleasure I have had from your good letter, and how interested I am in the excellent details about your current concern. You know well that no one offers your child more sincere good wishes for her happiness.... May God uphold you in your energy and activity. Be calm and happy. Your entirely devoted Chopin.[51]

Although written in the formal 'vous' — Chopin was rarely casual — this is hardly an embittered or furious missive. But Sand did confess to Grzymala that her sexual relations with

Chopin were a source of some strain. The gossips had accused her both of wearing Chopin out by her insatiable demands and of driving him wild with her frigidity — a contradictory but still very common pair of platitudes about Sand's sexuality. This cleft stick caused Sand some grief, despite her professed — or attempted — imperviousness to scandalmongering. Now it is perfectly true, according to the second letter, that Sand disposed — negatively — in the later stages of their relationship, whilst Chopin proposed to no avail. 'He complains that I'm killing him with privation, whilst I was sure that I would kill him if I acted any differently. You see what situation this melancholy friendship places me in. . . .'[52] How can we explain this abstinence if Sand really did possess a healthy libido? Are the maternal or frigid stereotypes correct after all?

Clearly it was Sand who proposed sex and Chopin who played hard to get when they first met. His reticence eventually went by the board, as a letter from Sand to the painter Delacroix in September 1838 makes plain: it mentions that Sand is enjoying 'the delicious fatigue of a happy love'. During the Majorcan stay that winter, and the next spring, when he was cured of his Majorcan illness but still emaciated, Chopin cannot have been up to physical exertion of this or any other kind. Although it is well-nigh blasphemous to speculate on whether this other-worldly seraph was good in bed, I cannot believe that Sand and Chopin were ever greatly compatible in sexual terms. Whether or not he had bisexual inclinations, it is certainly true that he had no other recorded affairs. Unless the syphilis story is true, he may have been a virgin at twenty-eight, when he met her. By this time she had slept with nine other men, by my count — Casimir, Grandsagne, Sandeau, Mérimée, Musset, Pagello, the actor Pierre Bocage, Mallefille, and the stocky, bald lawyer Michel de Bourges, whose departure from her preferred physical type seems to have been compensated for by his skill under the sheets. But if the relationship between Sand and Chopin was unsatisfactory in sexual terms, Chopin was the last man with whom she could have exchanged frank views on improving it. In a note written during the hot summer of 1846, Sand remarks humorously that the spiritual Frédéric was much embarrassed to find himself actually perspiring. 'Chopin is astonished to find himself sweating. He is mortified by it; he claims that wash as he may, he *reeks*. We laugh till the tears come into our eyes to see such an ethereal being refusing to sweat like everybody else; but don't breathe a word about this to him; it would only make him furious.'[53] Chopin took three or four baths a day, she laughed, to purify the flesh that smelt of mortality. But Chopin's asceticism — all too rational a distrust of his own treacherous, consumptive body — cannot really have been any cause for smiling. If he was too touchy to discuss his bathing habits, what outbursts would there have been if she had tried to discuss sex?

If there was no chance of improving sexual relations with Chopin, perhaps Sand preferred to do without. This would have come hard. When Bourges reproached her — wrongly, and hypocritically in light of his wife and his other affairs — with infidelity to him during her excursion to Switzerland with Liszt and Marie d'Agoult, she wrote:

> I won't hide the fact that my chastity caused me great suffer-
> ing. I had very troubling dreams. The blood came rushing to
> my head a hundred times, and under the hot sun, in the midst
> of lovely mountains, listening to the birds sing and inhaling the
> soft scents of woods and valleys, I often had to go and sit apart,
> my soul brimful of love and my knees trembling with voluptu-
> ous desire.[54]

But now Sand was approaching forty, weary of excessive passion and justly suspicious of its consequences. It might have been easier to tell Frédéric that sex was bad for his health — as it actually was after Majorca — than to occasion ructions by implying that he was not man enough for her. Perhaps it was also more tactful to play the motherly role. If he did have any homosexual leanings, he would have been even more sensitive, and perhaps this is also consistent with his later pleas to her: he may have been protesting his heterosexuality too much.

Whether or not Chopin was man enough for Sand, he con-
tinued to suspect that someone else was more virile, and his jealousy contributed in large part to their estrangement. The 'man-eating' Sand probably was chaste during her ten years with Chopin; there had always been a strain in her of seeing her own sexuality as a cross to bear. But reasoning, perhaps, that she had not found chastity attractive with her previous male companions, Chopin remained sceptical. Now Sand viewed possessiveness as

the worst of sins: in the earlier letter to Grzymala she had offered to share Chopin with Maria Wodzinska, if he did not object to having her as a mistress and Maria as a wife. In *Les Maîtres Sonneurs* the musician Joset — generally reckoned to be the closest likeness to Chopin in her novels, certainly more so than Prince Karol in *Lucrézia Floriani*[55] — drives himself into masochistic exile from the woman he loves, partly through jealousy. Later he supports a village campaign defaming her sexual reputation, much as Chopin gave aid and comfort to Sand's blackmailing relation, Brault. In *La Petite Fadette* Sylvinet is likewise afflicted by jealousy, which Sand describes as the invisible worm in love's bud, not as a proof of devotion. It is wrong to read all Sand's novels as autobiographical, but the *theme* of jealousy and its evil effects does recur consistently after the Chopin years — even if the *plots* are not true to life. Chopin was demanding enough even when he was not jealous, as his directive on shopping to Fontana shows. This sarcoma of distrust was probably fatal to the affair.

But it is a mistake to play down the genuine happiness which Chopin found at Nohant and with Sand for ten years. André Maurois believes that during his time with her — his only mature relationship — Chopin was as happy as his nature allowed him to be. It was a productive time for her, too, and perhaps his greatest composing years.[56] The couple's friend Delacroix sketched life at Nohant in words which still evoke a sigh: 'This is a delightful place. . . . Every now and then there blows in through your window — opening onto the garden — a breath of the music of Chopin who is at work in his room, and it mingles with the song of the nightingales, and the scent of roses'.[57] At the start, at least, Majorca, too, had been romantically blissful for Chopin, who wrote from there:

I am in Palma, among palms, cedars, cacti, olives, pom-egranates. . . . A sky like turquoise, a sea like lapis lazuli, mountains like emerald, air like heaven. . . . Huge balconies with grape-vines overhead; Moorish walls. Everything looks towards Africa, as the town does. In short, a glorious life! . . . I shall probably lodge in a wonderful monastery, the most beautiful situation in the world: sea, mountains, palms, a cemetery, a crusader's church, ruined mosques, aged trees, thousand-year-old olives. Ah, my dear [Fontana], I am coming alive a little. I am near to what is most beautiful. I am better.[58]

Even if both this trip and — much later — the love affair ended badly, it is exaggerated to view them as one long disaster, though of course that makes better copy. The relationship ended with a whimper, not a bang. Sand simply stopped trying to make it work: the onus had always been on her, and now, with Solange's marriage, she had other emotional business. The next year, 1848, was completely taken up with the Revolution, and Chopin was touring in England. She tried to find out the state of his health from his sister and to contact him through Pauline Viardot, but received no reply. By October of 1849 he was dead.

It is very revealing that Chopin was unable to muster up the energy or devotion even to keep his beloved sister Ludwika company when she travelled all the way from Poland to visit him in 1844. He spent some time in showing her the sights of Paris, true, but then he fled to Nohant without warning — so ill-equipped was he to persist in any relationship. In the summer of 1847 he simply failed to return to Nohant, as he normally did in the good weather, though he continued to use Sand's Paris flat throughout that year. Exactly why he avoided Nohant — except perhaps the indolence about relationships which I have suggested — is difficult to determine. His health was worse by then, and he may simply have been too ill to travel halfway across France. We cannot really know: most of the Sand–Chopin correspondence has been destroyed — some by Sand herself, supposedly to protect Solange's good name, after Alexandre Dumas *fils* returned her some letters which had undergone extraordinary peregrinations in Poland. Other letters disappeared during the Second World War, and some passages in the correspondence were actually struck out by Maurice.

Aside from their sexual differences, Sand and Chopin were leagues apart in politics. He leaned towards elitism and the aristocracy's right to rule; she had been republican from youth, feeling that her common blood demanded it of her. Since she was also impeccably aristocratic, whereas he was merely the son of an expatriate French tutor on a Polish nobleman's estate, he may have felt that her plebeianism came cheap, and she that his airs and graces were contrived. Her anticlericalism was ill-matched by his general acceptance of Catholic doctrine, and he may have retained qualms about 'living in sin'. In professional matters, it is also less surprising that the relationship broke up than that it lasted as long as it did. Chopin agonised over composing; it has been said that Schubert would merely scribble 'Repeat in the tonic key' to fill out the last five or six pages of a sonata, but even the most simple-seeming bass in a Chopin mazurka almost never repeats itself exactly. Even during his reasonably productive Nohant period, Chopin would revise a single bar a hundred times and spend six weeks on a page, Sand said — only to return at last to his first draft. In what must have been galling contrast, Sand wrote in easy haste, though she revised at leisure with great diligence. Nor did Chopin evince much interest in literature — in part, perhaps, because his French remained imperfect.

These disparities of social and professional outlook combine with Chopin's jealousy and the couple's sexual difficulties to make the final separation look inevitable. Such prescriptions for trouble seem sufficiently strong medicine without the last ingredient: both Sand and Chopin were 'men' of genius. As early as 1902, one of Chopin's biographers wrote:

> The world takes it for granted that the wife or paramour of a man of genius is in duty bound to sacrifice herself for him. But how does the matter stand where there is genius on both sides, and self-sacrifice of either party entails loss to the world? By the way, is it not very selfish and hypocritical of this world which in general does so little for men of genius to demand that women shall entirely, self-denyingly devote themselves to their gifted lovers?[59]

In fact, Sand generally did just that, breaking off her work on the four volumes of *Consuelo* to nurse Frédéric through his grief at a friend's death from consumption in 1842. (In fairness to him, he was also a good nurse when she was ill.)

But in any case, all this is hindsight. It is vital to remember that Sand had never lived so long as ten years with any one man before. Chopin never lived *any* time with any other woman, and Marie d'Agoult had predicted that the affair would barely last a month. (This was probably back-biting jealousy on her part, since her relationship with Liszt was in difficulties.) Afterwards Chopin did lend his backing to a pamphlet put out by the father of Sand's foster-daughter, Augustine Brault, who had been hoping for a larger dowry for his daughter than the 50,000 francs Sand gave her. Chopin also took Solange's part in the often violent altercations over money which shortly ensued between Sand and the Clésingers. This disloyalty, as she saw it, angered Sand into regarding Chopin as a child in a temper fit. Perhaps she was this maternal in her feelings for him, but not much more — and again, she only used the imagery of motherhood once the relationship was dead. Nevertheless, Chopin also kept a lock of her hair in the back of his journal until he died. In a letter of April 1839 he had called her his 'angel' — parallelling her exaltation of him to the same state in her letter from Majorca to Mme Marliani. On his father's death in 1844 he had locked himself in his room, and only she was allowed to comfort him, in the French which was always a rather weak second language to him. His Polish-speaking friends were barred. Earlier, in 1842, he hung onto her in the maelstrom of depression blown up by the death from tuberculosis of his boyhood friend Jan Matusynski. For her part, Sand always maintained that 1847, the year they separated, was the nadir of her days — in a life which never lacked for trauma. 'I was 43 years old when we last saw each other', she wrote to the publisher Hetzel in October of that year. 'Now I'm 86.'[60]

In a letter from Majorca, Sand did indeed say of Chopin: 'I am caring for him as if he were my child', which was nothing more than fact about her nursing duties. In another letter she added: '*He* loves *me* as if I were his mother' — which is, of course, no proof at all that *she* loved *him* as if he were her son. Chopin may simply have been grateful for her attentions:

> More than anything else, my angel's infinite good works have set me back on my feet. . . . I never saw her anything but concerned for me. She had to care for me all by herself; God preserve us from the doctors of the place! I saw her make my bed, tidy the room, prepare herbal teas, deprive herself of everything for me.[61]

Beyond these references, and Sand's remark in her autobiography that she thought of Chopin as a child now lost to her — perhaps intended to save Maurice's face and Chopin's reputation — I see little evidence that Sand's feeling for Chopin was any more motherly than her passions for Musset and Sandeau. Certainly the first letter to Grzymala suggests that her feelings were far from being exclusively maternal. If Chopin was as happy as he had it in him to be with Sand, their sexual relationship was also as normal as he could manage, I think.

It is a continuing irony of Sand's treatment by critics that a woman known almost entirely for her lovers is rarely credited with having loved them in the usual way. That she rarely repented her *amours* — though she did say she had sometimes been lacking in judgement — only angered society further. André Maurois believes that penitent Magdalens are quite acceptable, and Foucault might agree: they strengthen conventional morality. In 1847 Sand was older and sager than in 1834, when she assumed with perfect logic but great childishness that the world should pity her and blame Musset when her affair ended. Chopin would receive all the sympathy this time, she prophesied quite correctly in a letter to Mme Marliani in November. 'The general opinion will find it pleasanter to believe that I, in spite of my age, have got rid of him in order to take another lover.'[62]

Sand did in fact enjoy a long, compensating relationship with Alexandre Manceau, but they did not become lovers until the year after Chopin's death, 1850. Two years after Chopin left her, in 1849, she had a brief affair with the political writer and editor Victor Borie, and in January 1850 a short association with the German musician and academic Hermann Müller-Strübing. Of the latter she wrote to her friend and editor Hetzel:

It's the first time I have associated myself with a robust man in the moral and physical sense. [She may have forgotten that she described Pagello as strong.] Hitherto I have, as it were, sought out weakness through a maternal instinct which merely turned me into a spoiler of children, a mother whose weakness was too well known. One is always dominated by weak beings. Perhaps I shall find equality with a strong heart.[63]

It is perfectly true that Sand mentioned 'maternal instinct' in this letter. She never denied her motherly side, but she had learned by now how to fence it off from sexuality. It was no basis for adult heterosexual relationships, as she makes plain in this letter. And her wording conveys quite the opposite implication from that imagined by Pritchett and some biographers: that she controlled or dominated her 'sons'.

As in her earlier complaint that her maternal feelings — which she thought a powerful force for good in women — had been abused and exploited, Sand is giving vent to *dissatisfaction* with a motherly kind of loving where grown men are concerned. Clearly she is thinking of Chopin's 'negotiating from weakness'. She associates mothering men with *being dominated* by them, not with 'overpowering her young lovers'. In 1837 she had addressed a similar exasperated remark to the comic *alter ego* — a male one — of her *Intimate Journal*, Dr. Piffoël.

> Must one be as blind, devoted and tireless to the object of one's love as a loving mother to her firstborn child? No, Piffoël, there's no need for all that. . . . No. No. Piffoël! Doctor of physiology, but an idiot. . . . A man holds devotion cheap, reckoning it his birthright, by virtue of having emerged from the womb of Madame his mother.[64]

In any case, Müller-Strübing was younger by eight years than Sand, but the age gap alone did not produce maternal emotions here — or in the even clearer case of Manceau, thirteen years her junior.

Sand's letter to Hetzel ends plaintively: 'I don't believe in happiness. I'm not looking for it. I don't wish to live and I cannot live without loving'. These apparently inconsistent but moving sentiments again show Sand presenting her sexuality as burdensome. If so, at least by the end of her life she had learned to avoid letting it make a martyr of her. From the start Manceau took care of her. Chopin had been solicitous during her bouts of illness, but Sand had never enjoyed the constant consideration she had earned by her professional diligence, her breadwinning, her social philanthropy and political work, and her nursing of Musset and Chopin himself. In delight she made the highest comparison: Manceau was like 'a woman who is skilled, active, and ingenious. When I am ill, I am cured by the mere sight of him preparing my pillow and bringing me my slippers. I, who have never asked to be cared for, or accepted it, need his care, as though it were in my nature to be pampered'.[65] When she wrote *Les Maîtres Sonneurs* at her usual *prestissimo* tempo in 1853, Manceau helped her to relax in the evenings by reading Sir Walter Scott to her whilst she embroidered needlework daffodils. During the day he got through several hours of engraving, did the estate accounts, supervised the workers and servants, made copies for Sand or proof-read her chapters, washed her granddaughter Nini's face, and put up with ribbing from Solange. Sand's other lovers had either allowed her to pay their rent — like Sandeau — or maintained a separate but ungenerous financial existence — like Chopin — offering her no help when she needed cash for her political causes or Augustine's and Solange's dowries. But Manceau bought her a writing retreat at Gargilesse, in a hidden valley near Nohant where the mist rested on the rocks and the sun warmed them into retaining heat when the windy Berry plain was cold. He arranged and paid for a trip to Italy for her after Nini's death, which left her terrified at the inability to work which only beset her after her worst griefs. He tended her during a nearly fatal attack of typhoid fever in 1860–1, and in the convalescence she was able to write another novel, *Valvèdre*. Then as now, house-husbands gave cause for mirth. Théophile Gautier, who visited Nohant in 1863, complained sarcastically that Manceau had turned it into a printing factory, and that it was sadly fallen from the days when Chopin's and Liszt's playing floated out over the terraces. 'Manceau has really rigged up this Nohant place for turning out copy. She can't sit down in a room without the quills, blue ink, cigarette paper, Turkish tobacco, and lined writing paper appearing from nowhere.'[66]

Although he was supportive in a way that Sand's more famous lovers had not been, Manceau appeared unsuitable to her friend, the actor Pierre Bocage, because he was 'beneath' her. Now Bocage may have been a bit jealous: he and Sand had enjoyed a brief fling in 1837. But Balzac, whom Sand never found attractive and who claimed to see only one of the boys in her, also urged her in the 1830s to take up only with 'superior' men. Women needed to look up to their husbands and lovers, he warned her. Actually Balzac's own lady friends, Madame de Berny, the marquise de Castries, and the Polish-Russian countess Evelina Hanska, were all of a higher rank than he was. But that was almost inevitable, since despite the 'de' Balzac added to his name, his grandfather was a day-labourer, though Balzac may not have known this. In any case, as a woman Sand did face genuine difficulties in finding a man who was not threatened by her great fame. Her letter about Müller-Strübing may express not only her fear of equality, but her previous lovers' defensiveness about it. How better for them to trim Sand's success down to bearable size than to consign her to the innocuous maternal role? Although Manceau enjoyed some success as an engraver, he had no illusions about competing with Sand in the glory stakes. In this, perhaps, he *was* a *genuinely* 'superior' man.

Manceau was thirteen years younger than Sand, and had originally been one of Maurice's friends. Now no one suggests that Maurice's feeling for his wife Lina Calamatta was asexually paternal, although she was nineteen years younger than he — slightly more than the age gap between Maurice and his mother. In fact Maurice seems to have feared that his mother's feelings for Manceau were not maternal enough — and indeed, it is clear from the correspondence that the relationship was physical. Maurice was a rather spoilt dilettante who did not marry until nearly forty and enjoyed his mother's favouritism until then. (There is a revealing passage in the *Intimate Journal* in which Sand debates killing herself after Musset has thrown her over. She is stopped not by the thought of the six-year-old Solange — although she must have known what it was to lose a parent in early childhood — but by prospective sympathy for Maurice, who was halfway grown up.)

In 1864, now a *paterfamilias*, Maurice elected to force battle with Manceau by demanding of Sand whether he or her lover was the boss at Nohant. When Sand assured him that he was, as the son and heir, Maurice insisted that Manceau must go — just as he had managed to menace Chopin. No one, including Sand, seems to have considered the possibility that she was the master. (In fairness to Maurice, he had been taunted by his schoolmates when Casimir publicised his wife's affairs during the separation proceedings, and he had some reason to be sensitive about his mother's sex life.) With her essential meekness, Sand actually capitulated to her son's ultimatum. But Manceau put up a more tenacious fight than Chopin had done, and Sand changed her mind. Perhaps she remembered the sorry end of the previous altercation, which may have hastened Chopin's death, away from the clean air of Nohant and Sand's nursing. She and Manceau left Maurice and Lina in possession of Nohant — much as she had surrendered the field to Casimir thirty years before, when she left him enjoying her property while she struggled to get by in Paris on 250 francs a month.

The couple now lived together at Manceau's Paris flat; later, with half the proceeds from a successful play, they bought a small cottage near Paris at Palaiseau. It was there that Manceau died of tuberculosis in 1865. Sand had tried not to know how ill Chopin was — aided and abetted by her doctor, who had insisted that the composer was merely prey to nerves and would get over it once he hit forty. (It was precipitate of him to die at thirty-nine.) But now she recognised the same symptoms in Manceau, and her journal makes hurtful reading. 'I suffer as much as ever and cannot regain my courage', she wrote on 27 June. A week later this entry appears: 'How painful it is to see him so ill and desperate! What courage can I give him to overcome such crises? I haven't got it in me to see him suffer so'. On 21 August: '<u>Dead</u>' — she underlined the word to convince herself, perhaps — 'this morning at six o'clock, after a night that was seemingly completely calm. On waking up he spoke a bit in an already dead voice, and then came vague words as in a dream, and then a few efforts to breathe, then a pallor, and then <u>nothing</u>'. In all Sand's evocative prose there is no more horrible image than that phrase, 'in an already dead voice'.

Manceau's devout mother and sister disgusted Sand by refusing to kiss Alexandre's body because he had not received extreme unction. Sand was reclusive for some time afterwards. She made a reasonable sort of peace with Maurice and spent the remainder of her life at Nohant, but returned periodically to Palaiseau, even with its ghost. To Flaubert she wrote of this retreat: 'The absolute silence, which has always been rest and recuperation to me, is now shared with a dead man who ended there. . . . Never mind; sorrow is not unhealthy, it stops us withering'.[67] That she and Manceau loved each other is patent. She also made him happy, as he evidenced in his agenda book: 'During the fourteen years that I have spent here [at Nohant], I have laughed and cried and lived more than in the thirty-three years that preceded them'. Maurice pilfered the journal and scrawled under Manceau's entry: 'What a fathead! What a fool!'

There is some speculation that Sand enjoyed a last affair in October 1865 with Charles Marchal, but the evidence seems scanty. It is more likely that Sand took no more lovers after Manceau, although she tried to buoy herself up with the remark in her journal that she was still only a sweet young thing of sixty. This ends the chronology of her loves. I hope the maternal stereotype has been shown by now to be more truism than truth. Certainly she had a maternal side, but that alone is an insufficient characterisation of her sexuality. Indeed, the motherly stereotype is more often used to *deny* Sand's sexuality, and this is particularly unfair because she *was* quite liberated in asserting the existence of female desire. It remains for me to pronounce on the two conflicting interpretations of Sand's sexuality which I brought up at the start of the chapter, in discussing Foucault, and to draw together the threads of how they might relate to Sand's fall from fame.

The first interpretation was that Sand was vilified for her loose morals because her standards, perhaps inherited from the previous century, were below those of her own day. The second, closer to Foucault, is that the nineteenth century was actually lower-minded than the eighteenth. All in all, I find the second position more convincing. In a late-life letter to Flaubert, Sand stuck to her position in the 1837 Grzymala letter. There was far too much prurient fuss made about sex, she said, which ought to be perfectly natural and easy. It was an appetite — *for women as well as men* — which had to be fed, and in that sense a constraint. Reaction to *Lélia* and to Sand's own love life was suitably outraged by Sand's claim that women, too, had sexual needs. In this, perhaps, she *was* genuinely feminist.

Sand thought there was no chance of *mens sana* without *corpore sano*, and chastity was essentially unhealthy, although pleasure was open to abuse. Restraint was required to stop such 'sexploitation', but restraint also prevents pleasure. Beyond noting this paradox, she maintained that she still had no fixed theories about morality. 'I have spent my life asking questions and having them answered one way or another, but no one has ever given me a definitive answer that brooks no contradiction.'[68]

Sand saw the society of her time as pedantically confident that there were scientific answers about sexuality, and that this was a topic of great importance for theorising about. This suits Foucault's thesis that the period was obsessed with sex, although it claimed simultaneously to sweep sex under the carpet. If Sand had no strong feelings about morality, everyone else did — and still has — about hers. This bumptiousness helps to explain why Sand is now known almost entirely for her sexuality — though, ironically, in the most inaccurate, unscientific, and platitudinous terms.

When the French biographer Maurice Toesca encountered a Sand manuscript — 2,000 pages of fine handwriting — he was struck with the irrelevance of all the speculation about her love life. Simply to copy out over one hundred volumes, averaging 300 pages each, she would have needed to spend far more time at her desk than in bed. 'I asked myself, how could a woman who worked so assiduously be considered frivolous? . . . George Sand's life was not what legend would have it. Above all, she worked like fury; she was essentially a writer.'[69] This is true, even if we have been blind to it — and I have written more about her sexuality than about any other aspect of her — because we are still caught up in the last century's moral panic. Sand was not a particularly liberated woman, and may not even have thought of herself as a woman at all. But she certainly considered herself to be a writer — with every reason. In the final chapter I show that her century agreed, whatever moralistic bees it had in its bonnet. Next, however, I want to deal with Sand's writing methods and professional discipline.

Notes

1. Michel Foucault, *An Introduction*, vol. 1 of *History of Sexuality* (tr.) Robert Hurley (New York: Pantheon, 1978).
2. Vermeylen, *Idées politiques*, drawing on a point made by Sand's first biographer, Vladimir Karénine (a Sand-style male *nom de plume* for a woman, Varvara Dmitrievna Komarova).
3. Sand, *My Life*, p. 203.
4. Ibid., p. 87
5. Sand, letter to Charles Meure, quoted in Cate, *George Sand*, p. 191.
6. Suggested by Schor, in 'Reading Double'.
7. Suggested by Mozet, in 'Lord Byron and George Sand'.
8. Dale Spender, *Man Made Language*, 2nd edn (London: Routledge & Kegan Paul, 1985), p. 27.
9. This is one of the plethora of inaccurate and vicious legends put about — all too successfully — by books such as Gribbell's *George Sand and her Lovers*. Gribbell also concocts a death-bed scene between Sand and Chopin which never actually occurred. He then cites this as evidence that Sand forced herself on Chopin even in his last

moments, in order to create a sentimental legend.

10. Sand, *Journal Intime*, p. 14, translation mine.
11. Ibid., p. 14.
12. Ibid., p. 21.
13. Sand, *Corr.*, II, pp. 117–20, July 1832, translation mine.
14. Letter of same month, probably to Ladvocat or Fournier, ibid., p. 125.
15. Ibid., pp. 159–60, letter to Amédée Picot, September 1832.
16. The 'marginal man' concept in history would point out that Hitler, for example, had to present himself as a particularly dedicated devotee of German nationalism because as an Austrian, he was only marginally German.
17. Maurois, *Lélia*, p. 266.
18. Sand, *Lettres d'un voyageur*, p. 45, translation mine.
19. Ibid., p. 51.
20. Sand, *My Life*, quoted in Rambeau, *Chopin dans la vie*, p. 100.
21. Cate, *George Sand*, p. 86.
22. Sand, *My Life*, p. 179.
23. Quoted in Cate, *George Sand*, p. 110.
24. Quoted ibid., p. 142.
25. Quoted ibid., pp. 222–3.
26. Quoted ibid., p. 227.
27. Letter to Fournier, 14 January 1833, in *Corr.*, II, p. 225.
28. Quoted in Maurice Toesca, *The Other George Sand* (London: Dennis Dobson Ltd., 1947), translated by Irene Beeson from *Une autre George Sand* (Paris: Librairie Plon, 1945), p. 12.
29. Cate, *George Sand*, p. 291.
30. Quoted ibid., p. 297.
31. Quoted ibid., pp. 295–6.
32. Letter of 4 April 1834, quoted ibid., pp. 319–20.
33. Quoted ibid., p. 320
34. Quoted ibid., p. 321.
35. The title of a book by Paula Caplan.
36. Sand, *Journal Intime*, entry for 28 November 1834, p. 9, translation mine.
37. Ibid., pp. 25–6.
38. Quoted in Cate, *George Sand*, pp. 340–1.
39. The two letters are to be in found in Sand, *Corr.*, IV, pp. 428–39, and VII, pp. 699–702.
40. Quoted in Lubin's introduction to the first letter.
41. Quoted in Orga, *Chopin*, p. 104.
42. Quoted ibid., p. 90.
43. See, for example, Rambeau, Gerson, Orga, Maurois and Mallet, and to a lesser extent, Cate, and Adam Zamoyski (*Chopin: A New Biography*, Garden City, New York: Doubleday, 1980).
44. Sand, *Corr.*, IV, p. 437, translation mine.
45. Ibid., p. 439.

46. *Corr.*, V, pp. 692–5, quoted in Cate, *George Sand*, p. 517.
47. *Corr.*, IV, p. 434; translation mine. Note that Sand again uses 'brother' with insouciance, as with Sandeau and Musset. The tone of Sand's letters is almost infallibly warm and supportive. Family metaphors came naturally to her and her circle: Liszt addressed *her* as *his* brother, and Flaubert as *his* child. It is ill-conceived to make any more fuss over her use of 'my child' than over these equally frequent fraternal images, or her friends' use of paternal metaphors with her. It is also very indicative that Sand pronounces maternal love merely one type among many she has known.
48. Ibid., p. 435, italics mine.
49. *Corr.*, VII, p. 700.
50. Ibid., p. 69, quoted in Cate, *George Sand*, p. 537.
51. Ibid., p. 705, translation mine.
52. Ibid., p. 701.
53. Ibid., pp. 370–1, quoted in Cate, *George Sand*, p. 541.
54. *Corr.*, III, pp. 569–71, quoted in Cate, *George Sand*, pp. 407–8.
55. This view, which I share, is enunciated by Rambeau in *Chopin dans la vie et l'oeuvre de George Sand*.
56. Orga, *Chopin*, p. 102.
57. Quoted ibid., p. 94.
58. Quoted ibid., p. 103.
59. Frederick Niecks, *Frédéric Chopin as Man and Musician*, quoted by Enid M. Standring in 'George Sand, Chopin, and the Process of Creation'.
60. *Corr.*, VIII, pp. 238–40, quoted in Cate, *George Sand*, p. 575.
61. Letter from Chopin to Grzymala, 12 March 1839, quoted in Rambeau, *Chopin dans la vie*, p. 61.
62. Quoted in Maurois, *Lélia*, p. 317.
63. Quoted in Cate, *George Sand*, p. 619.
64. Sand, *Journal Intime*, pp. 56–8, translation mine.
65. Quoted in Cate, *George Sand*, p. 622.
66. Quoted ibid., p. 668.
67. *Corr.*, XX, pp. 196–7 (21–2 November 1866), translation mine.
68. Ibid., pp. 205–27 (29 November 1866).
69. Toesca, *The Other George Sand*, p. 5.

5 The Great Improviser?

> The great *improvisatrice* of French literature.
>
> Henry James on Sand

Only Balzac bested Sand's output, and he lacked the handicaps of a shabby education, a rash marriage, and early motherhood. Though he lived twenty years less, he was not troubled by the demands made on her time by political activity or the nursing of two consumptives. The only way to avoid admiring Sand's massive production is to call her a hack writer and lump all her novels into the 'pot-boiler' category. Barbara Cartland, after all, is prolific. This was exactly the hypothesis with which I began reading Sand, but I was dismayed to find that the novels were actually good.

With the exception of *Un Hiver à Majorque* and *Lettres d'un Voyageur* — though Pritchett thinks only her travel writing merits consideration — I found myself more impressed by each piece. Dostoevsky, Whitman, Heine, Flaubert, Matthew Arnold, Hugo, Turgenev and Balzac himself shared my expanding admiration for Sand's work, and so I felt myself to be in good company. Sand not only 'worked like fury' but learnt her craft in a journalistic apprenticeship and through informal tutorials in conversation with Balzac. She kept it in trim with extensive revision, careful research into locales, and an admirable lack of bigheadedness, even when overwhelmed with the fame which she actually found unwelcome. Perhaps because she was a woman — Emily Dickinson was also assumed, wrongly, to be a primitive, instinctive writer who never revised — Sand's professionalism has been played down by later critics such as Henry James. James is generally known as a Sand fan, but more frequently he proved himself the sort of friend who puts enemies out of work. This typical patronising attitude helps to explain why Sand has been so largely written off as a serious writer.

Nevertheless there seems to be a genuine enigma about Sand's professionalism: at first sight, she appears to have achieved it without any training. When Aurore Dudevant resolved to make her fortune in Paris — to show Casimir, and to live with Sandeau, neither of them professional motives — she was not even sure whether she would do it by writing. Painting snuffboxes seemed an equally plausible trade to her, and she also considered her mother's modest money-spinner, needlework. It was not until she reached Paris that she discovered that the bleakest quarters were stuffed with underpaid seamstresses, and that decorated boxes retailed for less than the cost of the paints. Instead she set to writing, and *Indiana* appeared eighteen months later, soaring to overnight success. Was this simply a fluke? And was Sand really no more than a lucky amateur in her writing?

Sand speedily abandoned any thought of strolling down the other narrow financial avenues open to gentlewomen. Needlework had given her mother the scantiest of livings, and as a governess — another possibility — she would have had to neglect her own children's education in favour of cultivating the minds of little strangers. At twenty-six she was actually too old for the stage, and the casting couch was already an august institution — as she may have suspected already, and as she certainly learned later from Marie Dorval. Like Mary Wollstonecraft, left to make her own living and provide for her sisters after the small family fortune went to her elder brother, Sand quickly learned that women's economic dependence was mandatory, not a free choice made in the name of love. To take up any career at all required great courage and all the inventiveness of her mother's stock, the birdsellers and tavern-keepers.

Even in literature there were obstacles. Although France had an atypically long honour roll of women writers, no females wrote for newspapers or magazines in Sand's time. Writing was the best of a bad lot; but once Sand had made up her mind to try it, she was far from amateurish in her perseverance. She arrived in Paris with two introductions to fellow Berrichons: one to Kératry — who gave her the magniloquent advice about making children rather than novels — and one to the *Figaro* editor Hyacinthe de Latouche. Although Aurore did her somewhat inadequate best to be polite with him — 'I curtsied, I took small pinches of snuff, scattering as little as possible over his fine white carpet, I didn't put my elbows on my knees, I didn't sprawl over his chairs' — Latouche was cordial but critical of the novel she had brought for his inspection. He announced that it made no sense, and she

127

brought herself to agree. He dictated that it must be completely redone, and she chimed in rather less assuredly: 'That's possible'. He ended by counselling her to start all over again and by offering Aurore her big chance: to write columns for *Le Figaro* at 7 francs each — less a princely than a minor-baronetish sum. Although she was not yet acquainted with Balzac, and unaware that he considered 25,000 francs a year to be the minimum income on which a woman could survive in Paris, Aurore was fresh out of the self-abasement required of her by Latouche. She left; with Sandeau she then submitted an article to the *Revue de Paris*, in high hopes. A fortnight of pestering other editors later, with no results, the article was returned on the grounds that the authors were too obscure. Aurore accepted Latouche's offer.

This journalistic training was the apprenticeship which enabled Sand to write to a deadline for the rest of her life, and to keep her own personality at an impartial distance from her work. These articles in *Le Figaro* were not her first pieces: after all, she already had a novel to show Latouche — probably *La Marraine*, which she finally destroyed on the perfectly professional grounds that it was too shoddy to publish. After her unconsummated flirtation with Aurélien de Sèze, she had written a 'confession' justifying herself to Casimir, even though she had little to justify. This early work has been praised as possessing some pages whose style prophesies sumptuous mature Sandian prose. At school she had written poetry and a prose piece of philosophy, 'Portrait of the Just Man'. As a child she had wearied her mother by concocting rapid-fire stories one after another. During the time before the publication of *Indiana*, she wrote most of *Rose et Blanche*, except the rude bits she left for Sandeau to do — ironic in light of her later lewd repute. She did literary essays, including one on Sénancour's *Obermann* which has been said to define the 'mal du siècle' more thoroughly than any other piece of Romantic writing.[1] (Later the breadth of her essay subjects covered Goethe, Byron, Mickiewicz, James Fenimore Cooper, and Harriet Beecher Stowe — an impressive range for a 'primitive'.)

In September 1831 she and Sandeau published one of the literary frauds then in vogue, in this Ossian-mad period: *Le Commissionnaire*, a Chatterton-style forgery of a supposed post-humous work by Alphonse Signol. She published a story called 'La Prima Donna' in the *Revue de Paris* — which seems already to

have revised its opinion about her obscurity — and one entitled
'La Fille d' Albano' in *La Mode*. Back at Nohant under the terms
of her agreement with Casimir, she wrote a volume of *Les Pauvres
Filles* — attributed to Sandeau — in five nights, from 7 p.m. to
6 a.m. daily. Besides all these, and her journalism, she began
several exercises which were to remain stunted and half-formed.
In May 1831 she wrote with her usual self-deprecation that she
was at work on a 'trifle', 'black as fifty devils, complete with
conspiracies, executioners, assassins, fisticuffs, agonies, death-
rattles, blood, oaths, and curses'[2] — *Une Conspiration en 1537*,
which became *Lorenzaccio* after she ceded her rights in it over to
Musset.[3] Although Sand laughed it off, she had actually to do
considerable research on this historical subject, and geographical
study of Sicily for another abortive work of the same period,
L' Histoire du Rêveur. If she was a great improviser, she was only
able to compose so spontaneously because she had already taught
herself theory of music.

But Latouche also played the role of preceptor to her — though
not always of the kindly sort. She described her ill-paid work on
Le Figaro as 'the lowest of callings': We aren't exactly free agents.
M. de Latouche, our worthy boss, is always looking over our
shoulders, cutting out all the good bits, making us go along with
his fads, his oddities, his caprices. We have to write his way: for
after all, it's his business and we're only his workers'.[4] Of course
Latouche was teaching Sand to revise, whether she liked it or not,
and the rest of her life she went on revising, as I shall document
shortly. The discipline of writing to a deadline was equally
galling to her. She complained that everyone in the office could
write faster than she — this from a woman who later finished one
novel at two in the morning and began another forthwith. Even
Sand's supposedly natural facility in composition was, at the
least, enhanced by her journalistic novitiate — and perhaps even
born there.

To conclude her frequent denunciations of this Gallic Simon
Legree, Sand usually shrugged that she only put up with Latouche for the money. But the money was minuscule, and eventually she admitted that she had been stung by the writing bug.
Decorating snuffboxes no longer held any attraction.

At the moment I am crushed by work, working like a dog, and

so far it's produced nothing. Nevertheless, I still have hopes —
and besides, it's a funny thing, literature becomes a passion;
the more barriers you run up against, the more difficulties you
foresee, the more determined you become to surmount them.[5]

That Sand was no Sunday writer can be seen from this odd
reversal of the time sequence common to amateurs. Far from
being romantically enamoured of the pen's might, she began
writing only to earn a living. This she went on doing, successfully
but never fulsomely enough to satisfy her financial commitments.
She paid Musset's gambling debts, bought a substitute for Sandeau when he was conscripted, financed a winter flat in Paris so
that Chopin would not be bored at Nohant, paid for most of the
Majorcan trip and the Venetian excursion, supported her children very nearly up to the time of her death, paid for her
nephew's education, owed Casimir 'reparations' for ten years
after their legal separation, took on a foster-daughter whom she
endowed with a hefty dowry, and fed forty Nohant families out of
her own pocket. The estate's income had always run short of its
expenses.

Only one commentator denies that Sand wrote for money, and
that she was a professional in that basic if rather crass sense of the
word. Ironically, this critic is a contemporary feminist, Nancy K.
Miller, who doubts Sand's repeated claims that she wrote to earn
her bread — and that of her proliferating dependents. But
Miller's evidence is circumstantial, based on Stendhal's misogynous comment that any woman under fifty will lose her lover if she
publishes — that is, says Stendhal, 'if she has the luck to have a
lover'. Therefore she had better swear up and down that she only
writes out of need.[6] Now it is true that taking up the pen was only
justifiable for early nineteenth-century American women if their
husbands were bankrupt or their families impoverished, as I have
pointed out in my *Emily Dickinson*. But those who did publish had
genuine financial need, and the same is true of Sand. Certainly
she made light of her own work in every sense, not least in terms
of its monetary rewards. When *Indiana* was published to riotous
acclaim, she undersold its success. 'For me, as you know', she
wrote to her friend Charles Duvernet, 'the writer's trade means
an annual income of 3,000 francs, enough to cover basic expenses
and to buy sugared almonds for Solange and good tobacco for my

confounded nose.'[7] But this is a piece of whistling in the dark: it comes from a letter which betrays her nervousness over forthcoming reviews. Even in her far more comfortable old age, Sand wrote to Flaubert with perfect truthfulness: 'I live off my day's wages like a proletarian; when I'm no longer able to do my day's fill, I'll be bundled off to the next world and I'll need nothing more'.[8]

Sand complained that she was a 'literary galley slave', and yearned to enjoy one solitary day when she could write for pleasure, not profit. This subservience to the almighty franc was an odd sort of self-inflicted bondage for an idealist like Sand. It was the price of her independence, but a confining sort of emancipation. She saw writing as hard slog — whereas amateurs generally do it for light relief. Convicts thought of their balls and chains with about the same affection she felt for pen and ink, she said, and no profession was less suited to her temperament. But the rack of her childhood handwriting lessons and the harrow of the Chinese chignon must have had the desired effect on her self-discipline. She wrote to Hippolyte that she was grateful for their grandmother's admittedly un-religious faith in the Protestant ethic. Work was Sand's greatest satisfaction, and she knew how to go about it with the required strength of mind. Of this no commentator is in doubt, even though most maintain — with potential contradiction — that she was tidy in her work habits but sloppy in what she actually turned out.

After *Indiana* Sand had a surplus of laurels she could have rested on, if she had really been as lazy as she made herself out to be. One reviewer thought her style immensely superior to Stendhal's. Another, with unconsciously ironic wording, called the book 'a chaste and delicious work, simple, true and touching, and written with an exquisite purity of expression'. A third elevated this first published novel by an unknown provincial to the ranks of the period's greatest works. A fourth lauded Sand in these terms: 'You have never seen a more detailed analysis, a more exquisite dissection of feeling, a more thoroughgoing anatomy of the human heart. . . . Expression is always at the service of thought: strong, elegant and simple'.[9] With her usual diffidence Sand wrote to her friends that she was surprised and even a little saddened by such full-throated singing of her praises. '*Indiana*'s success startles me. Till now I had imagined I could work for its own sake, happily ignored, but fate has arranged things differently. Now I shall have to justify this unmerited admiration.' [10]

Using the good sense she always demonstrated in professional matters — as opposed to her frequent misjudgements in affairs of the heart — Sand simply kept on writing. During the summer of 1832 she wrote a novella, *The Marquise*, and worked solidly on what was to be her second published novel, *Valentine*, despite attacks of fever and rheumatism. Indeed, she actually worked harder when she was ill — and her letters show her often poorly. To Emile Regnault she wrote in September 1832: 'The stupid thing is that this ailment, which hadn't cropped up during six weeks of hard graft, only returned after eight days of rest and brilliant good health. As soon as I'm ready to pick up the ball and chain again, I see that I've lost the habit. Well, I must do it, all the same'.[11] *Valentine* came out in the same year as *Indiana*, which had been completed in an equally brief time, speeded up considerably by the absence of Sandeau's assistance. Sand's standard output was beginning to average twenty to forty pages per day. *Gabriel* was to be written during the two months after her exhausted return from Majorca, in a hotel room in Marseilles, in between bouts of brewing herbal tisanes for Chopin. The year 1844 was also typically Stakhanovite: *Consuelo*, *Jeanne*, and *Le Meunier d' Angibault* all finished within twelve months. This was only possible because Sand wrote ten chapters of *Consuelo* in as many days. *La Mare au diable* was completed in four days in 1845. In 1848 she wrote endless bulletins for the republican government, edited and composed articles for journals, worked on plays, and carried on with the autobiography she had recently begun — oh, and dashed off *La Petite Fadette* during a ten-day summer 'holiday'. In 1852 she was still working overtime, now for a lower rate than before the 1848 Revolution. To her foster-daughter Augustine she wrote in June: 'Between now and September I have a five-act play to write, along with a two-volume novel and several articles to do with Maurice's drawings. . . . At the moment I earn exactly one-quarter of what I obtained with half the work before 1848'.[12] Hard times and inflation, combined with low grain prices, made her complaints plausible, and her need for money continually pressing. *Les Maîtres Sonneurs* — at 500 pages, not an unusually long novel for Sand — was made ready in first draft after four weeks in 1853. Not until the age of seventy-one, in the year before her death, did Sand yield to Maurice's pleas, and cut down to an anaemic production of a paltry two novels a year, not three.

As Toesca remarks, this left little time for orgies. Sand's work schedule was flexible in its actual hours but steely in its requirement of a certain number of pages to be completed daily. During the heyday of puppet plays and piano improvisations at Nohant, Sand would work in the small hours of the morning after the frolics were over. Whether or not she had one of her common migraines, she would never go to sleep until she had produced twenty pages. In the 1830s, when her children were young, she worked from the early evening until late at night, using the time after they had been put to bed. Sometimes, as in 1832, she extended 'late at night' until very early in the morning. While Chopin was living with her, she trained herself to write while he played. He went to bed early, and she continued writing. Waiting for inspiration — the amateur's excuse — was never a luxury Sand could afford. Like Musset, the Muses were required to call at the hours her work schedule permitted.

In this strict adherence to routine Sand was highly professional. The novelist Doris Lessing has said that her own work pattern may look whimsical — two hours sleep, two hours pottering about the flat and thinking what to write, two hours writing, two hours sleep — but it works *because* it is a pattern. Any format will do, but the professional writer is distinguished by having *some* format. Other writers were certainly struck by Sand's iron professionalism. Her collaborator Dumas *fils* was much impressed when she produced *Mademoiselle la Quintinie* in six weeks. Another younger writer, Flaubert, complained that he lacked her energy, often completing no more than a page a week. Sand replied with her general humility that he made her feel guilty about her speed: was it really only a sign of her tiro status, at sixty?

Of course this concern proves her professionalism: she had doubts about the standard of her work, whereas Sunday writers usually admire theirs unabashedly. Sand never reread her own novels, open-mouthed with self-congratulation, and her comments on her opus were always disparaging. But the comparison with Flaubert does raise a possible criticism of my insistence on Sand's professionalism. She may have worked regularly but not hard; she might have written easily but never revised. This is the brunt of James's comment about 'the great *improvisatrice*'. It is a slightly different point from the charge of amateurism against which I have defended Sand, but still constitutes a refusal to take her writing seriously. Often Sand's self-deprecation has been taken at face value, and used to patronise her. She insisted, for example, that Chopin was the greater genius — against the critical opinion of her own time. She was frank about her sexual needs in the well-known letter to Grzymala, and the world has declared such candour unbearable in a woman — proof of her frigidity or nymphomania, to taste.

In a much-discussed letter to Flaubert Sand again unwittingly lays herself open to scorn. Her only motive, however, was to cheer her friend with the advice he valued from the woman he called his 'chère Maître' — with the androgyny that so often comes up in Sandian matters. Sand's lengthy letter of November 1866 tries to deal with Flaubert's disgruntlement at his tortoise-like writing speed. He had written to her, with slightly green-eyed admiration: 'The idea flows from you broadly, incessantly, like a flood. With me it's a thin trickle'.[13] Sand is said to have won her handsome lovers in youth by her very feminine power of attentive listening, and she had lost none of this self-effacing sympathy in old age. Her letter to Flaubert likens herself to an old harp on which the wind plays freely, by way of encouragement to the blocked writer.

Now if Sand really was an old harp on which the zephyrs worked their harmonious will, somebody at least had to keep her in tune. Of course she did this herself, with her daily disciplined stint of work. But this image of Sand as a natural and instinctive writer — and through modesty she connived in it herself — is proved false by an examination of the *Intimate Journal*. When she did write straight from the heart, she wrote badly. The journal is pockmarked with clichés: 'I feel; that is all. I love him. That love might carry me to the ends of the earth'.[14] She likens herself to Mary Magdalen, in a fit of malapropism — 'without hair but not without tears', referring to the Magdalen's washing of Christ's feet, and to her own recent gesture of cutting off her hair and sending it to Musset in a skull. She wades through knee-high self-pity and swamps of platitudes. It could be said that the two largest chunks of diary were composed in great stress, after the failure of her affairs with Musset and Michel de Bourges, and that they could be expected to be soppy. Sand had not yet enjoyed any tranquillity in which to recollect her emotion. But she wrote *Mauprat* during the same period as the post-Bourges part of the journal, and that is a well-structured, dramatic novel. And she endured periods of worse crisis — after Chopin's, Manceau's and Nini's deaths — and kept on writing, with no visible ill effects on her work. Sand's off-the-cuff writing in the *Intimate Journal* is as bad as anyone else's. When she really did improvise, the result was less than harmonious.

Sand doubted that there was such an animal as literary improvisation, whatever musicians might achieve. After she and Chopin attended a meeting of Polish emigrés at which Mickiewicz extemporised a long poem, she described the Polish poet as an odd survival from a distant ballad-singing past. 'Nothing like that could happen today, and whatever Liszt and Mme d'Agoult have to say about it, only dilettantes show off like that. I have no faith in the improvisations of our philosophical and literary charlatans.'[15] Sand was just about willing to admit that Mickiewicz had worked himself into some sort of trance, but this, she said, was outside most writers' experience. Improvisation, outside of music, smacked of mysticism, and hypnotic states were the province of sleepwalkers, epileptics, and fakirs — not writers.

As her scepticism about naïve genius would indicate, Sand revised her professional work extensively. Commonly, Sand critics allege that she 'improvised' every novel except the one they are discussing. Of course when all these accounts are combined, it transpires that Sand reworked all her novels. The sum of the exceptions constitutes a rule. Commentators have found this hard to credit *because* Sand wrote so much. Yet the evidence indicates that she both wrote *and* revised with assiduous speed. Pierre Salomon, for example, concedes that 'her gift of facility does not show an absolute lack of effort'. He admits *Indiana*, *Spiridion*, *Maître Favilla*, *Le Marquis de Villemer*, *Mademoiselle la Quintinie*, *Mauprat* and *Cadio* to the pantheon of works for which Sand wrote more than one draft. Francine Mallet points out that Sand requested the return of *Spiridion* — with which her editor was perfectly content — so that she could make changes. She asked Sainte-Beuve's advice on deletions to *Le Secrétaire intime*, which she judged too drawn out for such a flimsy subject. Beatrice

Didier's introduction to *Un Hiver à Majorque* makes it plain that Sand tinkered with her style in the work without satisfying her standards for natural description. Maire-Claire Bancquart's preface to *Les Maîtres Sonneurs* shows that Sand spent almost as much time on corrections as on the first draft. Fluent composition, in a short space of time, does give *Les Maîtres Sonneurs* and many other novels a sense of unity, but the carefully structured plot also took trouble. Sand altered the outline of the plot and the corresponding numbering of the chapters, shifting the focus from the country girl's tale to the musician's story, which had originally been a subplot.

Many of Sand's works appeared in several altered editions: there are variants of *La Petite Fadette*, and the second edition of *Lélia* is two-thirds new. Originally Trenmor the convict was to be the central character. In the second edition he is (thankfully) off-stage, pursuing vague revolutionary ideals, for much of the time, and Lélia assumes the main role. This Sand did because she considered Trenmor too weak a character, she wrote with a self-critical professional attitude in the preface to the revised 1839 edition. This second version of *Lélia* — itself one long revision — numbers fifteen or more erasures and rewritings on a typical manuscript page. One or two errors do slip through: Sténio's hair changes from black to blond in both editions — perhaps because of his more-than-passing resemblance to the fair-haired Musset, whom Sand met when she was writing the first draft. But even if Sand missed out this mistake, there can be no doubt that she revised with proper authorial diligence. In the 1854 preface she made things worse for herself, as usual, by claiming that she had written *Lélia* purely for her own satisfaction, quickly and without a plan. Although it is best to take Sand at her word when possible, in the intervening twenty years she seems to have forgotten *Lélia*'s genesis. She was writing not for pleasure, but for a contract specifying a large first edition of 3,000, later doubled — best-seller status in those days. The great textual scholar Georges Lubin, who has spent over twenty years editing Sand's letters and autobiographical works, refuses flatly to believe that *Lélia* was anything but a professional proposition. At the time she began *Lélia* in the early 1830s, Sand had already taken on very business-like habits, delivering to her publishers only as much copy as she had been paid for. 'Otherwise I should run the risk of writing for the glory of it, and that's a slim salary for anyone as poor in spirit and purse as I am.'[16]

We may be forced to think the unthinkable: that Sand not only wrote enough to occupy all a copyist's lifetime, but that she also spent a considerable amount of her hard-won time in revising it. To strain credulity further, she put considerable labour into researching her books. *Un Hiver à Majorque* draws on geographical texts and travel books to flesh out the incomplete picture of the island, which is all Sand was able to sketch after a three-months' stay — much of it taken up with children's lessons, marketing, removal problems, and nursing Chopin. That she realised her little-travelled-traveller's reminiscences were insufficient is itself proof of her professionalism, although there is actually a bit too much fact in the book for my taste — and not enough about Chopin for the romance-hungry. She undertook some research on Czech history before writing *Consuelo* and *La Comtesse de Rudolstadt*; she read Virgil *in the original* before beginning the Berry novels. These bucolic tales are generally regarded as the most naïve of Sand's works, drawing exclusively on her childhood evenings listening to stable grooms and hemp-spinners. Balzac had tried the peasant novel and largely failed. The genre is immensely difficult because it must be kept free of the predictable and sentimental.

In any case, the Berry about which Sand wrote was already largely dead by the time she was a child. *Mauprat* and *Les Maîtres Sonneurs* feature characters born in the mid-eighteenth century. By the late 1830s and 1840s, when she was writing these *romans champêtres*, Sand had no option but to research and recreate the old bagpipers' costumes and the steps of the peasant *bourrées*. She also took pains with local dialogue, a notorious trap. Although her peasant novels are rather liberally sprinkled with 'Oui-da's', the rough equivalent of 'Ooh aar', she was aware that she trod a fine line between authenticity and staginess. Her Berry characters are given livelier lines than their Parisian visitors in *Le Meunier d'Angibault*, but they are never depicted in a patronising way as noble savages. They are stolid, generally trustworthy, but conservative and small-minded — bovine creatures of the fertile plain. In *Les Maîtres Sonneurs* the Berrichons are constrasted with the wild, inspired men of the Bourbon forests, only 20 kilometres distant but another country. Painstaking use of musical similes and a picaresque plot concerning the wandering Bourbon bag-pipers allow Sand to deepen her portrayal of the rural person-nages. In this fine novel the plain is said to sing in a major key, the forest in the minor — and the metaphor helps to elucidate the characters. This book — my favourite of Sand's novels — retains the lush style of *Lélia*, and includes a compelling but plausible *dénouement* in a Gothic secret society's underground chambers. To tie these very disparate strands together was the work of a solid craftsman. Hardy's *Tess of the D'Urbervilles*, which attempts the same rural realism, falls into bathos by comparison, particularly when it brings in the Romantic device of the blood-dripping heart-shape working its improbable way through the ceiling plaster.

In her restoration work on the Berry countryside, Sand had to use other paints than those already on her palette. Nor was she able to scrape through on autobiographical fact in her other novels — even though she had more than the average amount of incident to describe. Of course it is great fun to guess that Prince Karol in *Lucrézia Floriani* is 'really' Chopin, or Lélia, Sand. The personnages involved are comfortably dead; of such stuff cannot be made libel suits such as the recent one against Sylvia Plath's *The Bell Jar*. It is also pleasant to imagine Russian cannon in Chopin's 'Revolutionary' étude or raindrops in his D-flat prélude, but Chopin hated the titles bestowed on his works by publishers and public, and was prone to fury at any suggestion that his music was programmatic. He convinced Sand that this was a lazy low-brow interpretation, and in her autobiography she deplores the tendency to cheapen his music in this way. Why not accord her the same courtesy? Sand was unflaggingly self-abasing — except when rampaging against suffragists — and never thought her own life interesting enough for a novel. She always maintained that her relationship with Chopin was too pedestrian for fictionalising. Chopin — depicted by Heine and Mickiewicz, who knew him, as sensitive to the point of mania — made no objection when she read *Lucrézia* out loud to him and Delacroix. Being real, Sand said, Chopin was more inconsistent than Karol, and being only an amateur, Karol 'had not the rights of genius'.[17] The source of the myth that Karol equals Chopin may have been Liszt, whose biography of Chopin was often inaccurate — not least about the warm feelings he claimed that Chopin entertained for himself. (It is perfectly true that *Liszt* admired *Chopin*, but Chopin described his rival as a 'clever craftsman without a vestige of talent' and 'an excellent binder who puts other people's work between his own covers'.[18] As with most of his acquaintances, Chopin allowed Liszt's friendship with him to be very one-sided.)

It is now beginning to be thought that Sand's art at most anticipated her life, not described it in retrospect. The actual details of the plots rarely overlap with her life. Sand never became abbess of a convent, needless to say, and Chopin — to the extent that he is best depicted by Joset in *Les Maîtres Sonneurs* — was not a dreamy, rather stupid farm-labourer turned strolling bagpiper. If there is any effect of life on work or work on life, this interplay is in Sand's characters, not her story lines. But even here the resemblances are very loose, as Sand made clear in the case of Karol. Sand believed that character should determine plot — which again distances her from her post-Romantic contemporaries, with their rococo story lines, and accounts for the attention she devoted to dialogue. Her personnages reveal themselves through conversation far more than those in *Madame Bovary*, for example, which has barely a shred of dialogue in the first 100 pages. But with her psychological acuity she combined a conviction which reflects classicism admirably but suits modern taste not at all — that character should be idealised, though set off by a realistic background. If Sand's art anticipated her life, perhaps it was because she emulated — or thought she did — such highly idealised and idealistic characters as the monk in *Spiridion*.

Beyond this concession, I see little force in the argument that Sand merely wrote from life — her own. Once again I am struck by the unlikely parallel with Emily Dickinson, who had no life to speak of. Nevertheless, critics have wasted quantities of ink and breath on speculations about personal elements in her poems: an unknown 'Master', a 'love affair' with a Philadelphia clergyman whom she saw no more than three times in her life, a supposed jilting by a mysterious lover, lacerating miseries at the hands of a 'tyrannical' father who was only an ordinary small-town bigwig. Although Byron complained that his life was too often read into his work, generally the autobiographical parallels were glamorous. With Dickinson and Sand they serve only to overrate the sexual and to play down the professional in women writers.

In one unexpected respect Dickinson and Sand were exactly alike. In a minor French provincial château still laid out in the formal parterres of Louis XVI's time, the young Aurore Dupin had been taught Yankee industry by an *ancien régime* gentlewoman who took snuff. At sixty Sand still described work as 'my mainstay, my nourishment, my all', when she no longer thought love a fulfilment. After fifty novels, a lengthy autobiography, a career in journalism and fifteen stage plays, she still regretted that she did not work more. To Solange she wrote that she had been deluded in thinking her affairs with Sandeau, Musset, Chopin and the others would bring her freedom. It was work that had emancipated her — ball, chain and all. As a New Englander, Henry James should have been impressed by Sand's tenacious discipline; instead he wrote it off as a charming feminine grace. 'She was pressed to write because she had the greatest *instinct* of expression ever conferred on a woman.' [19] Creature of sexual appetite, instinctive maternal bosom, automatic writer: how did James and other critics succeed in peddling this forged portrait of Sand even to *cognoscenti*?

Notes

1. By Marie-Jeanne Pecile.
2. Quoted in Salomon, *George Sand*, p. 26.
3. The extent of Sand's neglect during the 1960s can be seen from the fact that the fortnight of university lectures on *Lorenzaccio* which I attended never once mentioned her rough draft and research. Nor did we read a single Sand novel during a year-long course on the French Romantic movement.
4. Quoted in Mallet, *George Sand*, p. 98.
5. Quoted ibid., p. 98.
6. Nancy K. Miller, 'Writing (from) the Feminine: George Sand and the Novel of Female Pastoral', in Carolyn G. Heilbrun and Margaret R. Higgonet (eds.), *The Representation of Women in Fiction* (Baltimore: Johns Hopkins, 1983), pp. 124–51, using a quotation from Stendhal by Claudine Herrmann in *Les Voleurs de langue* (Paris: des femmes, 1976).
7. Quoted in Cate, *George Sand*, p. 200.

8. Quoted ibid., p. 695.
9. This and the preceding three reviews are quoted by Georges Lubin in *Corr.*, II, pp. 114ff. The second is by de Latouche, the fourth by Félix Pyat.
10. Letter to Charles Duvernet, ibid., pp. 114–15.
11. Letter to Emile Regnault, ibid., pp. 160–1.
12. Quoted in Mallet, *George Sand*, p. 109.
13. Quoted in Cate, *George Sand*, p. 695.
14. Sand, *Journal Intime*, p. 6.
15. Ibid., p. 94.
16. Quoted in Mallet, *George Sand*, p. 103.
17. Sand, *My Life*, p. 16.
18. Quoted in Orga, *Chopin*, p. 68.
19. Henry James, *Notes on Novelists*, p. 130, quoted in Thomson, *Victorians*, p. 227. Italics mine.

6 The Extreme Conventionality of the Other Sex

> [Women writers] are impeded by the extreme conventionality of the other sex. For though men sensibly allow themselves great freedom in these respects, I doubt that they realise or can control the extreme severity with which they condemn such freedom in women.
>
> Virginia Woolf[1]

> I believe that fifty years from now I'll be completely forgotten and perhaps harshly misunderstood.
>
> George Sand

Vaunted by Heine as a greater 'prose poet' than Hugo, admired by Hugo himself, lauded by Balzac, venerated by Dostoevsky, loved by Turgenev both in person and for her works — George Sand was rated highly, and I think correctly, by the literary men of her day. After his father's death, Alexandre Dumas *fils* wrote to Sand that Dumas *père* — who had some experience of the sex — 'loved and admired you more than any other woman'. Although Sand's reputation remains a little more secure in the Soviet Union and in France — Proust and, surprisingly, Céline having been among her votaries — it has collapsed in English-speaking countries. The English Victorians all read Sand, and most thought her the greatest French stylist of her time. Today her translations, long out of print in England and America, have only recently become available in new editions. Curtis Cate suggests that Sand's star has dimmed — to black-hole state, I should think — because we no longer see it so clearly, not because of its intrinsic brightness. He believes that we are now separated from Sand by a 'Himalayan' range of great English-speaking novelists: Dickens, Joyce, Thackeray, and Hemingway. If she appeared on this topographical map at all, she would be a piddling foothill. But this rather begs the question of who counts as a 'great': in her time Sand was thought a greater writer than Dickens.

I do not think that Sand's near-complete oblivion can be explained by mere natural subsidence. In earlier chapters I suggested other grounds: the simplistic view that she incarnates the worst of an outdated Romanticism, misogynous neo-Freudian analyses of her only as a sexual creature, or the denigration of her writing as easy and instinctive. All these stereotypes are easier to apply to women, and in this chapter I shall suggest that to some extent this defamation has been part of a deliberate campaign. Drawing on recent work by Sandra M. Gilbert and Susan Gubar,[2] I argue that men of letters in James's generation and after were stymied by a Himalayan range of *female* novelists — George Eliot, the Brontës, Jane Austen, and George Sand — which now stood between them and their forefathers. Whereas Elizabeth Barrett Browning had complained that she sought everywhere for grandmothers and found none, Lawrence, James and other late-nineteenth- or early-twentieth-century writers looked for literary fathers and saw only 'thinking bosoms'.

Of these notable women Sand was the most threatening. She was the only one to enjoy constant and lucrative professional success from her early twenties, and the only one who led much of any sexual life. That this woman should have had her cake and eaten it too was almost unbearable. But luckily for the men of James's generation, she was more vulnerable to sexual slurs than the spinsters Jane Austen or Emily Brontë, the late-married Charlotte Brontë, or even the long-virginal George Eliot, despite her association with G.H. Lewes. Besides, Sand was a mother, as none of the others had been — and neither, in disproportionate array, are most modern women writers: Willa Cather, Gertrude Stein, Edith Wharton, Virginia Woolf, Elizabeth Bowen, Barbara Pym, Katherine Mansfield, Isak Dinesen, Katharine Anne Porter, Dorothy Richardson, Dorothy Parker, Lillian Hellman, Eudora Welty, Anaïs Nin, Simone de Beauvoir, Ivy Compton-Burnett, Christina Stead, Carson McCullers, Flannery O'Connor, Iris Murdoch, or Joyce Carol Oates. Sand was thus open to maternal stereotyping, particularly, of course, because her lovers were generally younger than she was. My argument is that Sand was extremely unlucky — and much victimised — in her post-humous critical reception. But I shall spend the early part of this chapter on her reputation in showing that she was greatly fortunate in beginning her writing career at a time of high literacy, rising sales rates for the novel, and considerable French cultural influence in other countries. She 'chose' the right time to live and the wrong time to die. This goes a long way towards explaining the paradox with which I began this book: the incomprehensible distance between her reputations in life and after her death.

It is often pointed out[3] that Sand was lucky to arrive in Paris just as a new platoon of Romantics was about to see action, the old guard being *hors de combat* through age. Her art may also have been stimulated by the sudden spotlight on Paris, which had now replaced Vienna as the musical capital of Europe and which attracted exiles from Poland (Chopin and Mickiewicz), Germany (Heine) and Italy (Mazzini). But what made Sand an instant financial success was not the undoubted artistic primacy of Paris, but its high level of popular literacy. This was revolutionary in two senses: unprecedented elsewhere in Europe, and a legacy from 1789. When Sand arrived in Paris just after 1830, roughly 85 per cent of men and 60 per cent of women were literate. By 1848 the ratio had increased in men's case to 87 per cent, and in women's to 79 per cent.[4] Literacy rose far more sharply among females than males between 1820 and 1848 — and much of Sand's readership was feminine. Between 1790 and 1870 distaff literacy rose by nearly half. Now literacy statistics are notoriously unreliable, but if sampling was done in the same way all during this period, the trend would be genuine even if specific figures might be off by a few points. The estimates are best for men because of conscription: almost all young Frenchmen had to register, even if, like Sandeau, they — or their lady friends — later bought them a substitute. In one of the poorest districts of Paris — whose rates were by no means the highest in all of France — 72 per cent of conscripts said they could read and write in 1829, and 85 per cent in 1845. Wealthier areas had male literacy rates approaching 100 per cent. These figures represent those who *said* they were literate, but they are probably not too great an over-statement. When claims of literacy began actually to be tested in the conscription procedures after 1850, fewer than 3 per cent of the draftees were found to be lying. Those who could write their names were almost certainly able to read as well, since literacy teaching put most emphasis on reading. Tutors actually charged more for writing lessons, and one's soul might be saved by reading the Bible but not by writing a neat hand. Literacy rates in Sand's Paris compare very well with modern British figures. A 1987 survey found that 44 per cent of the adults questioned could understand neither fire notices nor basic timetables, and the statisticians compiling the numbers put adult illiteracy in Britain as high as 7 million.[5]

The upper classes, both French and foreign, found this mass literacy decidedly improper. A writer for the *Universel* — who might have been thought to have some personal interest in literacy — grumbled in 1829:

> The rage to read has invaded everywhere. I learned this fact recently before the door to my kitchen and the lodgings of my doorman, where I threatened twenty times, without issue, to hang the culprits if they did not bring my dinner. Reading has now reached the blacksmith's shop, the quarries, the sheds of wood-joiners' apprentices, and the stoneman's closet under the stairs.[6]

It also penetrated to the servants' quarters, where literate maids or footmen would read to their illiterate work-fellows, and to evening family reading sessions in which the servants would often be included. Working women gathered for urban versions of the rural story-telling *veillée* which had inspired Sand, and reading became common in workplaces and shops, especially during the winter. An English traveller, Thomas Frognall Dibdin, was nonplussed in 1821 by his discovery that books were 'familiar to the middling and lower orders of society'.[7] A study of the book trade remarked that all of France had become 'an immense reading room'.[8]

Ascending literacy rates combined with technological improvements in printing, publishing and bookselling, as well as with a population increase and high demand for education, to create a reliably solid market for Sand's novels. The number of potential readers in Paris — literate adults — grew even faster than the expanding population, which mounted from under 800,000 to over 1 million in twenty mid-century years. In contemporary pictures the juvenile population — the next generation of Sand fans — is shown as queuing up for admission to schools. These new schools, begun during the Restoration, ran in tandem with the old *petites écoles*, once supervised by the Church but now managed by the State. In Paris alone there were over one hundred elementary schools by 1835, more than double the number in Napoleon's time. The population of the Department of Seine rose 50 per cent between 1821 and 1850, but the number of primary schools tripled, and the percentage of children attending for free quintupled. During the 1830s a system of primary schools for adults and apprentices was set up; by 1850 there were 66 of them, enrolling 4,500 pupils. In the seven years between 1827 and 1834 government spending on education performed an exponential leap from 50,000 francs to over 1.5 *million* francs.

Although many French workers scraped along at or below subsistence level, the 1830s and 1840s constituted a comparatively prosperous period for artisans and for factory workers with grown-up families. The years 1833–7 and 1841–6 — when Sand was at her most productive — were particular 'boom' times. Newspapers increased their circulation among the mass market: by 1847 they numbered 200,000 readers, at the height of the vogue for the serialised novel — the form of much of Sand's work at this time. Eventually the more elite Romantic journals and authors were bypassed by the workers in favour of their own writers and newspapers; but Sand also managed to be in on this development, sponsoring proletarian writers and editing socialist reviews.

Lending libraries gave great play to the post-1830 generation of authors. Fiction was more popular than drama or poetry, although even verse was well represented, considering its small run size. In general, the *cabinets de lecture* assured Sand and her colleagues a far wider readership than the limited edition sizes of their novels might suggest. The median run for Romantic fiction in 1834 was only 1,000 — when Sand had enjoyed a print order of 6,000 copies for *Lélia* — and still only 1,500 by 1841. But the professional authors of the time, such as Dumas *père*, Sand and Balzac, could boast slightly larger figures, around 2,500 on average. Serialisations in newspapers and eager booking in lending libraries for instalments of new novels or new editions from the great authors helped to broaden a writer's audience beyond what would now be regarded as an academic rather than a popular edition size.

To an English-speaking reader, accustomed to differentiate between 'good' literature and 'popular' fiction — or, from a less snobby point of view, between 'egghead' stuff and 'a good read' — it may be surprising that Romanticism was a genuine mass movement. Sand enjoyed both excellent critical notices and a catholic popular following among all social classes. In this she was lucky — and skilful in sensing readers' preferences for novels which ended with marriage between the lovers, as most of hers do except for *Lélia* and *Lucrézia Floriani*. But she was not unique in her good fortune; it has been suggested that Romanticism was the first genuinely popular literary movement.

> Here the intellectual values of elites filtered downwards to perhaps the most plebeian audience ever reached by a movement of ideas in France. . . . Modest shopkeepers, artisans, prosperous journeymen, domestics, as well as financiers, *rentiers*, and their families came to borrow books from the *cabinets*. . . . The movement's significance, then, goes beyond its literary revolt against the rationality, universality, and secularism of the eighteenth-century Establishment. It marked as well the first blending of social class interest in the development of a new literature for popular consumption. . . . Well before overtly hostile relations with the newer industrial classes developed during the 1848 revolution. . . . the humanitarian bourgeois . . . the socially aspiring master artisan . . . may have read the same books.[9]

The Romantic writers were often commercially minded — whatever picture we may retain of them starving in their garrets. Rather than being martyred for their convictions, they turned their sincere interest in the common man — or woman — into hard cash. This convergence between mass and elite cultures suggests that if Sand is to be condemned for having been a literary 'hack' who wrote 'pot-boilers', so should all the Romantics be judged.

France was the best place in which Sand could have written, and the novel was the best form she could have chosen — because of its especial closeness to women in other countries, too. In the late eighteenth- and early nineteenth centuries, middle-class women had a new unwanted leisure foisted upon them, and a new literacy made open to them. The rise of the novel coincides with both these changes. The novel came to dominate literature, and women began to dominate the novel. What could be more terrifying to literary men of the nineteenth century? Fanny Burney made the modern equivalent of over \$50,000 from *Camilla*; Charlotte Brontë earned £100 for the first instalment of *Jane Eyre*. As a governess she had earned £20 a *year*, minus £4 for her washing — indicating that educated women's earnings compared unfavourably with washerwomen's. Mrs Gaskell earned more than Brontë's £100 for a mere short story, her first published work — 'and William [her husband] has composedly buttoned it up in his pocket', she noted.[10] The lending libraries and newspaper serials also popular on the Continent were augmented in England by the system of subscription publishing, to novelists' great benefit. A payment of, say, $1\frac{1}{2}$ guineas would be obtained in advance from readers, whose names would be listed on the first edition's frontispiece. Publishers were thus enabled to predict a secure market beforehand, and novelists to receive correspondingly fat advances.

That many novelists should themselves be women was natural both in terms of the paucity of other occupations open to the genteel female and of the novel's nature and demands. The form rewards psychological acuity and detailed observation of everyday life, realms in which women excel. Unlike the drama, it requires no impresario or agent; male relatives could undertake the embarrassing public negotiations. Unlike poetry, it demanded no formal training or grounding in the classics, and unlike the epic it shunned macho bloodshed. It was new and not yet colonised by men, who in any case tended to dismiss it as less than intellectually rigorous. Women were practised in its antecedent forms, letters and journals, and its emphasis on conversation and dialogue required no other research than opening their ears to what was said to and around them. Sand went further by performing actual historical and geographical researches, but she also had the advantage of a sort of recording ear. She was generally silent in company, but could reproduce entire conversations years later in her novels. In her use of dialogue she is, I have argued, superior to Flaubert — and women could expect this sort of edge. For all these reasons, women have always enjoyed a special relationship with the novel[11] — and the novel was Sand's main form.

Sand's mass success can be explained by fortunate changes in demography and literary styles, but her critical success was equally extensive. In France only Baudelaire appears to have held out against the charms of her prose — and even he was fickle, admiring her work until his mistress was denied a role in Sand's play *Maître Favilla*. That Baudelaire had read *Un Hiver à Majorque*, and consciously or unconsciously plagiarised from it, is clear from the suspiciously fraternal resemblance between his most famous sentence and a line of Sand's. The preface to *Les Fleurs du mal* contains, of course, the resonant phrase: 'Toi — hypocrite lecteur, — mon semblable, — mon frère' ('You, hypocritical reader, my double, my brother'). In *Un Hiver à Majorque*, some fifteen years earlier, Sand uses the phrase 'son semblable, son frère' in a charged denunciation of the tortures which the Inquisition might have inflicted in the romantic-seeming dungeons of a remote monastery.[12] Perhaps this evidence is circumstantial, but the probability of the phrase simply recurring by chance in Baudelaire must seem low to anyone except a proponent of the theory that a million monkeys with typewriters would eventually produce the complete Shakespeare if they kept on pounding long enough. (A recent computer simulation by Richard Dawkins has demonstrated that they would need an almost infinite space of time to engineer the single phrase, 'very like a whale'.) Baudelaire's slanders against Sand — of the 'latrine' variety — are so hysterical that they must be personal and perhaps guilty, I think — unless, ironically for a man of Baudelaire's sexual habits, they simply stem from 'the extreme conventionality of the other sex'. Even Pritchett finds Baudelaire's hostility excessive, as in his accusation that Sand was 'stupid . . . ponderous . . . long-winded . . . in moral judgement the same depth of judgement and the same delicacy of feeling as concierges and kept women'.[13]

Most French critics of Sand's day were less emotional than Baudelaire, and perhaps less sexually conventional than those of the later part of the century — which fits in with Foucault's observation that the century became progressively more obsessed with sex. Virginia Woolf might have agreed: 'No age can ever have been as stridently sex-conscious as our own'.[14] I have already documented the generally favourable and frequently rhapsodic critical response to Sand's early novels, including of course Chateaubriand's encomium to her as the next Byron. By the time of her death the Realist movement had somewhat overtaken her work. Yet Sand herself was reasonably realistic in her portrayal of the Berry peasantry, and the Realist Flaubert predicted that she would 'remain one of the splendors of France and unmatched in her glory'.[15] Near the end of her life, he wrote to her that she would immediately recognise her own influence in his *Histoire d'un coeur simple*, but to his great desolation he failed to finish the book before she died. Flaubert also dropped a fascinating comment on Sand's androgyny: 'One had to know her as I knew her to realise how much of the feminine there was in that great man, the immensity of tenderness there was in that genius'.[16] Turgenev made a similarly gender-free remark: 'What absence of every petty, mean or false feeling! What a brave man she was, and what a good woman!'[17]

There was plenty of muck-raking surrounding Sand in her lifetime, as witness the pornographic ravings of Arsène Houssaye on Sand's friendship with Marie Dorval. But in France her generosity in sponsoring new writers, socialist causes and plebeian poets, together with the greater placidity of her personal life in the Manceau years and after, acquired her the reputation of 'The Good Lady of Nohant'. Until her death, at least, personal admiration and professional approbation concurred in French opinion. She is still somewhat less without honour in her own country than in the English-speaking world. Tourist guides set out an autoroute for Sandophile pilgrims to Berry. But even in France she is often considered a 'schoolgirl's' writer — the ultimate insult — known from her vast opus only for two stories exempted from the censor's prohibition, *La Petite Fadette* and *La Mare au diable*. The irony, of course, is that she has been relegated to this 'safe' status because the authorities considered her other novels to be dangerously radical.

In Russia the official censor also applied his blue pencil to Sand, although novels were in general better able to penetrate the frontier than non-fictional political works. Dostoevsky judged that the government had outsmarted itself in prohibiting all Western works except fiction: Sand's *Horace*, *Compagnon du tour de France*, and *Meunier d'Angibault* were more radically communist than less leftist writers' non-fiction. But in translation Sand's novels were nevertheless abridged and 'corrected'. Most Russian intellectuals read her in the original, and could admire her style with the same bilingual good taste shown by the English Victorians.

Meanwhile official St Petersburg yellow journalism detailed her sprees in male attire, during which, it was alleged, she not only swore like a dragoon but — yes — smoked cigarettes. This right-wing campaign to discredit Sand harped not only on her trousers, but also on her supposedly shrewish heroines — although they are no more 'domineering' than Sand herself was, that is, not at all. 'In these books there is something awesome and somber: a woman rebelling against man, her sovereign master. A rebellion filled with bitterness and vengeance, filled with regrets like pride itself, like the vengeance of Satan in *Paradise Lost*'.[18] Of the major Russian authors, however, only Tolstoy joined this state-sponsored witch-hunt, with his declamation that if Sand's heroines had been real, they should have been 'tied to a pillory for the edification of the populace and dragged through the streets of St. Petersburg'.[19]

Dostoevsky, Gorky, Turgenev, Belinsky, Herzen and Bakunin all disagreed ferociously; nor was Tolstoy in step with popular opinion. In 1847 Pauline Viardot wrote to Sand from Russia: 'Here all your works are translated the moment they appear. . . . Everyone reads them, from top to bottom of the social ladder. . . . Men adore you. . . . Women idolise you. . . . All in all, you reign more sovereign than the tsar in Russia'.[20] An entire school of novels originated in the 1840s — 'Zhorzhzandism'. Even conservative Slavophiles were greatly taken with Sand's depiction of the peasantry in *La Mare au diable*, in which they saw a form of peasant commune like the Russian *obshchina* whose rebirth they awaited. The most influential Slavophile except Dostoevsky, Alexei Khomyakov, even defended Sand from other right-wing commentators' sexual slurs. *Lucrézia Floriani*, the epitome of sluttishness to the reactionary press, would probably have been respected as a pillar of society had she been a man, remarked Khomyakov in a prescient attack on the double standard. Because it is men's depravity that causes women's, he said, 'the teachings of George Sand are justified'.[21]

On left-wing intellectuals, especially the Russian 'Men of the Forties', Sand had an even more profound influence. Mikhail Bakunin first read Sand as a student abroad, writing — in French — to his family: 'Each time I read her works I become better — my faith becomes stronger and greater. . . . No other poet, no other philosopher is as appealing to me as she is, none has so well expressed my own thoughts, my sentiments and needs. . . . Reading George Sand is like a cult, a prayer for me.'[22] Later Sand was to defend Bakunin against a charge of spying for the tsar — made by Marx's newspaper, the *Neue Rheinische Zeitung*. Sand's impact in Russia was initially far greater than that of the German Idealist tradition of Fichte and Hegel which influenced Marx. There she was not put down as a scatty female, but extolled as a practical sort of prophet.

Sand's doctrine on the justifiability of political violence altered after the failed 1848 Revolution, and even more so after the bloody suppression of the Paris Commune in 1871. In *Spiridion* the monk expiring under the rebels' blows forgives his assassins with a phrase that reverberated throughout Russia: 'Liberty can only be bought at the price of social cataclysm and revolution'. Later, however, Sand turned more pacifist, and the Marxist doctrine of inevitable class conflict is absent from her novels. As Sand was condemned by French radicals for her failure to support the Commune, so has she been to some extent by Russian Marxists for ignoring the class war which they feel confronted France directly. But Soviet historians and critics still admire her forthright, self-reliant peasant characters and her ability to tailor her works to readers of all social strata. Gorky called her 'the good, intelligent George Sand' and considered her both a valiant propagandist for avant-garde ideas and a genuine people's writer. That she was both popular and socialist carries weight in the Soviet Union — whereas both traits have been held as marks against her in capitalist countries, particularly Anglo-Saxon ones.

The 'woman question' reached Russia almost entirely through Sand's novels, even if she was not herself a feminist. Alexander Herzen's wife Natalie enthused in her diary that Sand was 'the Christ of the female sex'. *Jacques* roused more stir than any other novel for its depiction of the misery of conventional marriage. Sand's message was seen as the legalisation of divorce — though she actually argued against that if marriage could be improved — and as reform of the marriage contract — which was undeniably her great concern. Herzen predicted in his own diary: 'In the future there will be no marriage, the wife will be freed from slavery. . . . Has not the voice of George Sand proclaimed woman's opinion?'[23] When his wife began a liaison with the German poet Georg Herwegh, Herzen decided that Sand would be the only fair arbitrator. He intended to publish an account of the couple's affair and send it to Sand, 'the highest authority in matters concerning women'.[24] Herzen's novel *The Village* (1846), directly inspired by Sand's *Jeanne*, triggered a new Russian style.

Another 'man of the Forties', Vissarion Belinsky, wrote in an 1842 letter to Bakunin that George Sand was 'the Joan of Arc of our times, the guiding star, the prophetess of a great future'.[25] That Sand was somewhat less lily-white than the Maid of Orléans made no difference to Belinsky, who even likened her to the Virgin Mary: 'It's not the first time that a woman was the saviour of the world'.[26] In an earlier letter he, too, showed that he understood Sand to be at her most prophetic where women's liberation was concerned: 'I understand now how George Sand could devote her entire life to the war against marriage. . . . It is time to liberate the human person'.[27] Formerly Belinsky had most venerated Schiller, Goethe, Hoffman and Sir Walter Scott. All were second-rate, he said, compared to Sand.

When Dostoevsky first read Sand in his adolescence, he reminisced later, a fever of excitement afflicted him all night. In his *Diary of a Writer* he accorded her 'virtually the first place among a whole pleiad of new writers who at that period suddenly rose to fame and renown all over Europe'.[28] In the same work he related his dejection at her death: 'As I read the news, I understood what her name had come to mean in my life — how much enthusiasm and veneration this poet had produced in me at the time [when he first read her] and how many joys, how much happiness she had given me back then'.[29] Although Dostoevsky was also influenced by Schiller, Balzac and Dickens, he was particularly and deeply moved by *Mauprat* and *Spiridion*. These lodestars of his youth also guided his last novel, *The Brothers Karamazov*. Edmée de Mauprat, one of Sand's many morally-superior-to-the-average-male heroines, is thought to have influenced Dostoevsky's series of virtuous women who reform fallen men. The use of doubles, a recurring device in Sand, is also common in Dostoevsky. Even the Grand Inquisitor sequence in *The Brothers Karamazov* may be attributable to Sand, who wrote that Christ would hardly be welcome if he were to return. Dostoevsky retained a fascination for experimental forms, particularly those that shaded over into philosophy. Sand had attempted this sort of mix in *Lélia* and *Spiridion*, to her publisher's moans, in the latter case, that the book would never sell. That *Lélia* was *intentionally* plotless is indicated by the fact that Sand had published two perfectly normal 'plotted' novels before — *Indiana* and *Valentine* — and by Musset's crowing that his then mistress's new work had 'caused all visible novels to crumble' — those whose only interest was their narrative convolution and Gothic improbability.[30] Likewise, Dostoevsky believed the novel to be the best arena for gladiatorial combats between ideas. The myth that Sand wrote only pulp fiction obscures her philosophical bent, but her idealism was constant, and plain to a like-minded writer. 'George Sand is one of us, a Russian idealist of the 1840 generation. . . . Perhaps some people may laugh at the great importance I accord her, but the mockers are wrong.'[31]

Ivan Turgenev likewise eulogised Sand as 'one of *our* saints'[32] — with a loving possessiveness typical of her Russian admirers. He imitated Sand's *romans champêtres*, particularly in *A Sportsman's Sketches*. This work was thought mildly seditious — an apologia for the abolition of serfdom — because in it the peasants are generally more noble than the aristocrats. Now not all Sand peasants are noble savages: the soundly common-sensical Grand-Louis in *Le Meunier d'Angibault* is counterbalanced by the greedy rich peasant Bricolin. But for *any* peasant to be portrayed as anything other than a rural dolt — or to be portrayed at all — was largely Sand's innovation. Turgenev pronounced her novel *François le Champi* 'simple, true and poignant' and apparently drew on the 'holy fool' character of Patience in *Mauprat* for Kasyan in his story 'Kasyan from Fair Springs'. But he also felt that Sand had not completely solved the technical conundrum of how to make uneducated characters speak in a language intelligible to the literate reader. Sand was aware that she trod a tightrope: 'If I let the man of the fields speak in his natural manner, the civilised reader will need a translation, and if I make him talk like you and I, he becomes an incredible creature, to whom we must attribute a style of thought which he doesn't actually possess'.[33] Turgenev was to solve the riddle by using an educated landowner as his narrator — not an entirely original solution, since Sand had used a similar device in *Mauprat*, before *François le Champi*, for which she perhaps felt it was inappropriate.

Women in Turgenev are generally said to be stronger than male characters — another instance of Sand's influence, perhaps.

But Turgenev also complained to Pauline Viardot in words that recall the contemporary critics who begrudged women their comparative importance in Sand: 'Sand often spoils her most fascinating female characters by forcing them to be talkative, sober-minded and pedantic. . . . Even Fadette belongs in this category'.[34] Pritchett, too, objects that Sand writes description well, 'but the inevitable tutorial follows'. Women with ideas and wit are a centime a dozen in Sand, I agree, but this hardly seems a failing to me. Rather than forcing her women to be talkative, as Turgenev charges, Sand simply allowed them to speak — and I suppose that was heretical. Nevertheless Turgenev retained his admiration for Sand, despite these supposed flyspecks. To the novelist and critic Alexander Druzhinin he wrote: 'For you she represents a delusion to be uprooted. For me she represents incomplete truth when complete truth is unattainable'.[35]

Sand — whose novels, according to stereotype, are the opposite of Realism — is actually credited with *founding* Russian Realism by Prince Mirsky in his history of Russian literature, along with Gogol. She and he were the movement's mother and father, he says. If this is a large claim, it is no broader than Francine Mallet's insistence that Sand originated the idea of the 'useless man', Dostoevsky's 'smeshny chelovek', in the final letter of *Jacques*. This recurring type in Russian literature, the Oblomov character, could have been found in many other French Romantic books, of course, but since Sand was the most widely read writer of her generation in Russia, the claim is plausible. In politics, too, Sand's influence in Russia was perhaps disproportionate to the originality of her ideas. Although I reject the chauvinist line that Sand picked up her radicalism from her lovers, I would hesitate to call her an original political thinker. But she was an immensely powerful populariser of republican and socialist ideas.

In America the Puritan heritage ensured that Sand — like Shakespeare to Emily Dickinson's educators — was seen as a dangerous libertine. In the 1840s, Henry James wrote twenty years later, 'to read George Sand in America was to be a socialist, a transcendentalist, and an abolitionist'.[36] To be fair to James, he himself thought that Sand treated 'the erotic sentiment . . . with singular austerity'.[37] But the American writer most influenced by Sand was also the one with the shakiest moral reputation — Walt

Whitman, whom Emily Dickinson refused to read because she had been told that he was shocking. Whitman reviewed Sand's *Compagnon du tour de France* for his newspaper, the *Brooklyn Daily Eagle*, and was so enamoured of her picture of artisan life that he posed in his father's carpenter's costume for his portrait in *Leaves of Grass*. Her iconoclasm and socialism he found greatly refreshing. 'The talented French woman is nevertheless one of a class much needed in the world. Needed lest the world stagnate in wrongs merely from precedent'.[38] The *Compagnon*, her first major political tract, was his bedside reading, but he also admired her novels — preferring them to Hugo's because Sand, the woman, was less hysterical. 'I like Madame Dudevant better. Her stories are like good air, good associations in real life, and healthy emotional stimuli. She is not continually putting crises into them, but when crises do come they inevitably go to the heart. How simply yet profoundly they are depicted. You have to lay down the book and give your emotions room.'[39]

In this essay Whitman also compared Sand to Ralph Waldo Emerson and found the latter too dry. She occupied the *juste milieu*, that classical ideal which she attains with a frequency ignored in the received truth that she was 'all Romantic'. As I suggested in Chapter 2, Sand ultimately transcends the Romantic–classical dichotomy by refusing to elevate either heart or head over each other. This is also a common theme in Whitman: promotion of the body to the soul's nobility — or if one prefers D.H. Lawrence's words on Whitman, seizing the soul by the scruff of the neck and setting it down among the potsherds. Either way, Whitman rejects the ancient mind–body split which dates at least to Plato, and which recurs in modern philosophy in Cartesian dualism and the twentieth-century debates that has inspired. This theme occurs in *Consuelo*, from which Whitman copied out phrases and which he apostrophised as 'a genuine masterpiece: the most noble work George Sand has left us, the most noble in several senses, on its own ground and in all of literature'.[40] Whitman was as prodigal in his paeans to himself as in his praise of Sand, and his self-congratulatory tone owes nothing to Sand. Despite her self-dramatising stereotype, it was rare for Sand to 'loaf and invite my soul' as Whitman did in 'Song of Myself' — although he records of his visit to Emerson that he must have seemed very quiet and dull to the brilliant company, as Sand always feared she did at gatherings of the literary elite. But in Whitman's political and philosophical convictions, he certainly saw Sand as his kinswoman.

It is interesting that the other great Sand adherent of mid-nineteenth-century America was Margaret Fuller, also to be branded for loose behaviour when she produced an illegitimate son by an Italian count. Fuller, a very early feminist, influential critic, and co-editor of *The Dial* with Emerson, was able, like Whitman, to see beyond the 'shockingness' of Sand, even before her own much-condemned affair. *Consuelo*, the first novel to be translated in America, struck Fuller not as a plea for free love, but as a demonstration of 'how inward purity and honor may preserve a woman from bewilderment and danger, and secure her a genuine independence'.[41] Baudelaire may have likened Sand's standards to those of 'concierges and kept women' — which does give grounds for wondering what possible grudge he had against concierges — but Fuller credited her with

> the same high morality of one who had tried the liberty of circumstance, only to learn to appreciate the liberty of law, to know that licence is the foe of freedom. And, though the sophistry of passion in these books [*André, Jacques* and *Les sept Cordes de la Lyre*] disgusted me, flowers of purest hue seemed to grow upon the dank and dirty ground.[42]

Fuller admired Sand's style — 'not vehement, but intense, like Jean-Jacques' — and combination of intellect with sensibility — 'a manly grasp of mind, but not a manly heart'. She called Sand 'the best living French writer' — high praise from the most Europeanised of mid-century Americans, but not as fulsome as Fuller's reconsideration, 'perhaps the best living writer'. Although Fuller was even more shy than Sand, she called on the Frenchwoman during her 1847 visit to Paris. In that *annus terribilis*, Sand gave the lesser-known woman an entire day of her time, with her usual large-heartedness.

Sand was praised and imitated by writers of many other nations. Mickiewicz and she formed a small mutual admiration society. Zola, whom she helped to promote but who later turned against her work, did attribute to Sand a considerable impact on Ibsen, and thence on the modern drama. The second generation of Italian Romantics, in the late 1830s, held her second only to

Byron. Mazzini respected not only her politics but also her prose style. His notebooks are crammed with references to her novels, and the lyrical tone of his correspondence may owe something to her influence. Heine fell out with Sand over *Lucrézia Floriani*, as did Delacroix: both were insulted on Chopin's behalf, even though the usually irascible composer was quite placid about the book himself. But Heine was dispassionate enough to account *Lucrézia* 'infinitely superior' to Hugo: 'George Sand has everything Victor Hugo lacks: truth, naturalness, taste, beauty, enthusiasm, everything united in a pure harmony. Sand's genius has fine well-rounded curves to it, and everything gives off an air of grace and gravity. Her style is a mix of harmony and formal beauty'.[43] Heine also paid Sand a personal compliment: she was more beautiful than the Venus de Milo and, besides, several years younger.

But with the exception of the Russians, no entire national grouping of authors was more taken with Sand than the Victorian English. In Britain, as in Russia, Sand was fortunate during her lifetime: literate readers were fluent in her language, and the French novel generally esteemed. It would be mistaken, however, to overstate the ease with which the early Victorians were able to overlook Sand's sexual behaviour, so that I could heighten the contrast with James and other late-nineteenth-century writers. At the very start, in 1833, *Lélia* was called 'a monster, a Byronic woman' in the English press.[44] Indeed, Sand was alleged to be Byronic in more ways than one: an *Atheneum* review of February 1833 related with a straight face that she had tried to run away with Byron at the age of thirteen. Scurrilous gossip about her life was retailed before her books were reviewed in many of the notices. *Indiana* was dismissed as 'two volumes of all love and nothing but love'— jolly un-English of it. In the early years one or two reviewers were misinformed about Sand's sex, and in this mistaken judgement they were able to produce impartial reviews. In Chapter 2 I cited the *Edinburgh Review* article of July 1833 which fulminates against the excesses of the Hugo generation but exempts the novels of 'Monsieur Sand'.[45]

But by 1836 the truth was out, and the *Quarterly Review* elected to live up to its reputation for critical acumen by slamming Sand. (Previously the periodical had blithely predicted that Keats and Tennyson would be flashes in the pan.) Its review of Sand honoured what Patricia Thomson calls 'the best *Quarterly Review* tradition of vituperation and inaccuracy', and added snobbery for good measure. Much of the article was spent disputing the Dudevant title — actually new but entirely legitimate — and, in contradictory wise, enjoining Sand to espouse social ideas more appropriate to her aristocratic background. *Lélia* was lambasted because its cast included a convict and a prostitute. Blending Tory fear of revolutionary-minded France with patronising sexism, the *Review* lamented that Sand's novels were 'exhibited even in London in the windows of respectable shops . . . to be had in circulating libraries . . . nay; *ladies' book-clubs*'.[46]

But the characteristics which disturbed the High Tory press endeared Sand to many Victorian readers. Sand is always *engagée* and serious-minded, although the medicine goes down with a spoonful of humour and elegant style. That she was quite high-minded enough for English taste was suggested by a *Westminster Review* article of April 1838. 'It is against, and not for licence, that Sand is contending: for the right of a woman to belong to the man she deems worthy, and while she deems him worthy. How completely is the thing sought always a pure, unselfish, eternal affection!'[47] Although modern feminists might jib at the idea that a woman could 'belong' to any man, worthy or no, this reviewer — probably Francis Burdett — correctly identified Sand as an idealist. He also noted that English literature was then at a low ebb, whereas French writing was in a floodtide which would fertilise all other cultures. This forecast proved correct in terms of the notable authors who read and were influenced by Sand. Again she was fortunate during her lifetime: her novels arrived in England at a time of dissatisfaction with the old, but absence of much new.

Thackeray was one of the first Englishmen to rhapsodise over Sand's prose style. Although he made chauvinist fun of her 'philosophical friskiness' and deplored her immoral reputation, he was moved by her 'brief rich melancholy sentences . . . like the sound of country bells — provoking I don't know what vein of musing and meditation, and falling sweetly and sadly on the ear'.[48] This was fair-minded praise from one who believed that Frenchmen were inferior to Englishmen because they dined on vegetable soup whilst the English gorged on beef. Francophobia did colour other reviews far more than Thackeray's, however, as witness this gloating prediction in the *Foreign and Colonial Review* of April 1843: 'A few George Sands will soon reduce France to the level of the orang-outang or little better, possibly something worse'.[49] This was scanty repayment for the compliment Sand had offered England by dropping the 's' off 'Georges'. But G.H. Lewes, later George Eliot's cohabitee, reviewed her collected works more sympathetically in 1844:

> Never was there a more notable instance of giving a dog a bad name and hanging him. Mme. Sand has been known to travel in androgynous costume; smokes cigars; is separated from her husband, and has been the theme of prolific scandal. The conclusion drawn was that from such a person nothing but anti-social works could possibly be expected.[50]

He agreed with Thackeray about the excellence of Sand's style, which he called 'perhaps the most beautiful ever written by a French author'. But he also offers the first evidence of the mistaken assumption that because her style was gorgeous, it was effortless. 'Poetry flows from her pen as water from the rock; she writes as the birds sing, without effort, but with perfect art.' This is particularly inaccurate because Lewes was discussing *Lélia*, two-thirds revised between the first edition of 1833 and the second of 1839. Nevertheless, Lewes judged Sand both more chaste in her characters' ethics and more psychologically acute than Balzac. 'Sand, like a poet, has known and felt life; Balzac has observed it.'

As Sand approached the menopause, and as the last of the 'Boney'-haters died out, her work became more acceptable. The novels of the 1840s seemed to English reviewers to turn less on the 'woman question' and more on socialism; interestingly, the latter was perceived as less threatening. By the time the Berry novels appeared in translation, Sand was in her mid-forties and no longer categorisable as an oversexed hellion. Her professional industry and discipline appealed to none other than Samuel Smiles. By 1847 Sand wrote in a letter that she was now in great vogue on the other side of the Channel. Her earlier sins had not been entirely forgiven: Thomas Carlyle trumpeted against 'a strange new religion, named of Universal Love, with Sacraments mainly of Divorce, with Balzac, [Eugène] Sue and Company for Evangelists, and Madame Sand for Virgin . . . a new astonishing

Phallus worship'.[51] (It is noteworthy how much more lewd than Sand were her detractors.) But Carlyle had been judging by hearsay: when he actually read Sand's books, he recanted, telling Lewes that there was 'something Goethian about the woman'. Perhaps his initial remarks were also conditioned by his wife Jane's disobedience of his injunction against Sand being read in the Carlyle household — or by her new habit of smoking little cigars, albeit in private.

John Stuart Mill concurred in the universal delight at Sand's prose style. 'As a system of purely artistic excellence, there is not in all modern literature anything superior to the prose of Mme. Sand, whose style acts upon the nervous system like a symphony of Haydn or Mozart.'[52] Mill acted as a useful barometer of the state of critical opinion in 1842, when he wrote to Lewes: 'There are other admirers of her writing and of herself in this canting land — among which I am neither the only nor the best'.[53] This burgeoning admiration for Sand's novels irritated Dickens, who felt aggrieved because reviewers were beginning to take French writers more seriously than English. But Dickens's style is actually more prolix than Sand's. His inventive metaphors are often swaddled in layers of flannel, as in this excerpt from *A Christmas Carol*.

[Scrooge was] secret and self-contained, and solitary as an oyster. The cold within him froze his old features, nipped his pointed nose, shrivelled his cheek, stiffened his gait; made his eyes red, his thin lips blue; and spoke out shrewdly in his grating voice. A frosty rime was on his head, and on his eyebrows, and his wiry chin. He carried his own low temperature always about with him, he iced his office in the dog days; and didn't thaw it one degree at Christmas.

So far, so excellent, but Dickens will continue:

External heat and cold had little influence on Scrooge. No warmth could warm, nor wintry weather chill him. No wind that blew was bitterer than he, no falling snow was more intent upon its purpose, no pelting rain less open to entreaty. Foul weather didn't know where to have him. . . .[54]

And so on, and on. This determination to gild the lily in Dickens may account for Dostoevsky's preference for Sand's more spare style — although it has become another received truth that Sand is verbose.

Elizabeth Barrett Browning was another of the Sandian coterie in England — even though she had once been sceptical, fearing that Sand might be a 'naughty' writer. She branded *Lélia* 'a serpent-book both for language-colour and soul-slime',[55] but this phrase occurs in a letter to a friend who considered Sand to be Lucifer incarnate, and it may only be a form of polite agreement, despite the strength of its wording. Later she wrote to her cousin Kenyon that Sand's novels had been a lifeline to her in the enforced reclusion of her youth. 'When I was a prisoner, my other mania for imaginative literature used to be ministered through the prison bars by Balzac, George Sand, and the like immortal improprieties. They kept the colour in my life to some degree, and did good service in their time to me.'[56] Elizabeth's father considered Byron improper reading for young ladies and kept *La Nouvelle Heloïse* locked away. The furtiveness with which Elizabeth had to read Sand may have given her a particularly strong feeling for the Frenchwoman, whom she regarded as a fellow idealist and social radical. Sand described herself as a 'poet', and *Lélia* is sometimes referred to as a prose poem. Elizabeth Barrett's longing for 'grandmothers' — 'Where are the poetesses? I look everywhere for grandmothers and see none' — may have been partially fulfilled by Sand. Two sonnets invoke her, one beginning '[thou] large brained woman and large hearted man, self called George Sand . . .' Robert Browning was decidedly less enthusiastic about *Consuelo*, which he shrugged off in the manner which dominated later criticism as 'a woman's book, in its merits and defects'.[57] But Elizabeth rode roughshod over his objections and risked the chill of February to pay two calls on Sand when the couple were in Paris.

There has been some speculation that *Aurora Leigh* is heavily indebted to Sand, especially to *Consuelo* — whatever Robert's opinion of it. The similarity between 'Aurora' and 'Aurore' may only be a coincidence, but both Aurora Leigh and Aurore Dudevant were professional women writers making their way in a man's world. Perhaps Aurora represents an idealised, smut-free George Sand. Certainly Sandian themes occur in the book: 'Art is much, but love is more'.[58] And the expression of sexual matters is

franker than the ambiance of Wimpole Street would have suggested: 'With all that strain / Of sexual passion, which devours
the flesh / In a sacrament of souls . . .'[59] In another parallel with
Sand — though perhaps an unintended one — Elizabeth Barrett
Browning also found herself scolded for such candour by reviewers.

Charlotte Brontë, who spent two years in Brussels when Sand
was most adulated on the Continent, pronounced that it had been
worth learning French just to read *Consuelo* in the original. Brontë
was not uncritical of *Consuelo*'s defects or of Sand's 'masculinity',
as she saw it, but she found these faults redeemed by the 'poetry'
in the novel. Jane Austen, said Brontë, was 'only shrewd and
observant'; Sand was better, being 'sagacious and profound'.[60] Like
most critics of the time, she preferred Sand to Balzac: 'George
Sand has a better nature than M. de Balzac — her brain is larger
— her heart warmer than his. . . . Most of her very faults spring
from the excess of her good qualities; it is this excess which has
often hurried her into difficulty, which has prepared for her
enduring regret'.[61] Sand might have written the preface to the
second edition of *Jane Eyre*: 'Conventionality is not morality;
self-righteousness is not religion'. Brontë's aesthetic creed also
resembles Sand's aim of presenting idealised, symbolic characters
in a realistic setting: 'I hold that a work of fiction ought to be a
work of creation; that the *real* should be sparingly introduced in
pages dedicated to the *ideal*'. Two other common themes in Sand
also occur in Brontë and may be some proof of influence: the
sacredness of the heart's dictates, and the paradoxical difficulty of
carrying them out in ordinary marriage.

George Eliot called her namesake George Sand one of the
greatest influences on her own work. *Jacques* may have affected
Eliot's grim portrayal of marriage in *Middlemarch* and *Daniel
Deronda*. Unconcerned about Sand's morals, Eliot evinced a just
admiration for Sand's humour — which few other critics had
noticed — and for her psychological sensitivity. Being a man in
name only, Eliot was free of 'the extreme conventionality of the
other sex' as regarded Sand, even if she did insist in being called
'Mrs Lewes'.

> I don't care whether I agree with her about marriage or
> not. . . . It is sufficient for me as a reason for bowing before her

in eternal gratitude to that "great power of God" manifested in her — that I cannot read six pages of hers without feeling that it is given to her delineate human passion and its results and . . . some of the moral instincts and their tendencies — with such loving gentle humour that one might live a century with nothing but one's own dull faculties and not know as much as these six pages will suggest.[62]

Thomson suggests that Eliot may have been emboldened to run away with Lewes by Sand's example. Eliot's choice of pseudonym may be another instance of Sand's effect. Despite their own surface emancipation, both Sand and Eliot also attacked feminists. Both used masculine narrative voices — Sand in *Mauprat*, Eliot in *Scenes of Clerical Life* — and like Sand, Eliot began a slide into obscurity after her death — although she was saved by the ministrations of Virginia Woolf in *The Common Reader* (1925). Sand enjoyed the protection of no such knightess in shining armour.

Like Dostoevsky, Matthew Arnold was greatly affected by reading Sand in his youth. Although he hesitated to return to *Lélia* after he was 'past thirty and three parts iced over', Arnold attributed to Sand's novel an impact similar to that of Goethe's *Werther*. He made a pilgrimage to Nohant while he was an Oxford student and was still reading Sand in 1888, the year of his death — which cut short his intended projects of an essay on her serene old age and an edition of her selected letters in English translation. After she died in 1876, he wrote to his sister: 'Her death has been much in my mind; she was the greatest spirit in our European world from the time that Goethe departed'.[63] On the fly-leaf of his copy of her *Impressions et Souvenirs* he wrote a quotation from *Mauprat* describing Edmée's good influence, which he applied to Sand herself: 'In the impression she has made on me, there is mingled something so consoling . . . so good for the soul'.[64] Arnold's brother Tom went so far as to call Sand the interpreter of God's truth. Matthew Arnold admired Sand's discipline: 'She continued at work till she died. For forty-five years she was writing and publishing, and filled Europe with her name'.[65] In his turn he went on reading at least one new Sand novel every year. On the first anniversary of her death he wrote an article in the *Fortnightly Review* (1877), praising her dissent from social convention, her feeling for nature, and her humanitarian idealism. With an unfortunate lack of predictive accuracy, he forecast that '[the] immense vibration of George Sand's voice upon the ear of Europe will not soon die away. . . . There will remain of her to mankind the sense of benefit and stimulus from the passage upon earth of that large and pure utterance — *the large utterance of the early gods'.*[66]

These encomia are all the more startling in that Arnold normally displayed towards women writers 'the extreme conventionality of the other sex'. Of Harriet Martineau he said: 'What an unpleasant life and unpleasant nature!' Margaret Fuller's essays were sent packing with the comment: 'My G-d, what rot did she and the other female dogs of Boston talk about Greek mythology!' Charlotte Brontë he labelled 'a fire without aliment — one of the most distressing barren sights one can witness'. Harriet Beecher Stowe was, in his considered judgement, 'a Gorgon'. (Poor Stowe was either castigated as a domineering female by such as Arnold or patronised as a 'little woman', as in Lincoln's introduction of her as 'the little lady who started this great war'. Arnold's terminology was quite moderate compared to the epithets of 'termagant virago' and 'foul-mouthed hag' unloaded on Stowe by the justly forgotten George Frederick Holmes.) Yet in Sand's case Arnold was able to transcend masculine prejudice. Does this make nonsense of the argument that Sand has not simply fallen from favour, but been pushed by male critics? After all, female Victorians were also chary of Sand because she was thought improper; and men such as Mill, Arnold, Lewes, and, to a lesser extent, Carlyle were Sand advocates.

Lewes and Mill both conducted long-term liaisons outside marriage which earned them much opprobrium from 'good' Victorian society. Like Whitman, perhaps they already held unconventional sexual attitudes when they read Sand, and they could be impartially receptive. Even more important, it was the male *essayists, critics* and *poets* of the period who liked Sand best; a novelist like Dickens was likely to find her threatening. Henry James was both a critic and a novelist, of course, but his short stories — which I shall discuss shortly — indicate that he was most concerned with his status as a rising novelist. James and other men of his generation also had to contend — as, say, Thackeray, did not — with a matriarchy of notable female predecessors. The male French and Russian novelists who followed Sand faced no such threat: Sand was a unique token woman to them, and no danger. The Russian and French continued to read and admire Sand after her death — by which time the English-language novelists, in an evil coincidence, were combatting a 'monstrous regiment of women' captained by George Eliot and officered by Austen, the Brontës, and Mrs Gaskell, with Mrs Ward, Elizabeth Braddon, Harriet Beecher Stowe, and dozens of other female writers among the enlistees.

At the time of Sand's death in 1876, she was accepted as one of the greats — probably more so than any other woman writer. By no means all the male authors of this period were hostile to her. Robert Louis Stevenson began reading her just before she died, writing in 1873: 'I have found a new friend, to whom I grow daily more devoted — George Sand. I go from one novel to another and think the last I have read the most sympathetic and friendly in tone, until I have read another. It is a life in dreamland'.[67] Oscar Wilde condemned E.M. Caro's biography of Sand in a *Pall Mall Gazette* article of 1883 as 'the biography of a very great man from the pen of a very lady-like writer'.[68] Thomas Hardy, who was told to read Sand by Leslie Stephen if he was serious about the bucolic genre, rated her among the top ten French writers as late as 1899.

But none of these authors has been so influential in determining our low twentieth-century opinion of Sand as Henry James. It seems an indicative coincidence, then, that it is James whom Sandra M. Gilbert and Susan Gubar identify as having been most obsessed with the decline of male literary traditions in what *The Bostonians'* Basil Ransom calls 'a feminine, chattering, canting age'.[69] But other men of the very late nineteenth and early twentieth centuries — the period, oddly enough, when Sand's star began to dim — manifested a similar aggressive unease. Aldous Huxley's story 'The Farcical History of Richard Greenow' concerns a young writer emasculated by his female *alter ego*, a successful author of popular romances identified explicitly as one of the type including Sand, Elizabeth Barrett Browning, and Mrs Humphrey Ward. The woman in Huxley's story is depicted as a tigress and a vampire — exactly the images now current of Sand. The 'tigress of Armenia' — as Sand's Jewish publisher Buloz labelled her after a row in which she tactlessly called him a 'petty, pennypinching merchant' — is a bit of mud-slinging which has stuck to Sand, as can be seen from an account of the Chopin affair called *The Lioness and the Little One*. As for the vampire image of Sand, it will take more than my book to put the stake through its heart. Pritchett resurrects this old 'man-eating' bogeyman in his factually backwards claim that Sand consumed men's blood and pilfered their creative brains. The most damning characteristic of the woman in the Huxley story is her 'hideous industry'. Whereas 'the creation of a vast *oeuvre* is equated with noble potency when it applies to some of Sand's male contemporaries',[70] it has actually been held to prove that Sand was a mere hack. Now the nineteenth century expected prolific output from its male and female writers alike; it would not have been impressed by Philip Larkin's slim number of slim volumes, even though they were undeniably of the highest quality. But by refusing to accept that Sand wrote serious work, the twentieth century has been able to dismiss Sand as a writer, not just in spite of her professional discipline — but actually because of it.

Other male writers of this period also featured ugly female personages with all the nasty stereotypical traits which have been 'credited' to Sand. Max Beerbohm's Zuleika Dobson lures intellectual men to their deaths, intentionally or no. This *femme fatale* conceit can also be seen in the myth that Sand was a predatory spider and Chopin or Musset the helpless prey wound tight in the threads she spun from her body. D.H. Lawrence echoed male terror of an upcoming literary Armageddon — with women writers leading the charge of the Antichrist's battalions — when he lamented that the world had been taken over by 'Cock-Sure Women' at the expense of 'Hen-Sore Men'. In the 'Nausicaa' chapter of *Ulysses* James Joyce mocked women's style as 'namby pamby marmalady drawersy'. In *Miss Lonelyhearts* Nathaniel West prescribed strong medicine for women writers, particularly those who committed the sin of retaining their maiden name as a middle name: 'What they all needed was a good rape'.

Gilbert and Gubar speculate that male writers were offensively insecure in this manner because they depended on female patrons or publicists — Lawrence on Lady Ottoline Morrell and Mabel Dodge Luhan, Joyce on Lady Gregory, Harriet Weaver and Sylvia Beach. They suggest that this is one reason why Joyce hastened to welcome T.S. Eliot's 'The Waste Land' as a macho work which 'ends [the] idea of poetry for ladies'. Whether this personal jibe is justified or not, writers of this time — and later critics such as Leslie Fiedler, writing on nineteenth-century America — promulgated the claim that culture had become a battleground of the sexes, with unfortunate, genuine male geniuses condemned to failure by a world at once more capitalist and more feminine.

If this seems to be feminist 'paranoia', male writers have been prey to a phallic obsession far more than women's studies critics have. Even the spiritual Gerard Manley Hopkins thought that writing itself constituted a male sexual act: 'the begetting of one's thought on paper'. A writer most needs 'masterly execution', which is a male gift not bestowed on women. Norman Mailer puts it more crudely: 'The one thing a writer has to have is balls'. The critic William Gass has even implied that women cannot write because they do not have erections; they 'lack that blood-congested genital drive which energises every great style'.[71] If the capacity to write is equated with sexual potency, literature will only be suitable to 'mannish' females, as Sand was said to be. More important, male writing blocks will be seen as a disaster no less vast than impotence. Blaming women for both may be the panicked reaction.

In James's own work the theme of emasculating women and impotent men occurs in several stories. 'Greville Fane' contrasts the male narrator, a writer whose failure is 'admirably absolute', with a gallingly successful woman novelist 'who could invent stories by the yard but couldn't write a page of English'. 'The Next Time' likewise pits a high-minded male novelist against the gushing style, 'trash triumphant', embodied in a prolific woman writer. Born in America but resident in England, James could be expected to mirror the fears of male novelists in both countries. As early as 1855 Nathaniel Hawthorne had complained piteously of 'a damned mob of scribbling women'. James's youth would have been spent in the shadow of successful American poetesses like Lydia Sigourney and novelists such as Stowe. His mature years set him to compete — as he saw it — with women novelists of even more towering height: Eliot, Sand, Austen and the Brontë sisters. Although Gilbert and Gubar do not specifically mention James's defensive reaction to Sand, it seems to me that their ideas help to explain it. James's fears both rested on and further exaggerated stereotypes about the Frenchwoman. He was the major 'populariser' of Sand in the generation after her death; he wrote enough essays and reviews on her to make a novel as long as *The Europeans*. Thus his preoccupations with masculine writers' impotence and female domination of the novel were afforded much publicity.

As early as the 1860s — when travellers to Paris were turning back from the capital in the conviction that there was a revolution on, although the mobs were only queuing for Sand's plays — James was trying to write Sand off as over the hill. At this early point, however, he did praise her style and convictions, ranking her above Dickens and Thackeray, in line with the general evaluation of the time. Later, however, he dismissed her as 'a fictionist too superannuated and rococo at the present time'.[72] Unlike Arnold, the Brownings, Fuller or Turgenev, James never met Sand. He knew her only vicariously, through Flaubert, Turgenev, the Viardots, and Alphonse Daudet — as well as through Paris gossip. James never benefited from the calming influence which an actual meeting with Sand had on the most determined prejudices against her. He also had the disadvantage of having read the novels not in his youth — as Dostoevsky and Arnold did — but somewhat later, and of coming to grips with her last novels first. To him, then, she was an old woman, not the youthful fiery spirit of *Lélia*. Thomson also suggests that he had learned what he required from Sand by the time of her death, and that afterwards he outgrew her. Perhaps he projected his own certainty that she was outdated for *him* into his blanket assertion that she had nothing more to say to anyone else.

If James had merely admitted frankly that his own love for Sand was dead, there would have been no damage done. But he also entombed Sand's reputation in an iron casket of the worst prejudices. Like all women, he remarks, she had a habit of twisting the truth to suit her own purpose. Being a Frenchwoman, of course, she was doubly prone to tergiversation and truthlessness. Sand's lovers are presented with equal Francophobia as a string of 'so many more or less greasy males'. Chopin the ethereal is included in the general oiliness, but then excused: 'Poor gentlemanly crucified Chop! — not naturally at home in grease — but having been originally pulled — and floundering there at last to extinction'.[73] Arnold met both Chopin and Sand at Nohant and remarked on how well they got along. If anything, Sand and Chopin's contemporaries, such as Mickiewicz, say that *he* dominated *her*. But James presents malicious misogynous stereotype as fact, and this has become the accepted picture. Of course he is not wholly to blame for this unflattering official portrait: Chopin hagiolatry started with Liszt. But James appears to have been at best incurious about whether the myth was true, and at worst deliberately catty.

Similarly, he was inexcusably ignorant of the fact that Sand wore trousers only up until around 1840, and, more importantly, of the fact that Sand called Flaubert *her* father. What might be called the 'Mammy' myth of Sand's maternal sexuality was put about by James in second-hand, inaccurate stories about Sand and Flaubert. 'She offered her breast to his aggressive pessimism, had motherly, reasoning, coaxing hands for it, made in short such sacrifices that she often came to Paris to go to brawling ... dinners to meet him and wear, to please him, as I have heard one of the diners say, unaccustomed peach-blossom dresses.'[74] That neatly dropped little mention of being in with Paris high society does not eradicate James's ignorance of the facts that by this time Sand had worn these supposedly 'unaccustomed' dresses for thirty years; that Flaubert was actually more reclusive than she; that he had a perfectly good mother living with him at home; and that when Sand came to Paris it was more to spend time at Palaiseau with Manceau's ghost than to accompany Flaubert to dinner.

The maternal myth, and the domineering woman one, both occur in James; whether or not he originated them, he certainly gave them wider hearing. The supposed gospel truth that Sand merely dashed off her works, with no revision, also owes a good deal of its bogus currency to James. Finally, James's constant assertions that Sand's novels were dead constituted a self-fulfilling prophecy. When he began making this claim, his reports of their death were greatly exaggerated. The English journals which had condemned Sand as a harlot forty years before canonised her as a minor saint when she died. Details of her life were now told correctly, without prurience, and reviewers were magnanimous towards her sexual peccadilloes: 'Both in her life and in what she wrote [there was] a spirit of nobleness which, if sometimes obscured, was never absent. She strove to think and act rightly'.[75] The same periodical which had concocted a story of her running away to be with Byron now wrote that '[the] private life of an artist is, after all, but of secondary interest'.[76] An article in another journal the following year asserted quite plainly that at that time 'George Sand's fame continues to shine with a steady lustre'.[77]

Andrew Lang even stood the nymphomaniac myth — which informs James's 'greasy' accusations — unexpectedly on its head. 'No one can read her autobiography and her novels and continue of the opinion that love as between man and woman was one of the most masterful forces of her nature.'[78] Lang would not have had the contradictory evidence of the *Intimate Journal* available to him, and his analysis of Sand's sexuality risks lending aid and comfort to another enemy camp — those who call Sand frigid. Nevertheless, even given obituaries' rule, *de mortuis nil nisi bonum*, these reports and articles make it clear that Sand was highly rated — if only by the mere fact of their having been written. In 1876 — just before her death — James, in contrast, was dismissing Sand as 'an elderly diva who can get by on a thread of a voice comparatively'.[79]

In the obituary which James wrote for the *New York Tribune*, he did avoid undue emphasis on her 'greasy' lovers. Indeed, he made the opposite statement — and James's view of Sand is nothing if not illogical — that she was 'the most shade-loving and retiring of celebrities'. Emily Dickinson had replaced the *femme fatale*, it seems, which might be thought somewhat of an improvement. But James went on to note that 'her life was almost entirely in her books, and it is there that one must look for it'.[80] And so one has — not one, but many of Sand's critics and biographers. She has been variously and contradictorily equated with the 'frigid' Lélia and the courtesan Pulchérie, the dominated young wife Indiana and the 'dominating' Lucrézia. This autobiographical school of Sand interpretation — perhaps unintentionally — has further downgraded her work and reputation. As I remarked in my earlier study of Emily Dickinson, only very young or very bad writers make everything in their work conform to their own lives. If everything in Sand's novels is read as an unthinking borrowing from the life, she will be condemned as a terrible writer outright, before anyone bothers to read her.

James was not the first to read Sand's novels as autobiographical — recollect the fuss over *Lucrézia Floriani* — or to present her as a mere improviser, a maternal bosom, or a nymphomaniac. All these misogynous stereotypes were around while James was still in short trousers, and will no doubt continue in good health for many years to come. But James does appear to have accepted them uncritically and spread the rumours further. His interest in Sand — and the generous breadth of publicity which he gave her work — might have benefited her if he had only attempted to give a truer, less gossipy rendering. But of course he also insisted that Sand was already forgotten — despite the play he gave her in his essays. When Karénine's four-volume biography of Sand appeared in 1897, James reviewed it as factually helpful, but deplored its 'injudicious analyses of forgotten fictions'.[81] That Hardy ranked Sand among the top ten French writers two years later proves that Sand's fictions were not forgotten, although James helped to make them so.

My allegation that Sand was pushed, rather than being the victim of her own lack of balance, may smell of conspiracy theory. That there was a *conscious* plot among male novelists of James's generation I doubt; but I do accept that these and later literary men were obsessed by a deep fear, perhaps subconscious. James Agee enjoined us: 'Let us now praise famous men'; Sand's male English-language critics exhorted readers to make mock of this famous woman. Because Sand was more vulnerable to sexual stereotyping than other woman novelists — being a Frenchwoman, a mother, a divorcee, and a veteran of several affairs which she acknowledged with a frankness usually reserved, ironically, for the more conventional sex — averting one's eyes from both her life and her work was conveniently legitimate. If our age is more rather than less sex-conscious than the nineteenth century, as Foucault and Woolf assert, this process should cause little wonderment. Critics such as Pritchett do find good things to say about Sand, and James would doubtless resent allegations that his response to Sand was conditioned by her sex and sexuality. But here Woolf is a great help: one need not claim that male critics condemn female writers' sexual freedom and use it against them deliberately, she says. Indeed, she turns the tables on the masculine view of women as prisoners of their bodies by implying that the poor men can't help being so irrational.

A resurgence of interest in 'great women' — as witness this and other recent collections of critical studies — may simply replace a male First Eleven with a female one.[82] Perhaps some of the 'wrong' women will be included — but who would dare to argue that none of the 'wrong' men have crept into the literary canon? Unless Heine, Dostoevsky, Turgenev, Whitman, Balzac, Hugo, Arnold and Hardy are all there by mistake, we might at least consider their unanimous opinion that Goerge Sand was one of the 'right' women. I have tried to give a balanced portrayal which includes some of Sand's personal and professional weaknesses: her occasional sanctimoniousness, her vituperation towards feminists, the favourites she played with her own children despite her glorification of motherhood, and her rather outdated conviction that the novel's characters need to be idealised. If I have spent more time arguing for than against Sand, that is only what is required for balance. The popular image is still unfavourable, if there is any popular picture of Sand at all.

In the last century there was an American feminist series on lives of notable women. Who reads them now? All any 'great woman' biography and study can do is to set up a marker of genuine female achievement, in the knowledge that it will probably be knocked down again. As Germaine Greer says, there is plenty of work for devotees of these causes that have — at least for a time — been lost. 'Almost uninterruptedly since the Interregnum, a small group of women have enjoyed dazzling literary prestige during their own lifetimes, only to vanish from the records of posterity.'[83] Of no woman writer can this be more accurately said than of George Sand.

Notes

1. Virginia Woolf, 'Professions for Women', in *Women and Writing*, quoted in Mary Eagleton (ed.), *Feminist Literary Theory: A Reader* (Oxford: Basil Blackwell, 1986), p. 52.
2. Sandra M. Gilbert and Susan Gubar, 'Tradition and the Female Talent', in Miller (ed.), *Poetics of Gender*, pp. 183–205.

3. See, for example, Cate, *George Sand*, pp. xiff.
4. These and later statistics on literacy are taken from James Smith Allen's informative and pioneering study linking demography and Romanticism, *Popular French Romanticism: Authors, Readers and Books in the 19th Century* (Syracuse, N.Y.: Syracuse University Press, 1981).
5. *The Guardian*, 3 February 1987, p. 3. Other estimates of adult illiteracy in Britain range as low as 2 million, however.
6. Quoted in Smith Allen, *Popular French Romanticism*, p. 153.
7. Quoted ibid., p. 154.
8. Edmond Weroet, *De la Librairie française*, quoted ibid., p. 154.
9. Ibid., pp. 145 and 209.
10. Quoted by Ellen Moers in Eagleton, *Feminist Literary Theory*, p. 97.
11. Ibid., introduction, sect. three.
12. Sand, *Un Hiver à Majorque*, p. 105. As often, Sand takes an *anti-*Romantic line here.
13. Quoted in Pritchett, *The Myth Makers*, p. 115.
14. Quoted by Gilbert and Gubar in Miller, *Poetics of Gender*, p. 203.
15. Quoted in Cate, *George Sand*, p. 732.
16. Quoted ibid., p. 732.
17. Quoted ibid., p. 731.
18. An article by the reactionary journalist Senkorsky, quoted in Carole Karp, 'George Sand and the Russians', *George Sand Papers: 1976*, p. 153. Translations quoted from this article by Karp are her own.
19. Quoted ibid., p. 158.
20. Quoted ibid., p. 151.
21. Quoted ibid., p. 158.
22. Quoted in Carole Karp, 'George Sand in the Estimate of the Russian "Men of the Forties"', *George Sand Papers: 1978*, p. 180, translations Karp's.
23. Quoted ibid., p. 184.
24. Quoted ibid., p. 186.
25. Quoted in Mallet, *George Sand*, p. 419.
26. Quoted in Karp, 'George Sand in the Estimate', p. 154.
27. Quoted ibid., p. 184.
28. Quoted ibid., p. 180, from Fyodor Dostoevsky, *Diary of a Writer* (tr.) Boris Brasol (New York: Octagon, 1973), I, p. 340.
29. Quoted from Dostoevsky's *Diary of a Writer* by Isabelle Naginsky, 'The Serenity of Influence: The Literary Relationship of George Sand and Dostoevsky', in Glasgow, *George Sand: Collected Essays*, p. 115.
30. Letter to François Buloz, quoted ibid., p. 118.
31. Dostoevsky, quoted in Mallet, *George Sand*, p. 421.
32. Turgenev, *Pervoe Sobranie Pisem I.S. Turgeneva, 1840–1883* (St Petersburg, 1884), p. 292, quoted in Karp, 'George Sand and the Russians', p. 151.
33. Sand, preface to *François le Champi* (Paris: Garnier, 1962), p. 215.
34. Quoted by Lesley S. Herrmann, 'George Sand and Ivan Turgenev', *George Sand Papers: 1976*, p. 168.

35. Quoted ibid., p. 170.
36. Henry James, 1868 review in *The Nation*, quoted in Thomson, *Victorians*, p. 218.
37. James, *French Poets and Novelists* (New York: Macmillan, 1908), p. 173, quoted by Marie-Jeanne Pecile, 'George Sand et l'Amérique', *George Sand Papers, 1978*, pp. 176–7.
38. Quoted ibid., p. 174.
39. Walt Whitman, 'Genius: Victor Hugo, George Sand and Emerson' (1874), quoted ibid., p. 174.
40. Quoted in Mallet, *George Sand*, p. 409.
41. Article by Margaret Fuller in *New York Tribune*, 1 February 1845, quoted by Russell E. Durning in, *Margaret Fuller, Citizen of the World* (Heidelberg: Carl Winter, Universitätsverlag, 1969), p. 58.
42. *Memoirs of Margaret Fuller Ossoli*, (ed.) Emerson, Clarke and Channing, quoted ibid., p. 57.
43. Quoted in Mallet, *George Sand*, p. 407.
44. *Atheneum* review of *Lélia*, quoted in Thomson, *Victorians*, p. 12.
45. Quoted ibid., p. 14.
46. Quoted ibid., p. 15, original emphasis.
47. Quoted ibid., p. 16ff.
48. Thackeray, *Paris Sketch Book*, quoted ibid., p. 19.
49. Quoted ibid., p. 21.
50. Lewes in *Foreign Quarterly Review* article of July 1844, quoted ibid., pp. 21–2.
51. Carlyle, *Latter Day Pamphlets* (London, 1872), pp. 68–70, quoted ibid., p. 30.
52. Mill, *The Subjection of Women* (London, 1960), p. 509, quoted ibid., p. 34.
53. Quoted ibid., p. 33.
54. Charles Dickens, *A Christmas Carol* (London: Allen Lane, 1979), p. 11.
55. Letter to Miss Mitford, quoted in Thomson, *Victorians*, p. 45.
56. Quoted ibid., p. 49.
57. Quoted ibid., p. 50.
58. Elizabeth Barrett Browning, *Aurora Leigh*, IX, 656, quoted ibid., p. 56.
59. *Aurora Leigh*, V, 14–16.
60. *Letters of Charlotte Brontë*, I, p. 80, quoted in Thomson, *Victorians*, p. 53.
61. *Brontë*, II, pp. 172–3, quoted ibid., p. 65.
62. George Eliot, *Letters* (ed.) G.S. Haight (New Haven, 1955), I, pp. 277–8, quoted ibid., p. 154.
63. Quoted ibid., p. 117.
64. Quoted ibid., p. 120, translation mine.
65. Arnold, *Mixed Essays*, quoted ibid., p. 117.
66. Arnold, *Mixed Essays*, quoted ibid., p. 94, original emphasis.
67. *Letters of Robert Louis Stevenson* (ed.) S. Calvin (London: 1926), I, p. 116, quoted ibid., p. 205.

68. Quoted ibid., p. 206.
69. Quoted in Gilbert and Gubar, 'Tradition and the Female Talent', p. 187.
70. A very telling point, made by Naginsky in her article on Sand and Dostoevsky, 'The Serenity of Influence', p. 114.
71. The quotations from Hopkins, Mailer and Gass are from Eagleton, *Feminist Literary Theory*.
72. Quoted in Thomson, *Victorians*, p. 185, from *Letters of Henry James* (ed.) P. Lubbock (London, 1920), I, p. 363. Although I have found Thomson's detailed study enormously helpful — as can be seen from the number of references I make to it — I disagree with her assessment that James was Sand's 'friend' and her opinion that his prejudices are what we all really feel deep down. My argument is probably closer to that of Cornelia Kelley in *The Early Development of Henry James* (University of Illinois Press, 1965). She calls James 'at time condescending, at others vehemently condemnatory'.
73. James, *Letters*, II, pp. 235–6, quoted in Thomson, *Victorians*, p. 228.
74. Quoted ibid., p. 224.
75. *Saturday Review*, 21 October 1876, quoted ibid., p. 211.
76. *Atheneum*, June 1876, quoted ibid. p. 211.
77. *Nineteenth Century*, April 1877, quoted ibid., p. 212.
78. *Quarterly Review*, April 1877, quoted ibid., p. 214.
79. *The Nation*, 13 January 1876, quoted ibid., p. 220.
80. Quoted ibid., p. 221.
81. James, *Notes on Novelists*, quoted ibid., p. 227.
82. A point raised by Mary Eagleton in *Feminist Literary Theory*, p. 4.
83. Germaine Greer, 'Flying Pigs and Double Standards', *Times Literary Supplement*, 26 July 1974, p. 784, quoted ibid., p. 12.

Chronology

1773		Birth of Antoinette-Sophie-Victoire Delaborde (Sand's mother).
1778		Birth of Maurice Dupin de Francueil (Sand's father).
1797		Birth of Alfred de Vigny.
1799		Birth of Honoré Balzac (later de Balzac).
1802		Births of Victor Hugo and Alexandre Dumas *père*.
1803		Birth of Prosper Mérimée.
1804	5 June	Marriage of Maurice Dupin and Antoinette-Sophie-Victoire Delaborde, his mistress for four years.
	1 July	Birth at Paris of Amantine-Lucile-Aurore Dupin (George Sand).
	December	Napoleon proclaimed 'Emperor of the French' by himself, wresting crown from Pope's hand at ceremony and crowning himself.
1806		Birth and death of baby son in Dupin family.
1808		Heavily pregnant, Sophie travels with Aurore to Spain, where she joins Maurice with army there.
	12 June	Birth of son Louis.
	July	Return to France through great dangers.
	8 September	Death of Louis.
	17 September	Maurice Dupin thrown from Spanish stallion, Leopardo, on late-night ride; dies instantly.
1810	1 March	Birth of Frédéric François Chopin at Zelazowa Wola, near Warsaw, to Nicholas Chopin, who had emigrated to Poland at sixteen to escape the intellectual boredom of wealthy peasant life in Lorraine, and his Polish wife Justyna.

	11 December	Birth of Alfred de Musset in Paris.
1815		Fall of Napoleon, to Mme Dupin de Francueil's satisfaction and Sophie's chagrin.
1817		Aurore sent to Couvent des Dames Anglaises in Paris to finish her education.
1820		Aurore returns to family estate, Nohant in Berry.
1821	Summer	Aurore's grandmother Mme Dupin de Francueil (with whom she has lived since girlhood) suffers stroke. Aurore nurses her and takes over estate management with help of former tutor Deschartres.
	12 December	Birth of Gustave Flaubert.
	26 December	Mme Dupin de Francueil dies, telling Aurore: 'You are losing your best friend'. On the night before she is to be buried, Deschartres insists that Aurore accompany him to the family graveyard and kiss skull of Maurice Dupin, whose coffin has been exposed by grave-diggers.
1822	April	Aurore visits James Roëttiers du Plessis and family near Melun and later meets Second Lt Casimir Dudevant.
	17 September	Aurore marries Casimir; she contributes 400,000 francs to their common property, he 60,000.
1823	30 June	Aurore gives birth to son, Maurice Dudevant (later Dudevant-Sand).
1824	Spring	Visit to du Plessis family, perhaps to cure continuing post-natal depression. First recorded incident of violence against Aurore by Casimir, who slaps her face in front of hosts. *She* apologises.
1825		Visits to Gascony and Pyrenees. Platonic friendship with Aurélien de Sèze.
1826	20 February	Death of Casimir's father. Casimir inherits only his title of Baron; stepmother retains life possession of estate. Casimir now completely dependent on Nohant income and will therefore fight Aurore's later demand

		for legal separation.
1828	13 September	Aurore gives birth to daughter, Solange Dudevant (later Dudevant-Sand and then Clésinger), probably her child by Stéphane Ajasson de Grandsagne.
1829		Aurore writes first novel (*La Marraine*) — never published.
1830	July	Revolution in Paris; fall of Charles X, installation of Louis-Philippe.
	November	Polish uprising repressed by Russia, much to Chopin's grief.
1831	4 January	Aurore leaves Nohant for Paris, where she lives with lover Jules Sandeau and begins literary apprenticeship on *Le Figaro*.
	April	Returns to Nohant to see children and to fulfill agreement with Casimir by which she was to live half of each year at Nohant to sweeten provincial opinion.
	24 December	Publishes *Rose et Blanche* in collaboration with Sandeau.
1832	May	*Indiana* by 'George Sand' published to instant popular and critical success. Sand now living in Paris again, with Solange and Sandeau.
	6 June	Republican insurrection put down by National Guard.
	December	Sand's second novel, *Valentine*, published.
1833	Spring	Unsuccessful one-night stand with Prosper Mérimée after Sandeau liaison ends.
	Summer	*Lélia*, called 'the century's assessment of itself', published. Sand begins affair with Alfred de Musset.
	December	Sand and Musset leave for Venice, and share coach with Stendhal on the way.
1834	April	Musset returns to France.
	August	Sand returns to France with new lover, Pietro Pagello, who leaves about a month later.
		Publication of *Jacques* and first four *Lettres d'un Voyageur*.

1835	March	Musset and Sand make definite break after reviving affair briefly.
	October	Casimir batters Sand during her time at Nohant; dinner guests have to restrain him from shooting her.
1836	February	In separation suit, Sand is awarded sole custody of Solange and shared custody of Maurice, with possession of Nohant, to which she returns after her flight the previous autumn from Casimir's violence. Affair with her lawyer, Michel de Bourges.
	May	Casimir appeals decision but is unsuccessful.
	November	First meeting with Chopin.
1837		*Mauprat, Les Maîtres Mozaïstes, La Dernière Aldini, L'Uscoque* and *Lettres à Marcie* published. Affairs with Pierre Bocage and Félicien Mallefille. Death of Sand's mother. Solange abducted by Casimir and kidnapped to Gascony, where Sand pursues and recovers her.
1838		Balzac stays at Nohant. Sand begins affair with Chopin. Trip to Majorca. *Spiridion* and *Les Sept Cordes de la lyre* published.
1839	February	Chopin, Sand, Maurice and Solange leave Majorca and rest for some time in Marseilles to allow Chopin to recuperate.
1840		*Le Compagnon du tour de France* published.
1841		Sand sets up socialist *Revue Independante* with Pierre Leroux. Publishes *Horace*.
1842		*Un Hiver à Majorque* and first part of *Consuelo* published.
1844		*La Comtesse de Rudolstadt* (conclusion to *Consuelo*) published. Sand launches republican paper in Orléans, *L'Éclaireur de l'Indre et du Cher*. After finishing 1,200-page *Consuelo*, begins work almost immediately on *Jeanne* and *Le Meunier d'Angibault*. Death of Chopin's father. 'Young Europe' movement founded by exiles in Paris, headed by

		Sand's friend, Giuseppe Mazzini.
1846		*Lucrézia Floriani* published.
1847	19 May	Solange marries sculptor Auguste Clésinger at Nohant.
	Summer	Scenes between Clésinger, Maurice, and Sand, during which Clésinger punches Sand in chest. Solange intervenes on her mother's behalf but complains to Chopin that Sand is being unreasonable about money. Chopin fails to arrive at Nohant, for whatever reason, remaining in Paris until he goes abroad for last tour. Sand begins work on autobiography to raise dowries for Solange and foster-daughter Augustine Brault. 'Never have I known such agonising labour', she writes to Sainte-Beuve. Visit to Nohant by Mazzini.
1848		Abdication of Louis Philippe. Sand leaves Nohant for Paris to press new government for reforms in Berry. Becomes caught up in Revolution as unofficial minister of propaganda. After demonstrations in May Sand again takes refuge at Nohant, but even there mobs threaten her house. Nevertheless writes and publishes *La Petite Fadette* and stages *François le Champi* as play at Odéon. Daughter born to Solange but dies shortly afterwards. Chopin on unsuccessful concert tour in England, which worsens his health. In December Sand's half-brother Hippolyte Châtiron dies after drinking full bottle of brandy.
1849	January	Augustine (Brault) Bertholdi bears son, named Georges; Sand is godmother.
	May	Solange bears second and last child, Jeanne-Gabriel-Béatrice Clésinger, who lives with Sand after Clésingers separate in 1852 but dies of scarlet fever in 1855 after father places her in boarding school against Sand's wishes.

	October	Death of Chopin.
		Affair with Victor Borie.
1850	January	Brief affair with German academic Hermann Müller-Strübing.
	April	Beginning of Sand's most enduring relationship, with engraver Alexandre Manceau.
	August	Death of Balzac.
1851		Coup by Louis Napoleon, with whom Sand intercedes on behalf of imprisoned or exiled republicans. Plays: *Claudie*, *Le Mariage de Victorine*.
1853		*Les Maîtres Sonneurs* (novel), *Mauprat* (play form) published.
1854–55		*Histoire de ma Vie* published.
1856		*La Daniella*, anti-papist, pro-republican novel, provokes barrage of complaints. Sand warned by official censor, journal serialising novel suspended.
1857		Death of Musset. Manceau buys Sand a writing retreat at Gargilesse near Nohant.
1858		*Elle et Lui* published, taken at time to concern Musset affair, though not seen as autobiographical by all modern critics. Paul Musset defends brother's reputation in rejoinder, *Lui et Elle*. Louise Colet, Flaubert's mistress, produces even more vituperative *Lui*, which helps create myth of Sand as man-eater.
1860		Sand has near-fatal typhoid fever. *Le Marquis de Villemer*, *Valvèdre* published.
1861		Maurice marries Lina Calamatta at Nohant.
1862		*Laura: Voyage dans le cristal* published.
1863		*Mademoiselle la Quintinie*, anticlerical novel, proves enormously popular with new generation. Birth of Marc-Antoine Dudevant-Sand to Maurice and Lina.
		Deaths of Delacroix and Eugène Suë. Manceau's fatal illness begins.

1864	February	*Villemer* produced at Odéon; provokes pro-Sand riots of 5,000–6,000 demonstrators. Travellers to Paris so alarmed by crowds that they turn back in fear of revolution.
	July	Death of Marc-Antoine at Casimir's estate, Guillery. Sand arrives an hour too late.
		Maurice forces Manceau from Nohant; Sand goes with him.
1865	21 August	Death of Manceau from consumption at Palaiseau near Paris.
1866		Birth of Aurore Dudevant-Sand to Maurice and Lina. Growing friendship between Sand and Flaubert.
1867		Sand begins pattern of spending winters at Palaiseau and returning to Nohant in summer.
1868		Birth of Gabrielle Dudevant-Sand. Flaubert and Turgenev now frequent visitors at Nohant.
1869		*La Petite Fadette* (play form) and *Pierre qui roule* published. Death of Sainte-Beuve; Sand weeps at graveside. Suit against Casimir forces him to leave most of estate to Maurice and Solange, rather than to illegitimate daughter Rose Dalias.
1870		Deaths of Mérimée and Dumas *pére*. Only Sand and Hugo remain of 1830 generation.
	14 July	War declared against Prussia.
	15 September	Siege of Paris begins.
1871	March	Death of Casimir Dudevant.
		Paris Commune ends bloodily, with murder of 15,000 Communards and exile of 125,000.
		Journal d'un Voyageur pendant la guerre published.
1875		*Flamarande* published. Sand frequently ill, but continues to write. Republic estab-

lished. Hugo made a senator.

1876	8 June	Sand dies at Nohant of inoperable intestinal occlusion, working in the morning of the day on which she takes to her bed and never rises.
	10 June	Burial at Nohant. Prince Jerome Bonaparte, Dumas *fils*, Flaubert, and other notables attend; Turgenev sends sincere apology. Solange insists on religious ceremony, but secular address by Victor Hugo also read. Sand's American friend Henry Harrisse finds both less moving than 'this ill-tended graveyard, this throng of peasant women wrapped in their dark cloth mantles and kneeling on the wet grass, the gray sky, the cold drizzle which kept pelting our faces, the wind whining through the cypresses and mingling with the aged sexton's litanies'.
1889		Death of Maurice.
1898		Death of Solange, whose own daughters have been dead for over forty years. In 1871 she had written to her mother that her childlessness was 'a despair which lodges like solitude in the heart, and which burrows and spreads like a cancer as one grows older. To grow old alone is awful for a woman'.
1961		Sand line dies out with death of Maurice's granddaughter Aurore.

Select Bibliography

Primary Sources

Most of Sand's novels are available in French paperback editions. The principal publishers include Le Livre de Poche, Garnier Flammarion, and Gallimard Collection Folio. Sample titles are my own favourite, *Les Maîtres Sonneurs*, as well as *Mauprat, Le Meunier d'Angibault, La Mare au diable, La Petite Fadette, François le Champi*, and *Indiana*. Sand is not particularly difficult to read in the original, although she is rather free with dialectical and horticultural terms. Only in the French, however, can the reader understand why her style was thought to be the greatest in the language.

Her travel writing is represented by *Lettres d'un voyageur* (Paris: Garnier-Flammarion, 1971) and *Un Hiver à Majorque* (Paris: Livre de Poche, 1984). Both editions have useful introductions and chronologies, as do most of the paperback editions of the novels. Sand's political writing is exemplified in *Le Compagnon du tour de France* (Compagnonnage) and *Les Femmes et l'Académie Française* (Les Editions de l'Opale). The Musset affair is often thought to be documented in *Elle et lui* (Ides Calendes), though this is very much open to debate. The grim picture of the affair left by Paul de Musset's rejoinder, *Lui et elle*, and by Louise Colet's even more calumnious *Lui*, is mitigated by the light-hearted poem Musset wrote to describe the couple's Bohemian, happy life at the start, 'Stances burlesques à George Sand' (in Alfred de Musset, *Pages Choisies*, v. 1, Poésie, Paris: Librairie Larousse, 1959, p. 122).

The complete edition of Sand's correspondence is being edited by Georges Lubin, the foremost Sand textual scholar. This Pantagruelian endeavour, begun some twenty years ago and still incomplete as I write (March 1987), covers some twenty volumes so far, published by Garnier Frères at various dates beginning in 1964. Lubin has also edited Sand's *Journal Intime* and many other personal works as the two-volume *Oeuvres autobiographiques* (Gallimard, 1971).

Sand's autobiography exists in an edited English translation by

Dan Hofstadter, *My Life* (London: Victor Gollancz, 1979). English translations of the novels were copious in the nineteenth century, but except for Robert Graves's *A Winter in Majorca*, Sand has been rarely translated and generally out of print in English for most of this century. However, since the 1970s many of her novels have been published in English by American academic houses, and a translation by Siân Miles of *Marianne* is now available in Britain (London: Methuen, 1987). There is also an English paperback translation of the Flaubert correspondence by Aimee L. MacKenzie, *The George Sand–Gustave Flaubert Letters* (Chicago: Academy Chicago Ltd., 1979, reprint of 1929 edition). However, this does not draw on the authenticated Lubin editions of the letters.

Secondary Sources

A selection of *biographies*:

Caro, Elme Marie, *George Sand* (tr.) Gustave Masson (Port Washington, New York, and London: Kennikat Press, 1970, reissue of 1888 edn)

Cate, Curtis, *George Sand: A Biography* (London: Hamish Hamilton, 1975)

Gerson, Noel B., *George Sand: A Biography of the First Modern, Liberated Woman* (London: Robert Hale and Company, 1973)

Mallet, Francine, *George Sand* (Paris: Editions Bernard Grasset, 1976)

Maurois, André, *Lélia: The Life of George Sand* (tr.) Gerard Hopkins (London: Jonathan Cape, 1953)

Orga, Ates, *Chopin* (London: The Illustrated Lives of the Great Composers, Omnibus Press, 1976 and 1983)

Salomon, Pierre, *George Sand* (Paris: Hatier-Boivin, 1953)

Toesca, Maurice, *The Other George Sand* (tr.) Irene Beeson (London: Dennis Dobson, 1947)

Zamoyski, Adam, *Chopin: A New Biography* (Garden City, New York: Doubleday, 1980)

Collections of *essays* and *articles*:

Datlof, Natalie (ed.), *George Sand Papers: Conference Proceedings, 1976* (New York: AMS Press, 1980. Record of first George Sand conference at Hofstra University)

———, *George Sand Papers: Conference Proceedings, 1978* (New York: AMS Press, 1982. Record of second conference at Hofstra)

Glasgow, Janis (ed.), *George Sand: Collected Essays* (Troy, New York: Whitston Publishing Company, 1985. Proceedings of a 1981 conference)

Johnson, Diane, 'Experience as Melodrama: George Sand', in *Terrorists and Novelists* (New York: Alfred A. Knopf, 1982), pp. 41–51

Miller, Nancy K., 'Writing (from) the Feminine: George Sand and the Novel of Female Pastoral', in Carolyn G. Heilbrun and Margaret R. Higgonet (eds.), *The Representation of Women in Fiction* (Baltimore: Johns Hopkins University Press, 1983), pp. 124–51

Pritchett, V.S., 'George Sand', in *The Myth Makers* (London: Chatto and Windus, 1979)

Schor, Naomi, 'Reading Double: George Sand and Difference', in Nancy K. Miller (ed.), *The Poetics of Gender* (New York: Columbia University Press, 1986), pp. 248–69

Specialist studies:

Allen, James Smith, *Popular French Romanticism: Authors, Readers and Books in the 19th Century* (Syracuse, New York: Syracuse University Press, 1981)

Dolléans, Edouard, *Feminisme et mouvement sociale: George Sand* (Paris, Les Editions Ouvrières, 1951)

Marix-Spire, Thérèse, *Les romantiques et la musique* (Paris: Nouvelles Editions, Latines, 1954)

Moreau, Pierre, *Le classicisme des romantiques* (Paris: Librairie Plon, 1932)

Rambeau, Marie-Paule, *Chopin dans la vie et l'œuvre de George Sand*, (Paris: Société d'Edition «Les Belles Lettres», 1985)

Thomson, Patricia, *George Sand and the Victorians: Her Influence and Reputation in 19th-Century England* (London: Macmillan, 1977)

Vermeylen, Pierre, *Les Idées politiques et sociales de George Sand* (Brussels: Editions de l'Université de Bruxelles, 1984)

Vincent, Marie-Louise, *La Langue et le style rustique de George Sand dans les romans champêtres* (Geneva: Slatkine Reprints, 1978)

Index

People

Titles